D0962353

❧ PRAISE FOR HIJAS AMERICANAS ❧

"*Hijas Americanas* gives voice to the many influences that
go into making strong, talented, beautiful Latina women.
Molinary contributes to a much-needed conversation about
what defines Latinas as a community as well as what challenges
us as individuals, sending an affirmative message that is
bound to resonate with Latinas of all backgrounds and ages."

Julia Alvarez
author of *In the Time of the Butterflies* and *Saving the World*

"Molinary has written a powerful and meaningful book that
candidly explores the many stereotypes associated with growing
up Latina and the quest to accept this vital identity."

Marjorie Agosin
Professor of Latin American Studies, Wellesley College

"*Hijas Americanas* canvases the diversity of the Latina experience
frankly and compassionately. Molinary's subjects are candid
and generous, sharing the most intimate details of their
experiences. I was stunned by how many times I thought,
That happened to me, too!"

Michelle Herrera Mulligan
coeditor of *Border-Line Personalities: A New Generation of
Latinas Dish on Sex, Sass, and Cultural Shifting*

HIJAS
Americanas

BEAUTY, BODY IMAGE, AND GROWING UP LATINA

rosie molinary

SEAL PRESS

Hijas Americanas
Beauty, Body Image, and Growing Up Latina
Copyright © 2007 by Rosie Molinary

Published by
Seal Press
An Imprint of Avalon Publishing Group, Incorporated
1400 65th Street, Suite 250
Emeryville, CA 94608 .

Molinary, Rosie.
Hijas Americanas : beauty, body image, and growing up Latina / Rosie Molinary.
p. cm.
Includes bibliographical references.
ISBN-13: 978-1-58005-189-7
ISBN-10: 1-58005-189-8
1. Hispanic American women. I. Title.

E184.S75M62 2007
306.4'613—dc22
        2006038580

Excerpts from the book The Maria Paradox copyright © 1996 by Rosa Maria Gil and Carmen Inoa Vazquez are reprinted with permission. Permission granted by Lowenstein-Yost Associates, Inc.

"Monday" is an excerpt from the poem "A Week in the Life of the Ethnically Indeterminate" in Bardo by Elena Georgiou. Copyright © 2000. Winner of the 2000 Brittingham Prize in Poetry. Reprinted by permission of The University of Wisconsin Press.

Cover design by Gerilyn Attebery
Interior design by Megan Cooney
Printed in the United States of America
Distributed by Publishers Group West

To Latinas of every generation—

those who have traversed the beauty and body landscapes and

those whose journey has just begun—

because your presence is illuminating and your voice empowering.

contents

❧ AUTHOR'S NOTE ON LEXICON ❧

Language is a very complicated and personal thing. Words are like fingerprints: On the surface they may look the same, no matter who's using them—but if we burrow into the details, they are much less universal than we first thought. We use and interpret words in a way that speaks to who we are. They become our own, filtering into our consciousness in different ways based on how and where we've been raised, and how we see the world.

Because words are so powerful, it is important—particularly in a book that's sharing the experiences of such a diverse group of women—to clarify the choices I've made about usage in this book. Since we'll be talking about body image, beauty perception, and Latinidad—concepts that are highly individual—it needs to be said that my choices will not necessarily be the same as yours.

The women who responded to the survey and who participated in the interviews that contributed to this book often had very different takes on what it means to be Latina. They also used different descriptors and labels to describe their identity, their heritage, and their experiences. Though the majority of the women in this book self-identify as "Latina," I chose to retain the use of the word "Hispanic" when survey respondents, interviewees, censuses, and articles made use of the word. I did not feel it was my place to edit their use of identifying labels, and thus they will appear on occasion within the chapters.

Though I'm aware that the coopting of the word "America" by the United States is a point of contention among those who think of "America" in terms of the Pan-Americanism of all of the collective Americas, in this book, the words "America" and

"American" are used specifically in reference to the United States and its influences.

Below is a short glossary to shed light on what meanings I am working from when I use particular words or phrases, and to offer an understanding of critical diction and word usage throughout *Hijas Americanas*.

ACCULTURATE/ACCULTURATION: A gradual process in which people, without dismissing their native cultures, begin to adopt aspects of the dominant culture as a result of exposure. For example, being bilingual can signify acculturation, as it shows a desire to maintain one's native tongue while developing the language of the dominant culture.

AMERICAN: Many people in Latin America refer to the entire American Continent (North, Central, and South America) as "America." Therefore, for some Latinos, it feels redundant to say that they are, for example, Venezuelan American. However, in this book, I wanted to identify whether or not a person was born in the United States. To do this, in most cases I referred to people who were not born in the United States as "Peruvian" or "Cuban," for example, and to those who were born in the United States as "Chicana," "Latina," "Mexican American," "Cuban American," or "of Panamanian heritage/descent," for example. The one exception is that, given Puerto Rico's commonwealth status, women are described as Puerto Rican, and then their birth location, if it is of note, is identified.

ASSIMILATE/ASSIMILATION: A process in which people leave behind their native culture in order to adapt to the new culture (contrast with "acculturate/acculturation"). For example, those who are assimilated often make the choice to be dominant in the language of their new country and not their mother tongue.

BLACK/AFRICAN AMERICAN: When referring to blacks or African Americans, I am identifying the race of someone who is black but non-Latino.

BODY IMAGE: The subjective way that people perceive their own bodies and physical appearances in reference to themselves, their identities, their environments, and the reactions of those around them.

BORICUA: A woman of Puerto Rican heritage.

CHICANA/CHICANO: A person who is of Mexican descent but was born in the United States (at times, "Mexican American" is also used in this context).

HIJAS AMERICANAS: "American Daughters." This book title is an homage to both Latin American and North American cultures, which together unify each Latina.

HISPANIC: This word was first used by the U.S. Census Bureau in the late 1970s to identify people in the United States who have ancestral ties to Latin American countries, Spanish-speaking Caribbean nations, and Spain. Rather than identify a race, this term identifies a group unified through a commonality in culture and language. Not all people of Latin American descent approve of being called "Hispanic," and I opt for "Latino" and "Latina" unless I am directly quoting someone or referring to governmental figures, ideas, or policies.

LATINA/LATINO: A person who is of Latin American heritage and lives in the United States. Many people of the younger generations prefer "Latino" to "Hispanic" as a label. It's not uncommon to see the bisected usage: "Latino/Hispanic." As a reminder, this is a term that technically describes ethnicity and not race. If I want to clearly identify a person's race, I will differentiate by using such descriptors as "white Latina," "black Latina," "white non-Latina," or "black non-Latina."

LATINIDAD: This term indicates a pan-Latino identity for all Latinos that is rooted in a shared language and common immigrant experiences. This is the notion of a Latino identity that is not individual in nature.

MACHISMO: Behaviors among males in the Latino culture that display their masculinity. In today's context, it's often viewed as a negative behavior that is excessive in nature.

RETRO-ACCULTURATION: A process that happens when people who have assimilated to their new cultures begin to search for elements of their ethnic identities to incorporate into their new lives. They might embrace traditions they never had before, or learn to speak their native tongue for the first time as adults.

SELF-ESTEEM: The way people regard themselves. A person who has positive self-esteem has the ability to be authentic and is accepting of his/her skills, worldview, and cultural identity.

WHITE: In this book, when "white" is used as a descriptor of race without any other qualifiers, I am indicating that the person is a white non-Latino.

❧ INTRODUCTION ❧

Reconciling Two Realities

I never had Latina girlfriends growing up. I only knew two Mexican American girls at my high school. In college, there were two older Cuban American women whose beauty and classiness intimidated the hell out of me.

I have had Latino guy friends. Not boys I dated. Well, one. Almost. They were mostly just friends who understood me and helped me ease into a feeling of home. Two who stand out in my mind are Braulio and Christopher. Christopher was my almost (I'll share a little more about him later); Braulio was like immediate family. When Braulio and I first met, it seemed as if we had already been together for a lifetime. He came home with me during Thanksgiving and Christmas breaks. He completed our family, and the way he recognized me made me feel more complete. Before Braulio, I had no idea what feeling at home meant, really, because I'd spent so much time feeling like "the other."

Once, on a visit to New York City when I was in college, someone called out to me. "Hey, Boricua, over here!" a young man yelled from his apartment stoop. I looked around, wondering whom he was yelling at. Then it dawned on me: He was talking to me. Intimidated, I sped up. Later, I considered why I ran, why the Boricua in me did not march over to that stoop and ask, "*¿Qué quieres?*" But I had grown up in South Carolina. Besides my sister, I was the only Puerto Rican girl I knew.

In college, I was still the only Puerto Rican girl I knew—and the only Puerto Rican girl most anyone else knew. A counselor in the admissions office assumed I was a Spanish major; she looked at me with a knowing glint in her eye—an obnoxious look that told me she believed that studying Spanish might indeed be the only way I could succeed. She proceeded to tell me that I'd been granted admission not because I was an academic powerhouse, but because of what I could add to the campus. I felt the weight of needing to act polite, to be good, to play nice. I said nothing. Instead I let her offensive comment hang in the air between us. I walked away from her that day, just as I walked away from the guy in New York City. I wasn't sure where I fit in or what I was. I was someone who knew what it was like to be seen, but not valued or heard.

I'd also been told plenty of times that I wasn't Puerto Rican enough, or even Puerto Rican at all—despite Spanish being my first language, despite the fact that I had no relatives living in the United States. Once, in a college committee meeting about diversity, a woman I knew well looked right past me as she asked the group why we didn't have any Latinos on the committee. What I came to understand was that sometimes, despite my own reality, I was considered Latina enough to take care of every quota under the sun and other times not Latina enough to fulfill a single one.

Thinking back to that summer afternoon in New York City, I now realize that I hurried away from the guy who yelled out at me not because I was scared of him, but because I was scared of what he would find in me. *What if I had stopped and talked to him? What if he told me that I wasn't Puerto Rican enough? What if my own* compadre *chose not to claim me? Where would that leave me in my understanding of myself?* There I was, being recognized as Puerto Rican—perhaps for the first time without trying—but the possibility of being denied that I belonged was too much to bear. I've often wondered what would have happened if I had risen up and claimed an identity that was mine for the taking. But it would take a while before I could finally revel in the joy that the Latina in me had been so easily recognized.

My high school in Columbia, South Carolina, was diverse enough—despite the lack of Latinos—to keep me from feeling too isolated. I was relatively self-assured and had serious boyfriends, and while my home life was dramatically different from that of my peers, I felt more lonely because of my ideals and values than I did because of my ethnicity, class, and looks. Now I understand how much my ideals and values were shaped because I am Puerto Rican, and not in spite of it.

It was college that made me more sensitive to where I stood on the continuum of ethnicity, class, and beauty in America. Going to an upper-echelon liberal arts school in the South heightened my awareness about white America much more than I heightened anyone else's awareness about Latinos. I once had my intelligence both insulted and questioned by a professor who didn't even have me in his class. I typed my papers on a Brother word processor, and didn't learn the difference between a Mac and a PC until after college. Among my peers, I was thin, but did not feel thin enough. My hair was black, thick, and unruly in a sea of blonds with the popular Rachel (from *Friends*) haircut. A friend's father actually had an FBI buddy look into my family when he found out that we were hanging out. And my friend was the one who mentioned it.

Through college, I struggled with not belonging, with feeling alone. Some of my isolation was just the routine isolation that so many feel during a new stage of life, but most of it was about ethnicity, socioeconomic class, and being so distinctly different looking and different feeling from everyone else on campus. In those years, I wanted desperately to break the barrier I felt between myself and others. I wanted to leave a favorable impression on people. I wanted to matter.

My junior year, my college roommate—a close friend—watched me while I put in my contacts and said, "You would be so exotic looking if you just had different-colored eyes."

That comment, as much as it mortifies her now that she ever said such a thing, summed up how I felt in college. I was not exotic enough to be considered rare and worthy, and I was just different enough to not be considered.

I remember a letter I wrote that same year. A friend had written me and asked whether I felt I had chosen the right school. My response is still crisp in my mind. It wasn't the perfect school for me, I wrote. It wasn't a natural fit, and I didn't always feel comfortable, but it was the right school for exactly those reasons— because of what it taught me about survival, about standing up for myself, about existing in a world that I had never before experienced. Only now can I look back and recognize how precocious and accurate that assessment was. Because it was only later that I fell in love with the sense of *not* belonging, with the idea of not having just one place to call my own. Eventually, I could just be who I set out to be each day. Some people would like it, some people would not, but at the end of the day, I could still meet my own eyes in the mirror.

After I graduated and began teaching in the inner city, where my mosaic of students had last names like Rosario, Nguyen, Chang, and Perez, I experienced other difficulties. All of a sudden, boys found me sexy and beautiful, alluring and free game. Not because I was those things, but because I was ethnic—a girl from the Island, a Latina who could show them love in a whole new way.

In my twenties, as a teacher who preferred long skirts and baggy sweaters, the mention of my ethnicity sometimes elicited sexual reactions from students. When I was twenty-two, on my first day with a new class, a group of boys slapped high fives and affectionately started calling me their "Puerto Rican Pecan."

Later I overheard one male student whisper to another, "Man, our Puerto Rican Pecan makes me want to blow a nut." It stunned me, numbed my understanding of my ethnicity, made me wonder whether I should go on embracing my roots or ignore the part of my identity that made me seem sexy instead of intellectual.

As I became a bolder authority figure, I learned how to shield from my students the side of me that was hip, young, and vibrant. As a teacher, I wanted to claim my ethnicity in order to empower my students to celebrate their own heritages. Maybe I could pass as white, but I had never wanted to pass. I wanted to foster a forum where, with my lead, nobody would have to pass. We could all just be who we were, or who we wanted to be.

In the teachers' lounge, I started to hear the stories of the other young, single female teachers. These women were attractive, intelligent, and fun loving, but they never mentioned that their students called them by sexual nicknames, or that they were propositioned the way I had been on occasion. I was too embarrassed to mention my own experiences. Perhaps the delineation was based on race. My colleagues were white; my students, mostly African American, Asian, and Latino. In my students' eyes, it seemed I represented two things: the crossroads between the white and black worlds, and a local version of the sexy women they lusted after in hip-hop videos filmed on location across the Caribbean.

To them, I was a myth and not a woman, Wyclef Jean's Maria to all these wannabe Don Juans. It seemed as if my womanhood meant sex and sensuality more than other women's; as if I could simply exhibit my breasts and never my mind and no one would be the lesser for it; as if by merit of my ethnicity I was promiscuous and born to procreate.

I'm not certain whether they were enraptured by my ethnicity or by my candor. I only know that my experience with those propositions and chants, those questions and challenges, forced me to look at my Boricua in a way I never had. I learned that I can straddle multiple worlds, that I do not have to belong—and that I won't ever belong—to one place. "Belonging" is not what I was born into; it was not how I grew up; it is not who I have become.

The point is not that I belong now. It's that I'm free from the notion that I must. That maybe if I were more desirable or beautiful it wouldn't matter to people that I was Puerto Rican or poor. I came to terms with the fact that I have no control over how much my ethnicity, class, looks, or body size matter to someone else. I can only control how they matter to me. Where I used to think that belonging was a prerequisite for affection and care, I now realize that the only prerequisite for those things is my own willingness to give them to myself. Coming to terms with not belonging was indeed difficult for me, but through those difficulties and challenges, I found the best parts of me. I am better off knowing that I'm comfortable and capable most anywhere I end up. In that way, the isolation of being "the other" has been a provocative classroom.

Perhaps the most revolutionary part of my evolution is that I am no longer just looking at my own Boricua for answers. I am a woman who, until recently, had few Latina peers. I am a woman whose struggles with ethnic identity, beauty perception, and body image opened up a Pandora's box of questions. I am a woman who sought out the answers to my own questions by choosing to connect with the wider Latina community and by choosing to find out how other women have grappled with the same challenges I've confronted. This book has been my own reconciliation with that isolation, and through my interaction with more than five hundred Latinas, I've found comfort, solace, anguish, and, most important, understanding.

Among the topics of conversation I address with the women whose stories grace the pages of this book are the following: How do we Latinas in America straddle the inherent duality of our experiences? How do we reconcile what we hear our parents tell us in the home—to not get tan, to eat more *arroz con pollo,* to get curves but not get fat, to do chores they would never ask our brothers to do, to not use tampons because they're just for slutty girls—with what we hear in the America we live in, where the messages, opportunities, and experiences are drastically different? The answer is simply that we do—but each of us does it in our own way. Every day, we navigate a world not created with us in mind. We confront our two cultures, our varying traditions, the different values before us—and we try to carve out a place for ourselves.

For Latinas, there are many struggles in reconciling our two realities. But my own experience—growing up in a home in which the Puerto Rican essence opened out into an American playground of possibility—didn't just make my life harder. All the resulting bumps and bruises made my life better. Almost universally, the women who share their stories with me agree.

Hijas Americanas exists because Latinas share an understanding of the tension and complexities that result from the duality in our experience, and because there is a range of truths and experiences among Latinas in America that is not often explored by mainstream media and culture. My own story and the stories of the handful of Latinas I've come to know in my adulthood were not enough. I wanted a chorus of experiences. I wanted the volume to be loud and significant.

The result is more than I could have ever hoped for. Included here are the experiences (individual and collective) of hundreds of Latinas who grew up throughout the United States and navigated not just U.S. ideals, but also the ideals of their homes and home countries, to become the provocative, bright, passionate, and beautiful women they are today. This book explores the myriad ways in which growing up Latina and American has molded and impacted these women. Their stories show the significance of each individual's unique coming-of-age experience, but they also examine the universal truths that are part of all our experiences. As Latinas, we face our personal difficulties—and sometimes our impenetrable insecurities—with an individual honor and dignity that allows us to define who we are in the context of so many things: family, community, ethnicity, race, religion, culture, and more.

I used two methods of research to explore the themes this book addresses. First, with the support of two research assistants, I created a survey featuring 157 questions regarding body image, beauty perception, sexuality, and the influence and impact of family, faith, media, and social norms. This survey, which will be referred to as the Growing Up Latina Survey throughout the book, was completed online by 521 women who learned about the opportunity to participate through professional, educational, or women's organizations—or from other Latinas they knew. (The survey questions can be found in Appendix A, page 279.) In order to participate, the women needed to self-identify as Latinas and had to have lived in the United States since they were at least ten years old. Participants were between the ages of eighteen and forty.

In addition to the surveys, my research assistants and I conducted more than eighty interviews with women who reflected the same demographic. (These interview questions can be found in Appendix B, page 301.) All of the women were voluntary participants, and interviews were conducted in person or by phone. The interview participants are identified at first mention by name, age at the time of the interview, self-identified ethnicity, and hometown (sometimes a city, sometimes only a state). The survey participants are not identified; their voices contribute to the broader picture of what it's like to grow up Latina. The survey participants helped me gain statistical information, and oftentimes their stories are included because what they wrote moved me or served as a particularly interesting and/or universal example of the Latina experience.

My goal in conducting the interviews was to highlight the information from the survey with richer, more personal, and more detailed information. The interviews provided the context for how the lives of these women unfolded in America. Questions ranged from "What do you love about being a Latina?" to "What have been the triumphs of being a Latina in America, and what have been the challenges?" The interviewees gave voice to their self-conceptions, and to the perceptions they have and have had of themselves as they moved through a world that was sometimes familiar and friendly and sometimes foreign and cold.

Over the course of the research, my assistants and I marveled at these women. We were honored by their honesty and their ability to give voice to difficult experiences. Their contributions here will help someone else—some wonderful girl who is just approaching adolescence somewhere in middle America—know that she is not alone in her struggles. These women were forthright not because they themselves had something to gain from it, but because they wanted the world to gain from it. These are Latinas who see the world evolving and have something meaningful to contribute to that evolution.

As I wrote, I was struck by how my own sense of self and identity was changing in the process. My self-perception as a Latina was formed out of a fairly solitary existence. Often people have expressed things like, "I don't see you as a Latina at all"—a sentiment that's clearly meant as a compliment, as an indicator of inclusion and acceptance. I'm struck by the way people move toward connection by saying they do not see my color. After a lifetime of feeling like I do not belong, being accepted is a wondrous feeling. But by being told that I am not seen as a minority at all, I am denied a significant, difficult, and yet meaningful part of my experience. It's neither a favor nor a courtesy to ignore someone's ethnicity, culture, or reality. It's an omission, a negation.

So here is a book that gives me and the women whose stories are shared an opportunity to call it out clearly: We are Latina—in all our colors, styles, looks, mixed variations, heritages, and ethnicities.

Hijas Americanas gives you the opportunity to learn about and admire the women I was so privileged to get to know in the process of writing this book. And it does much more than that: It encourages you to acknowledge the way we beat ourselves up, and the way we're conditioned to do so because of the messages we get from the larger culture. And for Latinas, this is often coming from two, even three, different frames of reference. It's imperative that these voices be heard. These women's struggles are struggles that many of us are familiar with—born of the schism that results from living between two worlds, complicated by the ways that diverging cultures don't meet in the middle. When we can recognize this schism, see where it comes from, and take matters into our own hands to effect change, we can approach the world with a sense of confidence in ourselves as proud Latinas, in all our diversity.

In talking to the interviewees for this book, I have seen how far we've come, and though we still have far to go, the endless possibilities and openness of our future thrill and excite me. I hope that giving voice to these women's experiences will empower others to give voice to their own experiences. Here is an opportunity to reflect on whether you want to break out of limiting patterns and help our young Latinas grow into secure, confident women—not in spite of their race and ethnicity and body, but because of those very things. *Hijas Americanas* holds within it examples of what it takes to support one another, examples of what that kind of courage looks like and sounds like, and how speaking one's truth yields real beauty. Our interest in these issues can overhaul the low self-esteem and confidence we suffer by radicalizing the terms for beauty, and by setting our own standards for how we live and present ourselves in this culture. Listen to these women's experiences, consider their suggestions, and develop your own standards. Open your arms to embrace these *mujeres,* these *madres,* these *hijas* as they are, and as if they were your own.

ROSIE MOLINARY
APRIL 2007

one

Turning Gringa

My first kiss was over a chainlink fence. I didn't realize the significance of it then, but the fence that stood between my seventh-grade boyfriend and me was a metaphor for the otherness that marked my life. It separated homes that, back then, were worth more than half a million dollars from homes that were worth more like seventy thousand, and it divided an almost exclusively white neighborhood from a mixed neighborhood that was more minority than white.

The fence would come to symbolize the division I would feel in my life until I could finally comfortably settle into myself. But until that time came, there we were—a beautiful white boy on one side and me on the other. As I turned away to walk home, my mother drove by in her wood-paneled station wagon, and I wondered whether what I had just done was something that would make me more gringa than Puerto Rican.

In the fall of my sophomore year in high school, I spent many of my evenings sitting in the car of a boy named Wade while Jerry Garcia crooned about black muddy rivers. I'd stare innocently up at the infinite Milky Way while Wade whispered about the mighty Orion, my eyes trained upon the three-studded belt, more mystified by the boy than by the sky. On Saturday afternoons, he and I would curl up in the game room at his house and watch college football.

That fall, when Wade called to ask me on our first date, I felt a rush of warmth spread through my cheeks as I cradled the phone between my shoulder and my ear. I checked myself in my parents' mirror, my mouth gaping at this news: Wade Wilson was calling me.

"I was calling to see if you wanted to go to a movie tonight," he said casually.

I wanted to respond just as casually that yes, of course I could, but that wasn't how things worked in my house. I had to get permission from my parents first. "Can you hold on a second?" I asked.

"Hey, can I go to the movies tonight?" I asked my mom in a flurry, having rushed across the house and wanting to make it quick.

"*¿Con quién? ¿Qué película? ¿A qué hora?*" Mamacita's words came flooding over me with the heaviness of confession. I shook my head, forcing the overwhelming feeling to pass.

"Wade Wilson. Jonathan's brother," I responded, trying not to sound desperate. My parents had known Jonathan for years; we were enrolled in the same classes and shared friends.

"Why does Wade want to go to the movies with you? Is Jonathan going?"

"Mama, can you please just say yes so I can tell him, and then I will answer your questions?" My attempt at nonchalance cracked. I was keeping track of how much time I'd been away from the phone, and I was certain it had been at least three minutes.

"Why are you trying to *not* answer any questions; what are you hiding, Rosa?"

In that moment, I knew how this conversation would evolve. I could see in Mamacita's eyes that she was not going to give in easily. When she dug into a discussion, I had to commit myself to winning, and this one would take much longer than a few minutes. I turned, paced quickly back to my parents' bedroom, caught my breath, and then feigned being upbeat. "Can I call you back in a minute?"

God bless him for not reacting, for being gracious, for having a deeper awareness than the average eighteen-year-old boy. It was the same grace that I would see him demonstrate over and over again in the time we spent together, navigating first love and our very different families, cultures, socioeconomic classes, and experiences.

"No problem," he responded, and I found myself back in the kitchen with Mamacita. She continued with her questions, and I played the role of good daughter, answering each one as thoroughly as I could.

Then, "*Por favor,* Mami, please let me go. I hardly ask for anything."

This was always the final thing I resorted to, but it also nearly always worked. At fifteen, I worked and took care of my own expenses. I was also responsible for buying all my own clothes. I didn't ask to go away for spring break with my friends. I didn't party the way other teens did.

"All right, m'ija," she answered, "but just remember, you are not a gringa."

I nodded. Those instructions were an echo of an almost daily reminder she issued. "You are not a gringa" was my mother's party line, whether it was in reference to going out on a date, sleeping over at a friend's house, or cruising the mall. Each time she denied my requests with this phrase, I had to come up with a better excuse to give my friends for my inability to do things that they didn't even have to ask permission to do.

This reminder was in stark contrast to the other chorus in my life—one that I heard almost as regularly. In English class, a girl once told me I was not Puerto Rican because I wasn't like the other Puerto Ricans she had known in Boston. My face grew hot as I argued. I felt like I was arguing for my life, arguing for the only identity I knew. But she responded that I wasn't pregnant or strung out like those "Reekins," as if that disqualified me.

When I visited my cousins in Puerto Rico, they always called me La Gringa. I wanted to challenge them, but my explaining that some Americans didn't see me as gringa hardly seemed like it would elicit the validation I was seeking. I remember standing there in silence, wondering how I'd become an Anglo without any birthright.

In college, a friend once denied my ethnicity as we talked about my upbringing. I was telling her how the rules in my family were based on God, culture, and *machismo,* about how my mom's response to everything I wanted to do was, "You are not a gringa." Even as I repeated it there to my friend, I could hear the undertones of Mamacita's voice ringing in my ears.

"But you aren't really Puerto Rican," my college friend insisted. This denial rendered me silent, frozen on the borderlands between my Latina and my gringa, wondering which face to look to and which to turn from in order to find myself. Why did she believe this so absolutely? How could she determine what made up my whole? How was I betraying my truth?

Ultimately, I learned that the way people labeled me was often more about their own preconceived notions than about what I did or said. I slowly began to understand that the one thing I did have control over was how I saw myself.

In high school, Ryan—a boy I'd been friends with since middle school—turned on me. One night we were all hanging out at Wade's house. When I got up to leave, I found a pool of spit inside my shoes. I had noticed Ryan starting to throw out racist sentiments here and there, and this action was evidence to me that, despite our previous friendship, I was not exempt. Something arose in my normally mild, nonconfrontational nature that night, and I called him on his actions. I shook as I confronted him, terrified that I would not find the words to tell him that I had worth, that I did not belong in his kitchen, that I could participate in his world or any other that I chose.

At that point in my life, I was very aware that some people had an opinion about my place in the world and what opportunities I could access, and that these opinions rarely allowed me a choice or a preference. In ninth grade, my guidance counselor, after reviewing my perfect report card, wanted to remove me from honors classes and enroll me in work-readiness courses. Despite—or perhaps because of—the fact that I was the only Puerto Rican student in the Talented and Gifted Program, he wanted to reroute me.

I remember leaving his office in shock, my red face drawing the attention of another counselor, who listened to my predicament with compassion and added me to his own caseload. Years later, he encouraged me to apply to multiple colleges and helped me waive the application fees. "Let's see how we can do," he'd said. He smiled as I nodded and took on the challenge, fueled by a desire to prove my first counselor wrong.

For years, finding balance and settling into a peacefulness with my duality was difficult. But it was imperative to my identity and my development to figure out how my Latina and my gringa could share space in the mirror, how they could find union within the one reflection that stared back at me. And while I navigated these complexities in solitude for many years, I wasn't alone. My range of experiences is a representation of the experiences that so many Latinas in the United States have as they grow up in households with parents whose cultural and traditional values differ from those of the mainstream culture in which they are raised.

STRADDLING TWO WORLDS

Annabelle, a thirty-two-year-old Colombian American in New Jersey, recalls the dichotomy of her early experiences. "I grew up being the only Latina in my school and neighborhood, and sometimes I enjoyed being different, and sometimes I hated it," she recalls. At school, Annabelle's perfect English allowed her to blend in. "My peers forgot that I was Latina and would say racist things, and I would say, 'Hello, I'm here.'"

Annabelle's experience reflects a challenge some Latinas face when members of the dominant culture come to see them as one of their own. What do we do when racist jokes about our minority culture come out, or when we're told that we can't be Puerto Rican or Mexican or Colombian because we're not knocked up and strung out? What do we do when someone questions our worth, our intelligence, our soul? As young girls, more often than not our reaction is to withdraw into ourselves. When we are young, most of us don't have the wherewithal to insist that we be seen—that we are worthy and smart, and that we have value. It's only over time and through years of struggle that we're able to retrieve our true selves—selves that were lost, told to be quiet, or simply silenced.

Lucia is a thirty-eight-year-old who lives in Austin. She tells a story of sitting in a college biology class when the professor asked a question that few others seemed willing or able to answer. "I answered the question. A girl next to me told me that she was impressed that I spoke articulately and didn't have a Mexican accent," says Lucia. She is quiet for a moment, collecting some restraint, before continuing.

"We had a learning moment. When the professor finished his lecture, I asked her if she had a moment to talk. We agreed to walk to the student union for a Coke. Initially, the conversation centered on the class, the professor, and the academic work. Of course, I was angry and hurt by her comment. And I so badly wanted to yell, scream, and start name-calling so she would feel just as bad as I did. But I remember my mom always telling me, 'Don't ever pass up a chance to teach and to learn.' So I brought up her comment. I asked her about her life and her exposure to people who look like me. She told me about growing up in an upper-class area of Dallas, and how the only Mexicans she met were the wait staff and gardeners who worked for her family," Lucia recalls.

"I began to tell her about my life, growing up in a lower-middle-class Mexican American family in a small central Texas town. Once I knew that she was comfortable with me, I told her that her comment during class was bothersome to me. I told her that I didn't want her to think that anyone with brown skin, dark brown hair, and a Spanish surname would speak with an accent or not be able to use large words. I asked her if she had ever been pigeonholed or stereotyped for being a well-off, blond female from Dallas. Well, of course she had, and she did not like it. I remember her saying with tears in her eyes that people always called her a snob because of her family's wealth. I told her that, just as the generalizations that she experienced hurt her, her generalizations hurt me. I asked her to think about her words before saying them aloud. When we finished our conversation an hour and a half later, we both realized that the university was not only a place to develop our minds, but a place to nurture our relationships with others who are different—culturally and physically. Since my mom had always influenced me in broadening my life experiences and helping others do the same, I left the student union prouder that day. I was proud that I had helped someone to see beyond her comfort zone, beyond her life experience; proud to know that I was able to tackle life this way. I think the most important thing is to be true to who we are, and to go out and enjoy the differences that we all have," Lucia concludes.

I love how confident and able Lucia was at the age of twenty to graciously but directly confront a comment that had hurt her feelings. Her perspective, experience, and poise in this situation provides an amazing example of how much courage something like that takes, and how beautiful the results can be.

Many Latinas can relate to the experiences that Annabelle and Lucia had. We often have to confront hesitation on the part of others before we can prove what we can skillfully do. Many of us know that in order to get to the places we want to be, we have to assert ourselves and learn to speak up for ourselves. Speaking up to defend our heritage is a common coming-of-age experience for most Latinas in the United States.

I grew up on an Army base; my dad was an enlisted solider. My first friends were African American, and their culture resonated with my interests and experiences absolutely. But on any given day, I could move comfortably between my white and black friends, perhaps because my looks were ambiguous (in the South at the time, they could have been interpreted either way). Defending myself and my heritage meant giving up the cushy spot I had in both worlds.

Eventually, I had to start speaking my truth, sometimes not as eloquently as Lucia did, but enough to show myself that I was not settling. Once, my sophomore year of college, I sat in the lounge of a residence hall visiting with my friend Jeremy.

"What do you want to do after college?" one of his hall mates, John, asked me.

"I am going to teach high school in the inner city," I said, certain.

"Why would you come to a school like this and then waste it on being a teacher?" he asked, a look close to scorn on his face. I was laid back about most everything, but issues of privilege and justice were a trigger for me.

"The reason I'm at a place like this is because I believe that this type of education is valuable, and that it's the type of education that would make a difference in the life of any kid—especially a kid in the inner city. Maybe my students won't go to a top ten school, but my being there will help the kids I teach get that type of education every single time I walk into my classroom."

I was passionate and direct. I used the voice I would come to use in the classroom, the tone that one of my students once described as being an "I am in pain because of you" tone. Later, Jeremy told me, "Dude, John thought you were pissed. He was all like, *Damn, she got Latina on my ass.*"

"Did I seem pissed?" I asked Jeremy, wanting his interpretation of what that meant.

"Nah, man. I just don't think anyone has ever talked back to him."

I thought of John often when I was teaching, and most especially when two of my high school students enrolled at our alma mater.

Ethnic stereotypes are nothing new, nor are they going to disappear anytime soon. In September 2006, California Governor Arnold Schwarzenegger issued an apology for saying that the lone Latina Republican legislator, Assemblywoman Bonnie Garcia, had a "very hot," fiery personality because of her ethnicity—a comment that was captured on audiotape: "On the recording, Schwarzenegger . . . casually says that 'black blood' mixed with 'Latino blood' equals 'hot.' 'I mean, they are all very hot,' the governor says on the audio recording. 'They have the, you know, part of the black blood in them and part of the Latino blood in them that together makes it.'"[1]

If the immigrant governor of California—a state with one of the largest Latino populations—can think and say something so stereotypical and ethically ignorant about a group of people he interacts with on a daily basis, what does that say about the levels of awareness others might have in states where the exposure to Latinos is much more limited?

Jessica, age twenty-four, grew up in the northern suburbs of Los Angeles. She speaks about what it was like for her growing up in a neighborhood where she felt ostracized because she didn't look like everybody else. "I am white, so it's very complicated. When I was younger, Spanish was my first language. It was only when we moved out of a Cuban neighborhood and into a white neighborhood that I started getting conflicting ideas about my identity. The only Hispanic people were the house help and the gardeners. It was very difficult to figure out what I was. I had to argue with people and defend my heritage, even throughout college. Because of the color of my skin, I sense distrust from other Latina women. It's a constant struggle to prove myself to whites and Latinos both."

Jessica articulates what so many Latinas already know—that oftentimes we treat ourselves no better than others treat us. There is no single defining Latina experience. There are multiple communities within the Latino community and multiple layers of understanding, and many women I spoke to echoed Jessica's sentiments.

Magdalena is twenty-four and of El Salvadoran descent. She grew up in an Italian neighborhood in New York City. "In school, I was only one of two Latinas. I didn't fit in anywhere. In having to conform to the Anglo women, I feel like I had to let go of a little of my Latinness," she says.

Marie Isabel, a thirty-seven-year-old Puerto Rican in Pennsylvania, spoke of her conflicts in straddling the Latina world inside her home and the American world outside. "I grew up in an all-white neighborhood, which made it that much more difficult. I had to deal with the racism issue. I am very pale with blue eyes and straight brown hair. My parents were very Latino. I wasn't allowed to hang out with my girlfriends. I couldn't date until I was twenty-one, or go to my prom. I thought I was on a different planet. Although I was born and raised here and understand American culture, because I was Puerto Rican in my house, the transition between one and the other was difficult. We live double lives," she explains.

Marie Isabel's description of her parents as "*very* Puerto Rican" reveals how some Latinas perceive that there is a continuum as much as non-Latinas do. Marie Isabel remembers the shift that occurred when she became aware of her heritage, and reflects on her own awakening as a Puerto Rican woman.

"I was twenty-seven the year I became Puerto Rican. Before then, I didn't feel any connection to my country. Over there I was

a gringa, and over here I wasn't. It wasn't until I got older and became engaged with my community that I became Puerto Rican."

Though it was a long time coming, Marie Isabel's two lives
finally melded into one balanced life that she came to accept
and appreciate. She came to love being a Puerto Rican in the
United States.

Camille, a twenty-seven-year-old New Yorker of Colombian
and Dominican descent, had a similar awakening. As a young
woman, she hated her neighborhood and what it said about her. "It
was drug infested and dirty. People didn't care about the neighborhood. It was predominantly Dominican. A lot of kids dropped out
of school and sold drugs, which was the primary household income
for a lot of families I knew. I wanted no part of it, and at the same
time I started drawing my own stereotypes of Dominicans. I wanted
to get out," she says.

In college, however, Camille saw the way these stereotypes
played out for her personally. "One of my first jobs was working in a medical office. I had to go to the library to check out research books. The librarian looked at me and said, 'Are you one of
those people who calls it the li-barry?' She started laughing with
her coworker about me," Camille recalls. "They just think that the
Latinos around them are dumb. I still get that in the workplace. My
boss actually told me that I have a Latina attitude problem. What
does that mean? My friends from school, who are Latino, told me
that I sounded like a white girl, a valley girl. I still get that now,
even from white people. 'You don't sound Latina.' I didn't know
we had a sound."

Today, Camille's ethnic awakening is apparent in her career as
a fashion designer. She incorporates Dominican elements into her
clothing and jewelry designs.

WHITEWASHED

Some Latinas blend right into Anglo culture without realizing the complex questions this crossover might create for their identity later.

"Not until recently did I realize that I was a Latina," explains Joanna, twenty-two, a student of Mexican descent at the University of Texas in San Antonio.

"I grew up where the majority culture was white, and I was whitewashed. My parents didn't want me to learn Spanish. Then I came to San Antonio and joined a Latina sorority."

Joanna's involvement in her sorority and her participation in a La Fe conference, sponsored by InterVarsity Christian Fellowship, greatly influenced her perception of her Latinidad. "I realized that God created a unique array of people. I realized, *Hey, wake up, you are Latina.* You don't have to speak Spanish to be Latina. Look at the way you grew up. You had the *tías* and *tíos* around your house, and the *abuela* cooking in the kitchen. I realized that when I came to a function of any sort and I had at least one Latina friend around, I was home. I was with *familia*," explains Joanna.

With this knowledge, Joanna settled into being Latina—the type of Latina she had never quite been during her childhood, because her parents were concerned about her ability to make it in the world and thought that being seen as Chicana might limit her possibilities.

"I think it's a tremendous blessing to be a Latina," she says. "Four years ago, I would not be saying, *Thank you, God, that I'm Latina.* I would get embarrassed if I got too tan."

Joanna's embracing of her heritage, however, did not please her parents. In the summer of 2006, she traveled to Mexico, much to her father's disappointment. "My parents wanted me to be more assimilated and American," says Joanna. "When they found out that I changed my major from biology to Spanish, they were surprised. When my dad found out that I was going to Mexico, he said, 'Why? The good life is here.' He had a hard life there and wanted to protect me from that, but I needed to be exposed to Mexico."

In Mexico, Joanna fell in love with the people while witnessing what must have been a very hard life for her father. Her experience made her sensitive and even sympathetic to why her father did not want her to go there. "I learned many different things from my trip," says Joanna. "People work a whole lot harder; they embody the term 'manual labor.' I witnessed little boys about age ten carrying around huge bags of merchandise weighing at least fifty pounds. I learned that I can speak Spanish, and it doesn't matter how bad my language skills are. The important thing was the relationships I formed. I learned from Mexican families that spending quality time with each other is important in their lives. Growing up, my dad would talk about childhood memories—stories of poverty and how he would eat burnt potato chips just to get some food for the day. And yet in some ways, he didn't want his children to know where he came from. This didn't really hit me until I went to Acapulco and I saw this child, a boy around eight years old. He was just lying on the sidewalk, sleeping, and it was about three in the afternoon. I thought, *Man, that boy was my dad*. He actually lived off the street. It saddened my heart to see this homeless child, but it gave me a deeper understanding and appreciation for my father."

She goes on to talk about her father's protectiveness of her, something that she understands better having gone to Mexico. "At times, my father's opinion about my trip to Mexico was frustrating because you want your parents to be excited for you, but if I were to obey every little bit of 'honoring my parents,' then I would not be able to have any adventures. I know now that my father's protectiveness is cultural. I now understand this and must extend him grace and mercy."

Lola is a Mexican American, age thirty-four, who came of age in a part of Texas that was 90% white. Now she lives in San Antonio and works at an elementary school that is predominantly Latino. "My parents wanted us to be more Americanized. They didn't teach us Spanish because they didn't want us to have an accent. We were less Latino than others," she explains, reflecting this notion of a continuum of Latinness. "I had no Latina friends growing up," she says. "I didn't have any until I was an undergraduate. When I was younger, I hated being Latina and wondered why I had to be. I felt that way until I went to college."

Dahlia, twenty-five and of Colombian and Cuban descent, felt frozen between her cultures in a small suburb in New Jersey. She remembers yearning to be more like other girls around her. "When I was very, very little, I didn't get it," she explains. "I didn't get why we were different. Why couldn't we be like *Leave It to Beaver*? As I've gotten older, I can see the value of my culture. But when you're little and you're around white people all the time, there are things that you just don't get because your parents didn't grow up in the United States. I didn't know who Jimi Hendrix was. I didn't know any Beatles songs. It felt like I was missing something. It was a different cultural frame of reference."

HYBRIDS OF A NEW AMERICA

For every Latino family trying to create distance from the old country, there is another family trying to embrace their native culture despite their new address.

Claudia, a thirty-four-year-old of Ecuadorian descent who grew up in New York City, speaks to this point. "My father always tried to keep the traditions that we had back home, and we were very family oriented. I grew up with five girl cousins, and I never searched for friends outside of them."

As she grew older, however, Claudia did start looking at the world outside of her family. "There was a lot of tension, especially with my father. He didn't want me to do anything. I always had to fight with him and get older cousins to convince him that the things that I wanted to do were okay. When I wanted to go to college, my father almost had a heart attack. I had to get a Latina financial aid officer to call him and tell him it was going to be okay. He knew he wasn't in Ecuador anymore, and he had to change with the times. I got it the worst because I was the oldest and female. By the time my sister came along, he was modernized."

While many of the women interviewed lamented growing up almost solitary in their experiences as Latinas, others grew up with plenty of company.

"Growing up in Queens was a very different experience from being in other areas. I grew up not being the weird one, because everyone was an immigrant," reflects twenty-nine-year-old Josette, who's of Peruvian and Colombian descent.

Carolina, who's thirty and Puerto Rican, also grew up in New York City. "I grew up in a neighborhood that's eighty-five percent Latino," she tells me. "I didn't find it hard to find my place, because there were so many Latinos." But even given her comfort within her community in New York, Carolina is sensitive to the fact that there are discrepancies between the Puerto Rican experience she had growing up in the United States and the experience that women have in Puerto Rico. "It's two different cultures," she says. "You never grow up fitting into one place. You live in the margins, so you have to find your own identity. Growing up here in the U.S. changed my cultural experiences."

An important truth I recognized in talking to so many Latinas is that being surrounded by Latinos as you grow up doesn't automatically eliminate the sense of isolation or automatically create a feeling of place.

Yvette, twenty-six, says, "I was born in Lima and lived there until I was seven. It was hard coming here to Queens, especially being from Peru. Everyone thought that if you were a Latina, you were Puerto Rican or Mexican. I had to constantly explain why I looked different. I felt like I couldn't identify with anyone, even though we were Spanish people, because of the vast differences in culture."

Some families try to walk the line, living lives that in some way try to embrace both cultures. This would seem to have the effect of raising very adjusted daughters, but many of the women I talked to who grew up in situations like this say they ended up feeling confused.

"My parents were very strict. We had a very difficult relationship during puberty. I wasn't allowed to do much. I was always very obedient. I wanted to make them happy because of the family values instilled in me. It was difficult for me, because that meant I couldn't do what I truly wanted," recalls twenty-four-year-old Jessica, who grew up in the Los Angeles suburbs.

But there was a twist to the Cuban standards that guided Jessica's home life. "My parents were critical of my weight," she says. "I think they wanted me and my sister to be normal, to fit in and be accepted by everyone. Normal for them means white culture, though, which was impossible because of our genes."

For many young Latinas, one of the biggest struggles is figuring out how to deal with family members who have adopted certain principles of American culture in somewhat arbitrary or random ways. "Be skinny, but eat our full Puerto Rican meals," a mother might suggest. "Do well in school, but don't think you'll be more than a wife," a father might imply. These mixed messages have ethnic, gendered, and cultural implications and complicate the lives of young Latinas.

Penelope, a twenty-six-year-old Chicana from Texas, wrestled with this type of issue. "I have a complex relationship with Spanish," she says. "I spoke it until I was six years old. Then my parents wanted me to speak English perfectly and without an accent. They didn't allow my siblings and me to speak Spanish anymore," she recalls.

But she later made some decisions that led to her being reprimanded for being too American. "I have a clear memory of when I was in high school; I was very much into community service," Penelope explains. "Obviously, being Mexican American does not exactly mesh with being a vegetarian and a member of PETA. It came to a head when I was elected the president of the community service club. My mother told me that I needed to 'stop the Mother Teresa bullshit and get a job.' She thought I should be working and not bothering with extracurricular activities. All of these things that I was doing were not contributing to the family. I was seen as very selfish."

These kinds of discrepancies were apparent to many of the women interviewed for this book.

"I didn't grow up with any kind of ethnic pride," says thirty-year-old Sarah, who grew up in New Jersey. "I have it intellectually, but there's a place in your heart where your self-esteem resides, and I don't have it there. My dad used to pick me up in front of the mirror and ask, *'¿Eres Cubana, Colombiana, o Americana?'* I needed to answer *'Americana'* to get it right."

While Sarah's father expected that she would harbor American pride, it turned out that she simultaneously needed to act "other than American" to stay in her parents' good graces. "There was a tricky part: 'You are an American, but don't act American' was the message. It was so beautifully hypocritical. I learned that only sluts wore tampons, because there was one woman in our neighborhood who had an affair and everyone talked about how she wore tampons. 'Don't have sex before marriage.' 'Don't chase boys; boys chase you.' 'And don't turn out to be lesbian, bisexual, or gay identified.' I would come home and say, 'I want a bologna sandwich,' because that was what kids at school were eating, and my mother would look at me and say, 'You don't eat that.'"

Sarah's parents chose to cut off the family's contact with Colombia and Cuba by never going back and by talking very disparagingly about both countries. "Had I not grown up Colombian and Cuban in America, I would not have seen myself as 'the other,'" reflects Sarah. "I feel a very strong alliance with other people of color, especially African Americans, and my parents don't understand that. I've always been very conscious of not belonging. Sometimes I am envious of not having grown up in Colombia or Cuba, because I don't have nationalistic pride. I have never really been proud of being American, because I know that I haven't always belonged."

While some women embraced, understood, or were accepted by one culture of their upbringing over another, and while others struggled to figure out how to meld their parts, some women settled right into the duality of their lives from the very start.

"I am very aware that I am Latin American. I feel very blessed to be American as well. I always say, 'Latina by birth but southern belle by the grace of God,'" explains Diana, twenty-one and Puerto Rican, who was raised in Georgia.

Frances, thirty-five and of Colombian heritage, came of age in New York City. "Ever since I was very young, I knew that I was American born, and I was proud of it. I always felt connected to the American idea that women can do whatever they want to do, whereas my family had more of a traditional understanding of women. I thought that coming from the United States gave me a free pass. It was very liberating for me. When I was in my twenties, my dad told me that I was the Madonna of the family, because he thought I was very rebellious," she recalls, referring of course to the pop star and not the Virgin Mary. But to say she "turned gringa" would only simplify the truth. Instead, Frances illuminates the complexities and beauty of being dual-cultured in America. "I love being a person of color. I feel such an affinity for any other person of color. I love the history of being a Latina and the historical narratives of all of these cultures coming together. I love that sense of lineage that comes from different parts of the world. I love the flavor, fire, spirit. I have freedom of movement and the ability to see the world from various cultural perspectives."

The truth is that none of us "turned gringa," like some of my friends tried to insist and like my mother still worries. But none of us are *pura* Latina Americana, either. We are hybrids of a new world order, multiethnic children of Latino parents and an American upbringing, learning to take what we need from our cultures to balance what we want for ourselves.

two

Double Lives

Having a sense of what is feminine and beautiful, and at what age different types of femininity and beauty are appropriate, is a significant part of the coming-of-age experience for all young women. But for Latinas in the United States, reconciling the standard we are presented at home with our own desires and with what we see in mainstream culture can lead to additional conflict and pressures—especially during adolescence, an already tumultuous time for most.

I had my first bouts of pre-adolescent tension with my parents the summer before sixth grade. I was not an early bloomer. My best friend, Jenny, wore a training bra before I even started developing, which caused me to resort to "willing" my breasts to arrive. That summer I studied Jenny's bra straps through her shirts and observed with envy what I didn't have. I felt stunted, behind, all wrong.

And so I begged my mother for a bra. I was ready to offer my money from dog-sitting; I was ready to cry if necessary. But my mother did not hesitate, saying that we could pick one up that very afternoon. Thrilled, I invited Jenny to join us, wanting to show her that I too had reached young womanhood and was in need of a bra.

I entered the local mall with one hundred percent dedication to the pursuit of the training bra that would coax my chest into blossoming. But before we could head to the teen department, my mother insisted that we look at summer sandals. Standing at the register, my mother said to the saleslady, at a decibel level loud enough for all Saturday shoppers to hear, "Could you hold these for me, sweetie? I need to go get my daughter her first training bra."

I froze, and then regained my senses. I was nearly strangled with mortification. Desperate, I turned to Jenny and declared, "Did you hear that? Mom says you're getting a training bra!"

It was my attempt to direct the unwanted attention Mamacita had forced upon me to my fair-skinned friend. I did not want anyone to know how much I wanted breasts and how much they mattered to me. I wanted to ponder them in secret, while reading chapters from *Are You There God? It's Me, Margaret* and studying my older sister's bras.

But secrets were not Mamacita's way. For the Latin American women of her generation, there is pride in being a mother; there is a way in which their own identities can seem to be consumed by their children's. As I grew older, I came to understand that Mamacita's inability to keep a secret was not a matter of her wanting to intrude upon my privacy. Rather, it was about her beaming with pride over her children—and the more she told, the more points she earned for her sacrifices. And in many ways, that seems fair to me now, though it didn't then. She did sacrifice a great deal for us to be raised in the United States. Six of her brothers and sisters, along with her mother and father, still lived on the Island. She made a trade to ensure that my siblings and I got an education, and in the deal, she sacrificed the closeness of her family. Whenever I reached a milestone, it was a validation for her of a choice well made. I was coming along, and she was partially (largely, in her mind) responsible for it. I didn't have to like that my life was broadcast, but I came to understand that my life was what it was because she made a hard choice to settle in a new country, learn a different language, and deal with a wholly different culture.

PUBERTY. PERIOD.

It wasn't until the following summer that I got my period. At an amusement park. With my friend's youth group. Standing in the hot bathroom under dim lights, I stared down at my underwear and understood that the stomach cramping I'd felt earlier wasn't anxiety about getting busted for hanging out with some boys we'd just met. I grabbed a handful of toilet paper and folded it into a makeshift Maxi pad. As I washed my hands, my eyes flashed over to a tampon dispenser. Tampons weren't used in my house. After all, wasn't that almost like having sex?

Everything I knew about my period had come from my girl-friends and Judy Blume.

I stepped out into daylight, my face red with embarrassment. I forced foot after foot forward, willing the time to move faster so our trip would end. Even then, I still had to suffer through an hour-and-a-half ride home. In a van. With other kids who could probably sense that I had just started my period.

Back home, I called my mother into the bathroom. I needed help, desperately. She scrounged around for a Maxi pad, and I begged her not to tell anyone.

"Who would I tell?" she pleaded earnestly.

Dinnertime came, and we gathered around the small table in our kitchen. My uncle and several male cousins were in town from

Puerto Rico, and we were enjoying a typical Puerto Rican meal. I ate without muttering a word, my usual effervescence tempered by the day's development.

"I have an announcement to make," my mother said, commanding the room's attention. We all looked at her expectantly. "Rosie became a woman today."

I dropped my fork, felt the heat rise so dramatically on my neck that I thought I would pass out. My cousins covered their mouths, shielding their laughter. My uncle applauded. I ran outside without comment.

So that was what "telling no one" meant to my Puerto Rican mother. Silly me, I thought it meant telling *no one*. My uncle came out after me, telling me it was only natural for families to share in this news.

"No, it's not," I insisted. But, of course, it *was* natural for my Puerto Rican family to share this news. But it was the American me who was going through puberty, and I wanted all of the developments—training bras, periods, acne, and leg hair—kept under wraps. In that moment, I saw clearly how my two cultures could clash, how they were in fact not mutually exclusive but, rather, inclusive and overlapping at all times. I sat outside until night fell, at which point I slinked into the house and back to my bedroom without being noticed.

In their book *The Maria Paradox: How Latinas Can Merge Old Traditions with New World Self-Esteem*, Rosa Maria Gil and Carmen Inoa Vazquez write, "Once in North America, many Latinas develop a new identity, which we will call the American self. We have to develop this identity in order to survive. . . . Until that American self becomes a natural part of us, we Latinas sometimes suppress our real selves and emotions, behave in a manner we feel is expected of us, and end up trying to act much more American than we feel or vice versa."[1] I would argue that this phenomenon is not just true of Latinas who move to the United States after being partially raised in their home countries. For second- and third-generation Latinas, their homes often mimic the rules and expectations of their parents' or grandparents' homeland, and so a conflicting American self might emerge to substitute for the Latina self when it seems appropriate.

Feeling alone and embarrassed as I did in the rose garden that summer night, I had no idea that across America, other young Latinas were going through awkward puberty-related experiences quite similar to my own.

Enid, who's thirty-four and of Puerto Rican and Colombian origin, recalls what happened when she got her period while growing up in Massachusetts. "In terms of sexuality, the only thing that was ever talked about was our period. My mother called all of her friends when we got our periods. We were so embarrassed."

Sandra, thirty-seven and of Dominican heritage, grew up in Queens with a single mother. "She never talked to me about sex. She was very private. Her idea was that it came naturally and that nature would take its course. She never told me about my period. So it was traumatic for me when I got it. I thought I was dying."

Thirty-seven-year-old Katarina, who grew up in Chicago and is of Colombian descent, recounts that her mother never talked about sex or periods. "You would hide any signs of Maxi pads and tampons, because she was embarrassed by them," she said.

"It was frowned upon that I used tampons. I grew up with these old wives' tales, like you can't wash your hair or walk barefoot when you are menstruating," says Lucy, a thirty-nine-year-old Puerto Rican in New York City.

INVITING AMERICA HOME

For those of us who grow up in two cultures, it sometimes seems impossible to figure out where we stand on issues of tradition, values, and life in general. In many cases, mine included, it's the children who bring America home, who invite her to dinner with their Latino family. And sometimes, as many of us have experienced, our families just want the guest to go away.

Enid, who was mentioned earlier in this chapter, went to a private Catholic high school in Massachusetts that was predominantly white. Her father, who had grown up in Puerto Rico before moving to the United States, had an old-school mentality that countered his children's emerging American values.

"I wasn't allowed to spend the night with friends. We grew up in a working-class community and carpooled to school with a good family friend. My sister even had to convince my mom to let her go to that friend's daughter's sleepover party. But Papi ended up going to the house after he got home from work and made my sister come home, because you don't sleep in anyone else's house. You sleep where your bed is."

Initially for thirty-six-year-old Eva, who grew up in Spanish Harlem, the disparity between America (where she lived with her mother) and Puerto Rico (where her father still lived and where she sometimes visited) was disconcerting.

"I would arrive back in New York City from Puerto Rico on 'island time.' And New York City is one of the fastest and most aggressive places in the world. It was like going from the womb to some industrial maze. All of a sudden, though, I was able to do both. I could walk that fast pace in the city and then go home and speak two languages."

Soon Eva had melded the two parts of herself in a way that sometimes startled her family.

"I was the first to get a tattoo and the first woman in my family to drive a car. That is part of my assimilated, side and not my family side of me. Getting a tattoo was just something that young Latinas don't do. This many years later, I'm still the only female in my family with a driver's license. My father had a hard time with my tattoo—saying it was boorish and vulgar. But my assimilated self really thrives off of freedom. Self-definition comes with freedom."

Within some Latino families in America, there are expectations that the youth will do things differently from other kids their age just because that's the way the family wants it to be, or insists that it be. My sister and I didn't drive until we were in college, even though the majority of our friends were driving at sixteen. We had to rely on our friends to take us anywhere, or on our parents to drop us off and pick us up. My mom would invariably forget, and I could often be found on the curb outside school, waiting for her to come.

In their aforementioned book, Gil and Vazquez discuss the conflict between acculturation, assimilation, and embracing roots. "No two cultures and no two people within those cultures go through the process in the same way or at the same rate. Some may even try to turn their backs on the new culture, while others may rush to embrace it. Either way, the truth is that we simply can't avoid embracing the new culture if we want to survive and prosper. A second truth is that acculturation is experienced as a series of changes and choices which includes new forms of how to live, what to eat, what language to speak, how to behave toward your relatives and peers, whether or not to follow certain patterns of behavior which pertained in the Old Country but which may be not useful at all in the new culture."[2] These tensions run deep within many Latino families in America.

"My parents think I am a traitor because I refuse to conform to the way they think a girl should be—like wearing a skirt. The constant thing I hear from them is, 'I would never have said *that* to my parents.' But I don't think I am being rebellious," says Cassandra, twenty-eight, who was born in Honduras but moved to Miami when she was four. In many ways, Cassandra tries to protect her parents from an America that they might find difficult to understand.

"I try not to tell them what I need, and fend for myself," she says. "I guess that is very American. But I've learned to not conform. My parents believe that a woman is supposed to get married and become a baby factory. I hear my mom's stories, and she had an adventurous spirit, but she learned to conform and gave up her dreams."

THE TIPPING POINT

Inside our homes, many of us learned that there were rules and expectations, sometimes said out loud, other times just implied, inferred, or suggested. We grow up learning to read our families the way we read our peers; in between all these messages we sometimes come up against a tipping point that can be challenging for any Latina.

Sonya, thirty-two, is half Peruvian and queer identified. She grew up in Boston. "We were a family who watched television together, and there were different messages we were receiving via TV," she remembers. "There were a lot of slurs used in my household. My mother referred to other Latinos as spics, faggots, dykes. My mother often commented on what other women were wearing in public."

But some of those same women her mother derided on the streets of Boston helped Sonya develop her own sense of style. "I have always been a naturally feminine person," says Sonya, "but what I found sexy was based on what I saw in Puerto Rican women. It was this effortless and yet put-together look. It appealed to me and showed me how you could use your femininity to gain power or as an asset." So, carefully, Sonya figured out what she wanted for herself while weighing the expectations she felt from her mother.

Natalia, Puerto Rican and thirty-eight, grew up in South Carolina and recounts the problems she experienced when her perception and her mother's perception of what was permissible were at odds. "Mom was always very careful to make sure that I wasn't dressed too promiscuously, because it would relay the wrong image. You just had to have a sweet, unassuming appearance. Nothing sexy, nothing spicy, because being Latina was spicy enough. She had definite opinions about femininity. There were definite things that girls should and shouldn't do. She was against me running track in high school, because boys did track and not girls. When I was in college, she had definite opinions about me lifting free weights. She told me I was going to be too *macha*. She never said anything about my weight when I was growing up, because I was always thin. The second I started putting on weight, she told me that I was getting too fat. She still has lots of opinions about my weight and body shape."

These tensions between parents and teenagers may seem typical across cultures, but it gets more complicated when the disagreement is culturally charged. Gil and Vazquez cite psychological experts in their book, noting, "[P]sychologists Jose Szapocznik and William Kurtines have found that Hispanics tend to develop self-esteem problems if they're finding it hard to integrate two cultures. . . . Unquestionably, the struggle to weave Hispanic tradition and North American innovation can make for a great deal of unhappiness and self-doubt if it isn't understood and dealt with for what it is."[3]

Clothing and makeup were lightning rods in many of the homes of the women who participated in the Growing Up Latina Survey. While some women said they were able to dress as they chose, other women's answers varied when it came to the question: "How did your family expect you to dress and present yourself in public?"

One woman wrote, "I always had to wear makeup. I was raised by my grandparents, and my grandmother does not leave the house without putting on her makeup. She always makes sure I put on lipstick before leaving the house, too."

For some, lipstick was not enough. "My mom always told us that when stepping out, even to the corner store, to put at least lipstick and some perfume on," one interviewee wrote.

Another noted, "I would get upset about not having enough variety of clothes, and my mother accused me of wanting to attract male attention. At times, I would change at a friend's house before going to clubs, because my parents felt that clothing that was too exposing was inappropriate."

One woman was allowed to choose her own clothes, but she paid for that liberty. "I would be shunned if I wore anything trendy, or told that I looked *loca*. My dress, they felt, reflected poorly or positively on my parents."

Another commented on the lengths she had to go to in order to achieve the look preferred by her family: "When I was younger,

I wore dresses. When I got older, as long as I was presentable—meaning pants pressed, shoes shined, hair neat, nails clean—I was fine."

The notion that a woman's dress reflects on her whole family was prevalent among the survey participants. "When I was a kid, my mother used to dress my sisters and me in the exact same fluffy dresses. Most times, we were way overdressed for occasions, and that was a bad thing in the eyes of other kids, because we couldn't play as freely. It was a pretentious detail on my mother's behalf," wrote one of the women. Another shared, "I was expected to dress and present myself properly, neatly, ladylike, and most importantly not to embarrass my family."

One woman echoed this sentiment, writing, "We never left the house without being *bien planchada*. It was from my mother's fear of what the public would think and say if we were to leave the house without being presentable."

Some parents worried about the negative stereotypes attributed to Latinos. "As long as I didn't look like a gangbanger, with the baggy pants and bright red lipstick, they were fine. I could even wear short skirts, as long as it looked decent and not slutty. I was always expected to act proper with everyone, and especially around friends and family," one survey participant wrote.

In addition, there was pressure to be feminine, but it sometimes came with the message that there was a tipping point. Several women wrote that they were expected to wear makeup every day. They had to make sure to accentuate their best features, while also being cautious not to put on too much.

One woman noted, "My female cousins and I were always taught to carry ourselves like *muchachas serias* and to dress appropriately for our age. I wasn't allowed to wear makeup until I was sixteen, and even then it could not be any loud colors. My mom did not mind me being fashionable, but I had to wait until I was mature enough to wear grown-up clothes."

Another woman said, "My jeans should be tight enough to show off my curves, but not so tight that everybody noticed it."

One woman recounted how she discovered hairspray at the age of twelve. "The style at the time was to tease and spray your bangs straight up, almost like a brick standing on your forehead. My mother was incensed, telling me that I would never, ever look like a *chola* in her household. She wanted my sister and me to be ladylike at all times. Light makeup (pinks and mauves), hair pulled back in neat buns, pearls. She didn't want Sandra Dee daughters, either, but my mother certainly would never allow baggy jeans or T-shirts. Ever."

For some of us, that tipping point was actually a tipping place. Many women, regardless of their country of origin, expressed that they were allowed to wear whatever they wanted in their home countries, but as soon as they came back to America, whether because they moved here or because they were returning from a vacation, their parents (most often their fathers) would take issue with how they were dressing. When they asked their parents why they could dress one way "back home" but not "at home," their parents replied that they were expected to comport themselves like *muchachas decentes*. Among the women I interviewed, there were countless things that were deemed just too extreme or inappropriate.

"We were discouraged from wearing revealing clothing or getting tattoos or multiple piercings," wrote one woman. For several women the number one no-no was a tattoo. Indeed, that was true in my house as well, which we found out the hard way when my sister got a vine tattooed around her big toe.

"Why'd you get it there?" I asked her when she called me at my college dorm room to tell me about it.

"So I can hide it when I need to hide it," she answered.

For almost a year and a half, her plan worked. But then my parents dropped by Sonia's house unexpectedly on an afternoon when she wasn't feeling well. Sonia, barefooted, led Mom into the kitchen to find bowls for the homemade chicken noodle soup she'd brought, while Dad settled into the couch to watch baseball.

It wasn't long before Mom let out a shriek. *"¡Por amor de Dios! ¿Qué tú has hecho?"*

Sonia saw Mom's eyes staring at her feet, but she acted as if it were nothing. That strategy didn't work at all, so finally she conceded what Mom already knew.

"It's just a tattoo."

"¿Solo un tatuaje?" Mom yelled back at her. "I don't know why you think that is okay. Your body is a temple. I didn't raise you this way. You are turning into an American."

This was the lowest of Mom's criticisms. Becoming an American in our house was tantamount to becoming a Satan worshipper. When Sonia walked back into the living room, she put her foot on Dad's leg.

"Papi, I have a tattoo."

He glanced down at it and simply responded, "I heard."

"Are you surprised?" Sonia pressed.

"Nothing you do surprises me anymore. Go make up with your mother," he said with the patience of Job and the focus of a man who wanted to get back to the ball game.

In the kitchen, Mom was crying at the table.

"When did you do it?" she asked Sonia.

"Over a year ago."

"You were hiding this from me?"

"Of course I was hiding this from you."

"You have been lying," my mother challenged.

"You call it lying; I call it hiding." Sonia answered.

"I just don't know, Sonia. You move out and you're not married; you find a male roommate; and now you get a tattoo. What's next?"

"Telling you I'm pregnant?" my sister answered sarcastically.

"This isn't funny. I can't talk to you anymore. We are leaving."

And for two weeks, my mother and sister, who talk several times each day, did not speak. When I think back on my mother's reaction to Sonia's tattoo, I know it was affected by several things. First, many Latino parents of my parents' generation want and hope to have a tight rein on their children. There is not a distinct line where "parent" ends and "child" begins. Autonomy is not an important value. Instead, there is an emphasis placed on the collective. Expressing your autonomy with a tattoo might be perceived as a threat to the whole. Moreover, there are risks associated with getting a tattoo that went far beyond disease in my mother's eyes. The tattoo was a desecration of God's temple. Depending on who saw it, it could also be assumed that Sonia was involved in illicit or illegal behavior. Many Latino parents want control over their children for safety reasons, but also to have some degree of say in how other people perceive both their children and their families as a whole.

Sandra, the thirty-seven-year-old Dominican who grew up with a single mother, speaks to this when she describes what it was like to grow up as the only child of a single mother. "There were a lot of tensions. I wasn't able to wear tight clothing or expose my body in certain ways. I wasn't allowed to wear makeup. Through high school and into college, I had a curfew of four o'clock in the afternoon. There was no such thing as eighteen being an adult. It doesn't matter how old you are: If you aren't married, you live with your parents. I live alone now, and I don't think my mother has forgiven me for it," she says, her voice heavy with a sadness that accentuates the fact that Sandra and her mother have not worked through this disagreement.

Katarina, thirty-seven, hails from Colombia and grew up in Chicago. "My parents, unfortunately, are divorced, and my dad is very *machista*, so my mother never advanced in terms of her education. My mother realized that she didn't like the path that she took, so she encouraged us. But she was struggling, too—with her identity as a Colombian and as a conservative—while encouraging us to be educated. She pulled the reins when we showed too much curiosity. We grew up not really trusting her point of view, because her world was quite small."

Many Latinas struggle with their mother's viewpoints. Daria, thirty-three, grew up in Oregon with parents who pushed her to move past what her Mexican roots might imply were her limit. Now a college professor, Daria sees the encouragement as bittersweet. "My mom was always pushing for education in a way that was self-degrading to her. 'You don't want to be like me,' she would say. 'You have to get a real job where you work inside a building.' They were so proud of me when I got a job at Dairy Queen, because it was inside," she says.

Twenty-nine-year-old Josette, who's of Peruvian and Colombian descent and who grew up in Queens, was troubled by her mother's actions. "I had a close but love/hate relationship with my mother because she was too weak," Josette recalls. "She let herself be stepped on."

But it was also hard for Josette—and many other women I interviewed—to engage with their fathers. "My father and I fought often. He was more typically *machista,* and abusive. I was most offended by him because of his actions toward my mom," says Josette.

Tamara, a thirty-year-old Cuban American from Miami, spoke about the distance between her and her father. "We had a typical household. Our mom nourished us and did everything, and Dad worked and came home. There wasn't too much of a relationship with him. I got into sports to find something to relate to him more," she shares.

SPREADING OUR WINGS

After coming of age in homes that had one standard for beauty and trying to reconcile it with the surrounding American culture, which idolizes all things youthful, bony, and blond, many of the interviewees pushed themselves toward college and the possibilities it might provide. But for some of them, the collegiate experience led to tensions they did not anticipate.

"Going away to school, I had a coed hall, and that was a really big problem. I was very strongly given the message that if anything happened, it was the woman's fault. If a woman received any sexual advances, it was because she wanted them. You had to show men that you were someone to respect," recalls Paola, who's twenty-eight years old and is half Cuban and half Puerto Rican. Furthermore, her parents required her to come home to Queens, New York, on the weekends, because, as they put it, "You go to college to study, not to make friends and party." That became a major battle. "Why does she want to go away when she has a family?" they'd ask. But Paola had grown up surrounded by an American culture that encourages leaving home and going away for college.

Paola's experience is not unusual. A policy brief released by the Tomas Rivera Policy Institute stated, "For most prospective college students, choosing a school to attend involves more than balancing considerations of curriculum, location, and cost. Students come from a community, a family, and cultural traditions. For Latino families especially, there are expectations for young people to rely on the family for emotional support, to contribute to the well-being of the family, and to stay physically engaged by either living at home or visiting often, participating in family events, and staying in touch. For example, in a recent national survey, it was found that 78% of Latinos felt that it was better for children to live in their parents' home until they get married, compared to 46% and 47% for whites and African Americans, respectively."[4]

Regardless of the tensions within many families, none of the women who went away to school regretted their decision.

"In our home, you only leave the house when you're getting married. Just because I chose to live on campus for college, I was called the Americana. There was never a moment where I questioned my decision, though," says Blanca, a twenty-eight-year-old Dominican American in New York City.

Attending college was not just about achieving a standard course of study. For some young women, going to college changed their relationship with their own ethnicity.

Gloria, age forty, who was born in Puerto Rico before moving to New Jersey, says, "My dad had a mentality that I didn't need to go to college. He told me that all I needed to know was how to read and write to get married and have kids. I had a vision: I wanted to go to school. When I moved to college, my parents didn't come with me. My dad didn't speak to me for two years. I had to do everything on my own. My parents had never been to college. My dad always said that I was going to kill him, and my mom always said, 'She should have been a boy.'"

But Gloria's choice to go to college opened her parents' minds in positive ways. "Once my father saw that I wasn't living with some guy and I was still in college, he was okay. I made it a little easier for my siblings."

College also led Gloria to a new understanding of the ethnicity with which she had struggled. Speaking of her high school years, she remembers, "I was the minority, and that made a big difference in my life. I wanted to fit in with all my friends who were not Hispanic." After high school, things changed. "And then, when I went to college," she says, "I realized that being different was okay. That was when I decided to learn to read and write Spanish. Once I went to college, the big difference was that I had a different circle of friends. Hispanics were just one percent of the population, but I went to work at the Puerto Rican Institute and found myself very comfortable there. I realized, *This feels comfortable, this feels good,* and this was the way it should feel. It was an awakening."

Sonya, the half-Peruvian woman who grew up in Boston, now works in higher education. She considers the education of Latina women to be one of the great triumphs Latinas have achieved in the United States.

"There is still a level of sexualizing and exoticizing of Latinas. And we are able to succeed despite that. Look at how many Latinas are getting degrees and postgrads. I am excited for that. All of these things will contribute to a lifting up of our people here," she says.

But do the numbers support Sonya's enthusiasm? In fall 2001, the National Organization for Women drew attention when it published an article revealing that Latina girls drop out of school at a much higher rate than any other group.[5] Another survey, administered by the Academy of Educational Development, cited pregnancy and marriage as the two most common reasons for dropping out among Latina girls. Other reasons included gender expectations and stereotyping, economic strains, and family demands.[6] Given this information, the future may seem grim for Latina women, but there are other numbers—including my own research, gathered from the Growing Up Latina Survey and the U.S. Census of 2004— that seem promising.

The Growing Up Latina Survey is skewed toward people who have access to information technology, an angle that might naturally encompass women who have achieved higher education. But still, in the sample of 521 women who answered the survey, 37.9% had completed some college, including those who were currently working on completing a bachelor's degree. Another 32.7% had received a bachelor's degree. An additional 10.6% had completed some graduate work, with another 15.6% holding master's or doctorate degrees.

These numbers are promising but are hardly representative of the whole population of Latinas in America. Without regard to gender, statistics for Latinos in the U.S. Census of 2004 revealed that 58% of Hispanics age twenty-five and older had a high school education, while 12% of that same group had a bachelor's degree or higher (compared to 9.2% in 1990).[7]

The increase in the number of Latino college students is what most justifies Sonya's excitement over the improvement in Latina education. The 2005 American Community Survey revealed that Hispanics comprised 14.5% (41,870,703) of the total population of the United States.[8] In 1990, 782,400 Latinos were pursuing some sort of postsecondary education.[9] In 2002, that number jumped to 1,661,700.[10]

While some Latina women had to risk creating tension within their families by choosing a collegiate education, others had their families' support from the start. In some cases, that support existed because the parents were college educated and were not concerned about the exposure their daughters would have while away at school. Other times, the parents were aware of what a difference a good education would make for their daughters.

"I was fortunate that my education was my parents' number one priority. My parents went to college, and it was very important that their three daughters go to college. Marriage was never pressed upon us. My parents are a hell of a lot more progressive than a lot of other parents. It was important for their daughters to be independent and passionate. I have the full support of my parents behind me as a working artist," says Delia, a twenty-nine-year-old Chicana living in New York City as a poet, actress, and teacher.

Alejandra, now twenty-two, moved to the United States from Cuba when she was nine. She spent her formative years in North Carolina, but her family's experiences in Cuba had a profound impact on her coming of age in the United States. "I was born under the communist regime. My mother was involved in the anticommunist movement and was jailed. It's made me much more aware of how lucky people are in the United States. We had to start our lives over from nothing. The really triumphant people are my parents, who never strayed and made sure we were educated."

TAPPING AT THE GLASS CEILING

Social expectations from home countries can play an interesting role in family dynamics. Many Latino countries favor a conservative

social structure, perhaps because of Catholic and Evangelical influences, which can feel limiting to young Latinas being raised in the
United States. While most women feel that the glass ceiling has yet to
be shattered for women in America, most Latinas feel that the ceiling
is much closer than it would have been had they grown up in their or
their parents' home countries.

Angela moved back and forth between Puerto Rico and the
United States until she was twelve. Ultimately, her family settled in
New York City. At sixteen, she returned to Puerto Rico for a family
visit. She recounts, "I was about to finish high school, and people
were so concerned about when I was getting married. The pressure
there for women is on marriage and children. You are almost defined
by whether or not you are married and have children. My friends
from there are really impressed that I went to school. I love Puerto
Rico, but I am very thankful that I am not caught up in that."

Angela is now twenty-seven, has an MBA, and has completed
a semester of doctoral work. She is keenly aware of how different
her choices could have been, especially if her family had stayed in
Puerto Rico.

"My triumph has been going further with my education and career. I beat the statistics. I always said to myself that I wouldn't be a
statistic, and that I would avoid the social stigma that exists in America
for Latinas. I've proven to people that Latinas can succeed."

In traversing a difficult path, Angela has become self-reliant—a
trait she thinks she may not have developed so fully had she stayed
in Puerto Rico.

Many Latina women in the professional world understand that
there is a stigma that they must deal with.

"The biggest challenge of my life is my wanting to be taken
seriously as an academic and professional when people look at me

and just see a Latina girl," says Penelope, the twenty-six-year-old Chicana from Texas. Now pursuing a Ph.D. in American studies, she tells me, "This might be true for all young women. You get dismissed as being a young, pretty thing. But for Latinas, people have a set stereotype of what we are." And, Penelope notes, the people holding these stereotypes about Latinos are not just non-Latinos.

"I was volunteering at the immigration office recently when two older Latina women walked in while I was talking to a male coworker. My friend walked over to them and asked if they had been helped. One of them answered, 'No, we haven't. Your secretary over there hasn't helped us.' Culturally, they understood the man to be the director and the woman to be the secretary. I try to defy stereotypes, but it's difficult to change people's opinions from a dominant to a nondominant perspective. Other Mexicans often don't see me as educated."

Penelope's experience with stereotyping within the Latino culture had deep roots. She told me another story from earlier in her life. "When I was a high school student in Texas, I was the leader of an organization for Latino students. So much of my problem was the involvement of very macho men—the fathers of some of the kids. They had a hard time with me leading things. They would talk over me at meetings, and it was okay because I was a woman."

Tensions in both undergraduate and graduate education, misunderstandings among family members, misconceptions among friends or other outsiders—all these things happen in everyone's life, no matter their ethnicity. But for a Latina who is coming of age in the United States, these experiences are amplified, doubled simply by the fact that the young woman is dealing with two cultures while trying to find her own way. Despite this fact, the women I interviewed, for the most part, revealed that they feel fortunate;

they would not trade the hard work of growing up biculturally for another option—and I am with them on that.

When I look back at my youth, I can remember that we were poor, or at least poor compared to my peers. I can remember that there were tough days filled with emotions and differences and growing pains for all of us. But I can also remember that our financial status never kept my mom from making my sister and me the most beautiful dresses for the prom. My dad took me to the library every Saturday morning and patiently waited as I walked by every single shelf, checking out a whole stack of whatever books caught my eye. It's true that they did not want me to become a gringa, but I am the woman I became—some hybrid of Americana and Latina mixed into a pressure cooker of choices, cultures, and chance—because of their courageous decision to move stateside and raise their children in a culture that held no promises, only hopes and dreams.

three

In the Name of the Father

For much of my early life, I followed the rules of my religion without question. Everything was clear and simple and good. But then, like so many young Latinas, I reached a point where I started to synthesize and evaluate my experiences with faith based on what I was going through as I matured.

The doubt, confusion, and anger I experienced are more often than not inevitable in a faith walk. Life forces the questioner to arrive at a place of understanding that makes sense of conflicting situations. In this case, a young woman might move from a relationship with religion that's delivered as a package by her family or culture to one in which she chooses the parts of religion—or in some cases the whole—that work for her.

When I was a sophomore in college, I was enamored of a young man named Trent. I was shy and he had bravado, something I loved and wanted. But I was also deeply curious about him, and that interest seemed to encourage his movement toward my soul, allowing him to climb into my thoughts. Still, I was hesitant. Back then, I operated in only the most veiled ways. I was a naive little Catholic girl on her way to womanhood—a whisper of the woman I am today.

One night early on in our courtship, we wrapped ourselves around each other under a blanket and lay on the dorm room floor to watch *Star Wars,* so drawn to each other that the movie seemed to be there only to provide background noise. Captivated as I was, the temptation paralyzed me, and so I told him that no one could know about our attraction for each other. I insisted that we really couldn't go anywhere or act on our impulses, because there were other people we needed to think about. My heart raced as I told him this, as I watched his face grow dark with something like anger, as I felt my own desire plummet.

Other people we needed to think about. The idea of protecting, considering, prioritizing other people was inherent in me. My Latino and Catholic upbringing had taught me duty and responsibility to others in ways that I couldn't explain to Trent in that moment, and in ways that would haunt me more over time. Duty. Obligation. Expectation. These were words that hung heavy on me like rosary beads, sentiments I heard other Latinas echo in their interviews. For a significant part of my coming of age, obligation and duty kept my own desire, my own dreams, in check. I couldn't pursue anything that possibly threatened anyone else, or even my own understanding of myself. I was good, a *muchacha buena,* and being *buena* meant not tumbling into Trent with the intense desire that bore down on me. Intense desire was something I was supposed to avoid. And so I shelved my attraction, pushed it out of reach, because there was no room for it in the life of a Catholic Latina.

And then, inevitably, Trent challenged me, by climbing into my dorm room bed one night. I didn't protest. We kissed, first shyly and slowly, earnestly. Then his face moved toward my ear, and in a breathy whisper, he asked, "Would you like to lose your religion tonight?"

My heart tripped over itself in the pause that followed. In the background, the Allman Brothers CD took up too much space as it filled the silence.

You're my blue sky.

You're my sunny day.

I'd never talked about religion with Trent; it wasn't my way. Sure, I was raised Catholic. But my Catholicism was a silent thing, a thing between God and me. Not something that anybody noticed (except for a couple of high school boyfriends who realized what *wasn't* on the agenda for our weekend dates). Not something I ever talked about aloud. I wondered what Trent thought he knew about me in that moment. Did he assume I was a virgin because I was Catholic, or did he just know that I was a virgin and thought maybe religion played a role in that choice?

During that long pause between us, I considered his offer, considered the larger question of losing my religion, knowing that Catholicism had not been the only thing keeping me chaste. It was as much about my own search and desire for integrity in intimacy. I didn't want to be foolishly vulnerable. I wanted to matter to someone for reasons more than just sex; I wanted to matter because of who I was.

Now I don't remember how I answered him. I don't even remember what happened next. But I know that we never had sex, not that night or any other night. This, despite the fact that there was something definitively carnal about our attraction, and something so sweet about our familiarity. And yet there was something so painful about our guilt—or at least my guilt.

Guilt. It creeps into the soul of Latinas in a way that's practically imprinted in us at birth. We are raised to be part of a larger whole, to be devoted to something—family, men, religion, housekeeping—

other than ourselves first. Lose that sense of obligation, and you lose yourself and your way. Veer off course, and your stomach plummets, reminding you just how far you have strayed from the compass of self-understanding that your culture and faith have ingrained in you.

I didn't know myself—didn't trust myself—enough to move beyond that imprinted message when it came to Trent. He was new to my world, and my obligation to him did not trump my duty, my obligation, my expectation. More important, my obligation to myself was confounded by faith-based rules that had been drilled into my mind from a very young age. I didn't owe Trent an explanation as much as I owed God certain right actions. And the God of my understanding, at that point, was still the God that had been handed to me in my childhood. Back then I was still a Buddhism class, a summer internship in a faith-based program, an Anne Lamott book, and several life experiences away from meeting the God of my own understanding—the God that would provide me with comfort and gentler, more yielding guidance in my adulthood. So it was that religion shaped a significant part of my coming of age—and the coming of age experiences of many Latinas, though each of us traveled our own very different path.

ROOTS IN FAITH

Generally, people think of Latinos as Catholics. And that's not completely off base. Many Latinos are Catholic, but not to the extent that it's assumed. In my own family, only my mom's side of the family is Catholic. My father's side, with the exception of my grandmother, is mostly Presbyterian.

Among the women I surveyed for this book, 72.6% listed Catholicism as the faith or spiritual practice that influenced their upbringing; 4% were Protestant; 4% did not practice a faith; 3.4% were evangelical Christians; and 1.9% listed Santería, a hybrid of Catholicism and traditional Yoruba beliefs. Small numbers were attributed to the Mormon, Jehovah's Witness, Baha'i, Baptist, Seventh Day Adventist, Buddhist, and Jewish faiths. Many women said that their faith is still a significant part of their life journey, and 32.7% said they are members of a religious community today.

Serena, who's twenty-five and grew up in Charlotte, North Carolina, dreams of the day when she will be married to a fellow Catholic in a cathedral in Nicaragua, where she was born.

With pride, Serena tells me, "I grew up praying the rosary in the morning, at lunch, in the afternoon, and at night. We went to church every Sunday. It played a huge part in my life." For her, one of the principal factors in finding the right partner is finding someone who can share in this aspect of her life experience.

Joanna, the twenty-two-year-old Chicana from San Antonio, Texas, grew up Catholic and is now an Evangelical. "I grew up Catholic, but stepped away from the Catholic faith to be a more evangelical Christian," she recalls. In college, she attended and was significantly impacted by a La Fe conference—a Latino fellowship ministry sponsored by InterVarsity Christian Fellowship.

"We learned about our awareness of being Latino," says Joanna, "of carrying that with pride. We learned there is a specific reason why God created every individual at that conference to be of Latino heritage. Leaving the conference, we were reminded that it was important to pass this gift on to others who were Latino. It affected me a lot, knowing that we are wonderfully made. In that Christian community, I am respected as a woman."

Before college, Joanna's Latino heritage was not important to her. This conference sparked in her a greater awareness of her culture, helping her to embrace her ethnicity. And it also gave her a jumping-off point for her faith walk. In fact, the two went hand in hand: It was having the space to own and revel in her religion that allowed her to find connection to her background.

Frances, who's thirty-five and Colombian American, was raised Catholic in New York City. And while she remains a Christian, she also feeds her interest in other faiths. She credits her upbringing in Catholicism and its belief in good works for her continued sense of compassion.

"For as long as I can remember, my mom has been really strong in her Catholic faith," she tells me. "We went to church as a family. My mom has always been about caring for people. We were always giving things away, and not because we had a lot. Her care and compassion really made an impression on me."

Many women noted how Catholicism, with its emphasis on good works, encouraged their investment in their community. In fact, one of the benefits of being encouraged to be other-focused is the way that it allows people to move past themselves and feel empathy for the suffering of others. The altruism encouraged in Catholicism and other faiths is invaluable for living a compassionate life, but, like anything done in excess, taking it too far can starve someone of her own necessary care.

Thalia is a twenty-seven-year-old Chicana who also hails from San Antonio. She self-describes as a "very strongly practicing Catholic." Her familial history and circumstances are ingrained in her devotion. She is the single mother of a two-year-old daughter who was born out of wedlock. "By the time I was three years old, I was leading the rosary at church. I was a Eucharistic Minister and Lecturer in high school. Truthfully, I started to get turned off from it because of the way we were pressured to tithe. When I came to college, I started going to a student Mass, but then I got away from the church. After the birth of my daughter, I circled back around."

When I ask Thalia about the circumstances of her pregnancy, given the fact that she'd been raised so devoutly, she tears up. Her experience highlights a truth that some young Latinas experience: Because they are taught to be giving to others, and even to yield to them, many make the choice to please and trust their partners by forgoing the use of protection, believing this will increase their partner's enjoyment. Many even believe that their partner knows more than they do when they promise—or insist—that nothing will happen. Months later, these women can find themselves pregnant or with sexually transmitted diseases.

Thalia says, "I started experimenting with who I was outside of the house and away from the boundaries that had impacted me growing up. I had been with someone for four years, and we didn't use protection. I got into a relationship and believed I was going to be a homemaker, but then, when that didn't work out, I found myself making the best of what could have been a bad situation. I feel guilt, but I am lucky that I have a forgiving God."

WALKING THE WALK, TALKING THE TALK

Many women addressed the fact that their faith, whether Catholic or not, directly influences how they live their lives.

Selena, twenty-two and of Honduran descent, was raised in Minnesota. She grew up in the Baha'i faith, a Persian religion that emphasizes the oneness of God, religion, and humanity. "I grew up with very good morals. My religion believes in racial harmony, and that men and women are equal—and those are things I apply to my life," Selena says.

One of the women who responded to the Growing Up Latina Survey is a Buddhist. She offered the following: "My Buddhist principles had a huge influence on me in high school and college. I became a lot more self-assured, more outgoing, more thankful, and positively in tune with the environment around me."

For Latinas like these two, who grew up with less common faiths, the female experience is influenced by ideas that aren't necessarily promoted in the Catholic religion. Their coming of age experiences had unique spins that made them different from the more male-dominated Catholic faith, although not all respondents felt limited by the standards within Catholicism. Several survey respondents, many of them Catholic, had strongly positive experiences with their faith or spiritual practice over the course of their preadolescent and adolescent years.

One of the survey respondents wrote, "I was very gung ho. I wanted to do my First Communion, Confirmation. I wanted to go to church. My mom went but never pressured me, so there weren't really any expectations. My faith influenced my decisions a lot. I chose to be abstinent because of it. I chose not to drink or do any drugs."

Another woman shared, "My Catholic upbringing made me feel like God was always watching me, and it served as my backup conscience. During my adolescent years, I did my Confirmation, which solidified my relationship with God and also helped me through some difficult times. I carry my faith with me to this day. It continues to help me believe that I can achieve anything, and that life takes you through various struggles. So in the end, the road well traveled will be there, waiting for you to continue your journey."

Esme, twenty-four and Puerto Rican, was born in Long Island and now lives in North Carolina. When asked to describe what she loves most about herself, her faith is the first thing that comes to mind. Her voice lilts with her conviction. "My faith is the number one thing in my life. I have inner peace about salvation and what I am doing in my life. A lot of times when I feel bad, I pray or read my Bible," she says.

In fact, Esme credits her journey as a born-again believer, an evangelical Christian practice, with positively shaping her self-image and her idea of women in the home. "God thinks I am beautiful, and he looks at your inside, not your outside. I appreciate the way the home is set up, where the husband is the head of the home and the wife is the helpmate. I never saw women as doormats. I see being a woman as a high calling to be a wife and supporter of a husband," she says.

For these women who grew up with a close bond with the faith tradition of their upbringing, the conflicts they felt as they came of age may have seemed less dramatic, because some of their actions and options were tempered. Their faith kept them from doubting some of their decisions and acted as a guide during times when options could be overwhelming.

Religion even had a significant impact on some of the women who felt their family members were more casual in their relationship to faith.

"Coming from a Catholic family that was not very religious (but one that believed in morals and ethics and being a decent person) influenced me a lot in not being sexually active at a young age and not being tempted to do drugs or any wrongdoing or violent act. My family's expectations are very high, and I tried my best to meet them out of respect for what they had taught me and respect for what Catholicism teaches us," wrote one survey respondent.

LOSING OUR RELIGION

While some women feel that their faith shored up their confidence and helped them make decisions during their coming of age, other Latinas took exception to the control and gender differences they found in their childhood faiths as they matured.

Twenty-six-year-old Yvette was born in Peru and moved to New York when she was seven. She shares, "I was raised Catholic, and that helped me not rebel and follow the strict principles which were enforced by my mom. Hispanics try to fit certain ideals when they come to America. When you are growing up, you are more impressionable, and you take everything to heart. People tell you not to be a certain way, so you change. I decided not to be Catholic when I was in college. I was religious because it was a cultural thing, yet a lot of things in that religion made no sense to me. There are a lot of contradictions. It favors men, and I have problems with that. When I took theology classes in college, I realized that I did not believe in religion. I believe in God. I just don't support any religion."

Elsa is a twenty-one-year-old of Venezuelan descent who grew up in Florida. Her critique of Catholicism led to such tension in her family that she doesn't feel comfortable telling them where she stands on the issue now. "I haven't told my parents that I am atheist or agnostic," she says. "My parents are both Roman Catholic. When I started to ask questions, my father told me, 'You just need to believe.'"

Some families stop practicing a faith because of how it conflicts with other things that take priority in their lives.

Clara, twenty-nine, who's Peruvian American and lives in New York City, was raised Catholic, but then the challenges of being part of an immigrant family meant prioritizing other things over religion. The family dropped their religious practice and stopped going to church, realizing they needed to take control of their financial situation. Today, Clara is converting to Judaism, as she prepares to marry a man of Jewish descent.

Clara is not alone. Many Latinas find a new way of incorporating faith into their life as a result of relationships or political interests.

Brenda, fifty-four, is of Mexican decent and grew up in Texas. Religion, once a major force in her life, became a source of conflict and tension. While she mourns the fact that some of her family's rituals are no longer a part of her life, she is confident of who she has become.

"Religion was a major force in our home when I was growing up. My mother prayed the rosary all day and required her family to kneel at the end of every day to pray the rosary together. All of us had to attend catechism and achieve Holy Communion and Confirmation. Attending church and going to regular confession were expected of each and every one of us, except our father, who got away from having to do these regularly, being that he was the 'man of the house.' My mother always gave her children *la bendición* and continued this practice into our adult lives. This was something I came to love and appreciate, and now that both of my parents are dead, this practice no longer survives. Once in a while I find myself giving a rote blessing to my sons and my grandbaby.

"My mother raised her seven daughters with a belief that vanity was the devil's work, and that we should not love ourselves to the point of obsessing over our appearance. Also, we were taught that sex was something to be done only for child-producing purposes, and that it was a woman's God-given *duty* to 'satisfy' a man's 'needs.' So, we had to look good to attract a man, but not look good for vanity's sake. Due to the negative experiences I had growing up Catholic, I quit practicing Catholicism when I moved away from home to attend college. Today, I do not pray the rosary, attend church regularly, or practice confession. Sometimes when I travel, I will say a little prayer for our safety, and I do pray silently to myself on a regular basis. I am a very spiritual person, but not a religious one."

Josette, the twenty-nine-year-old from Queens, New York, identifies as bisexual. The gendered associations she saw in Catholicism were difficult for her. "There was always a sense of feeling guilty, and the guilt made me want to do what was right. I had this idea of a woman's sexuality being pure and something we needed to protect, and men's sexuality as his nature and something he couldn't help. It stressed the importance of being a good girl and told me what I should do," Josette tells me.

"When my mom died," Josette continues, "I tried to find a place to fit in, and I read a lot about religious institutions. I didn't want to associate myself with that. I believe in something beyond us, but I don't practice."

Today, Josette is married. Her husband is Chilean, though he was raised in France. His European sensibilities and her decision to turn away from formal Catholicism have liberated her from some female sensibilities and stereotypes that she found limiting.

Joselyn, who's Chicana and twenty-three years old, grew up in Brooklyn and now lives with her boyfriend, something that would be frowned upon in many Catholic households. "I stopped believing in Catholicism when I was twelve or thirteen," she says. "Going to Catholic school, there are so many restrictions on how you can behave and how you dress. I thought it was so strict. It didn't make sense to me that if I didn't go to church every week and died, then I wouldn't make it to heaven. I don't believe in going to confession to get forgiveness for my sins. I believe in a God and an inner light, but Catholicism didn't make sense for what I believed in my heart."

Thirty-year-old Carolina, who's Puerto Rican and grew up in New York City, started experiencing her own criticism of Catholicism when she went to college. "Religion reinforced that part of my family's culture that believed the role of the woman is to be a good wife, cook a good meal, and serve her husband. Religion had a lot to do with how I first perceived a woman's role. When I went to college, I realized that this was not fair. As women, we have to work twice as hard."

The survey respondents had profound insights to share as well. One respondent felt manipulated by Catholicism. "Being Catholic was difficult, because so many traditions, beliefs, and dogmas were unexplained. It was just so, and we had to accept it. Any deviant behavior was said to be against God, the Bible, and Jesus. That never made me feel good. I had no spirituality, just faith, hope, and fear—and a desire to maintain religious traditions, because our family life and events revolved around them."

Another respondent wrote, "I stopped attending all church-related activities at the age of thirteen because I could not stand the hypocrisy. I did not want to be a part of something that made me feel so ashamed of myself and think of myself as a sinner all the time. It didn't do much for my self-esteem."

And a third confessed that she "hated growing up Catholic. Childhood was bad enough without being part of a religion based on guilt. I always felt nothing I did was good enough. Growing up, my religion was a burden, instead of the support system I feel church should be."

GETTING BACK TOGETHER WITH GOD

As I listened to these women's concerns, my mind turned to Mujerista Theology, a movement derived from Liberation Theology. Originally conceived in the late 1930s and sometimes called Christian Sociology, Liberation Theology's main premise is to examine and execute theology from the perspective of the poor and the oppressed. Although its initial influence was among Catholics, especially in Latin America, an admonishment by Pope John Paul II and opposition from Pope Benedict XVI have diminished its appeal to Catholics, although it's still influential among some Protestants.[1]

Mujerista Theology takes Liberation Theology and considers it from a Latina perspective. First conceived in 1987 as Hispanic Women's Liberation Theology, it identifies its three main goals as the following: (1) creating a valid voice for Latinas while providing a platform for the voices of grassroots Latinas; (2) developing a theological methodology that seriously considers the religious understanding and practice of Latinas as a source for theology; and (3) challenging theological understanding, church teachings, and religious practices that oppress Latinas.[2]

I was twenty-six and heading to live in the Amazon region of Brazil for a month, with ten students in tow, when I first heard of Liberation Theology. The more I learned about it, the more I felt a deep relief that some practice among formalized religions was acknowledging, embracing, and championing the poor. It affirmed the God of my understanding and gave me a language for my views. Much like the way in which Liberation Theology revolutionized the faith walks of people in poverty, I believe that a wider dissemination of information about Mujerista Theology would help many of the women I spoke to reconcile the disparities they feel in their faith traditions.

Some women spoke of experiences in which their families revisited or began a faith practice as a result of their difficulties.

"The thing about being Cuban is that Castro did away with a lot of traditions. I am a practicing Christian, but that was something my family had to come to on our own. We didn't belong to a church in Cuba. We didn't celebrate Christmas or Easter until we came to the United States," says Alejandra, a twenty-two-year-old living in Charlotte, North Carolina.

Some Latinas returned to faith after going through periods of doubt in their youth.

"My mother was very religious and still is. We had tension about that, because I wanted to do everything the opposite. She wanted us to be virgins until we got married, but then if you went to church and confessed, you were forgiven. I felt like the Catholic Church was hypocritical, because it wasn't very good to women. Now I feel better when I pray. It's important to me," says Claudia, thirty-four, who's Ecuadorian and grew up in New York City.

Blanca, the twenty-eight-year-old Dominican American who lives in New York City, had a different take on religion once she went to college. "I honestly did not become religious until I went to college," she says. "I was in a completely different environment and was exposed to things I had never been exposed to up to that point. I always said I was Catholic, but it was because my family was. Being away from home, I prayed more."

Ava is twenty-four and also Dominican American. She was raised in Rhode Island, and changed her faith from Catholicism to evangelical Christianity. "Growing up, I went to church because I had to, so it didn't really influence me. Now, as a born-again Christian, my faith has everything to do with my life—the way I dress, talk, think. My confidence grew after becoming a Christian.

I learned to look at myself the way God looks at me, and I was finally able to tell myself that I was beautiful. With my sexuality, I've learned how to respect myself a lot more by deciding to practice celibacy. None of this was the case when I was a Catholic."

Lisette's confidence also grew when she embraced her faith. As a child, she was raised Catholic, but it is only as an adult that she has embraced its meaning in her life. "Faith was never that important to me when I was growing up, but now that's changed. These days, it guides my life. I respect and value myself because of my religion. I truly believe in it, as opposed to believing in it because I was told to. I am so much more myself. I am the way that I am because God made me that way," says the twenty-year-old Puerto Rican from Manhattan.

Religion helped Lisette come to a sense of clarity, and as a result she exudes a confidence that wasn't with her in her teens. Asked if she considers herself attractive, she answers with an emphatic yes, and then proceeds to detail how she made sexual choices she wasn't proud of when she was younger in order to feel attractive to men. Her faith, however, now makes her feel a greater responsibility to herself and her values, rather than to the wants of a partner.

One survey respondent felt that choosing to have faith can be empowering: "Of course there are expectations. I had to be a good Catholic Mexican American daughter. My behavior was a reflection of my soul. I was expected to attend Mass on Sundays, and Holy Days of Obligation, church events, choir, catechism; to be an altar server; et cetera. I was expected to not bring shame to my family name. At first I resented it, but then I realized that I own my faith; it does not own me. As I've learned more about my Catholicism, I have come to love my religion more."

Jesse, twenty-seven and of mixed European and Mexican descent, lives in California. Today she can discuss her choices with her mother more openly than when she was younger.

"She wants me to be Catholic, and it doesn't resonate with me anymore," she says. "I feel more connected with spirituality and Buddhism. My mom has placed an importance on remaining connected to what our families have been taught over generations. Whether it's food or songs, she tries to keep traditions alive. She is okay with challenging some of the patriarchal traditions in the Latino community, though. She doesn't think you have to have kids. She has a lot of consciousness around being an independent woman and not depending on a man. That's somewhat different from what our culture typically expects from Latinas."

This openness in dialogue between Jesse and her mother has created a space where Jesse doesn't feel the need to turn stridently away from the faith of her upbringing. Instead she feels like she has options. She is incorporating traditions that informed her upbringing, taking pieces of what she grew up with and mixing them with her new understanding of faith, thus forming a mix of religions and values that honor the woman she is today.

SEX, SINS, AND SACRIFICE

While she has benefited from her mother's attitude, Jesse has not told her mother about her bisexuality. She does not yet feel that her mom is progressive enough for that. And she's not alone. There are other women who wonder how their sexuality can have a place in their spiritual practices.

One of the survey respondents noted that her religious upbringing "led to the internal shame that I feel about being gay. It truly thwarted my self-perception. I still struggle with this, even though I've come a long way."

Camille, the twenty-seven-year-old New Yorker who's of Colombian and Dominican descent, struggles with the guilt she sometimes feels being Catholic but is not ready to give it up. "I practice my faith more than my mom, sisters, and aunts," she says. "There were certain things that were expected of us ethically—to be a good girl, a respectful girl, and not to throw yourself at guys or be provocative around them. I always felt guilty about how I acted around the opposite sex. To this day, I still have a guilty conscience about doing things sexually. It doesn't allow me to enjoy anything."

It is interesting to consider Camille's position and her language. She doesn't compare her faith practice only to the practice the women in the family. And she has internalized the feelings of guilt that seem to riddle Catholic-raised women more than Catholic-raised men.

Others shared a pro/con approach to reflecting on their religious upbringings.

"There was definitely a Virgin Mary complex planted in my upbringing that screwed me up. However, there was an expectation to be a good person, which I think had a positive influence," one survey respondent wrote.

Another shared, "Because the Catholic faith and tradition was such a huge part of my upbringing, it's interwoven into every piece of my life. I was encouraged to go to catechism classes, and I participated in a number of Catholic teen retreats that brought me closer to my faith and introduced me to other Catholic teens. I eventually became the president of my youth group organization. The lessons I learned through my catechism classes focused very much on abstinence and gender roles. As a female, I was expected to be chaste until marriage. It was a pretty conservative parish, and I soon real-ized that there were some ideals I did not agree with. In particular, I recognized that women did not hold positions of power in the church, although they could be nuns. Yet, in our church, most of the women were the movers and shakers. When it came down to business, our pastor was a *machista,* and that really bothered me."

The respondent found a way, however, to use these troubling issues for empowerment. "Although it did not turn me away from my faith, the whole experience did make me a feminist, determined to stand up for my belief that women should be treated equally and given the same opportunities. I took to heart the lessons about be-ing respected by men. And in the end, it made me realize that my body was a temple that I should protect and only share with some-one I was comfortable with and who respected me."

The guilt felt by some of the women brought up with strict faiths was palpable.

A survey respondent wrote, "We three girls were not to have sex until we were married. My brother was an exception, but that was unspoken and understood. I repressed my sexuality, my sexual everything. I wasn't supposed to feel pretty, because I might encour-age lascivious thoughts—my own and those of dirty pedophiles."

Some women made deals with their faith. One survey respon-dent wrote, "Though I went to Catholic school, I didn't let that stop me from doing what I wanted to do. In high school, the times when I thought I was pregnant, I made promises to Jesus or the Virgin Mary, saying that if I wasn't pregnant, then I would go to Mass or be eternally grateful."

Eva is a thirty-six-year-old New Yorker of Puerto Rican de-scent who felt frustrated with the gender differences she noticed within her faith. Her sometimes difficult home situation made her question the very existence of God. When I spoke to her, I could hear that she still bears wounds from her early experiences in the Catholic Church. "I went all the way up to Communion, and it supported all the messages that I was getting at home. Worse than that, I felt a strong male presence in the Church, and the males in my family weren't present. They were either out drinking or working, but predominantly drinking. I got the message that women were volatile and sinners. I started to feel like there was no God with what I was going through at home."

One survey respondent shared an experience of coming to a crossroads, where she was faced with an especially difficult situation. "Religion was in my life every single day. I went to Catholic school all my life, and my parents took us to church every Sunday. I spent a good amount of time praying and, most especially, feeling guilty about everything. I tried to keep my virginity until marriage. That was my cherished goal, but I was date-raped, and blamed myself for it. Losing my virginity in this way, and because I had vowed to wait until marriage, traumatized me."

This is one of the places where faith becomes a slippery slope. It's like a geometric proof, and the givens in the equation state: 1) To have sex before marriage is a sin; and 2) Fail to repent for sins, and you will go to hell.

For this survey respondent, trying to prove that she did nothing wrong while grappling with the rules she had been taught about expectations was impossible. This is where religion can defeat young Latinas who are trying to reconcile with some of their coming-of-age experiences. If the rules are hard and fast, there's no room for the gray situations we often encounter. And the guilt that sometimes comes with religion can become too much for a teen or twentysomething (or even a thirty- or fortysomething) to bear.

I know many women, of all backgrounds, who offered a deal to God in order to avoid the punishment they felt was inevitable for their sin of having intercourse. Perhaps if they were willing to bear the responsibilities of their actions in another way, they would escape the fate of a more public consequence: pregnancy.

I wonder how many young men in general, and Latinos specifically, make those same deals—how many toss and turn through the night after sex, feeling both sick about their God and sick over whether or not the woman they were with will call them. By criminalizing sex among young women and glorifying it among young men (all while we encourage girls to be pleasing to boys), we create an absurd double standard that fails our girls, boys, and communities in so many ways.

FACTS, FIGURES, AND FAMILY

While most people have a tendency to automatically slot Latinas as Catholic and religious, I found that the range of religious experiences among these women is vast. It seemed to be common that women came to terms with their religious experiences as they came of age. While 67.3% of the survey respondents said they are not active members of a church or religious community today, 86.7% said they are somewhat or deeply spiritual and influenced by their faith. Many women who suffered at various points due to their faith later found peace in a practice or belief that sustains and affirms them—even if it doesn't happen within four concrete walls and beneath stained-glass windows.

I am no different. My own relationship with Catholicism is filled with difficult memories, like the night Trent asked me if I wanted to lose my religion, or the sadness I felt when I realized at a young age that I couldn't be a priest—no matter how much of the Mass I had memorized. But it is also filled with moments of real clarity and hope, like the way I feel most connected to the sacred when I'm engaged in my community, when my life is about something other than myself. My religion, my faith, have made me alternately feel guilt, devotion, and duty in relationships with men, my family, friends, and even in my relationship to institutions like schools and nonprofits.

Like many Latinas, I had a spiritual role model at a young age. My *abuelita* was devoted to the Church like no one else I knew. When arthritis ravaged her knees so badly that she could no longer kneel in devotion through a full Mass, she stood instead.

As a child, Abuelita periodically visited from the island and stayed for months on end, caring for us. My earliest memory is from when I was three years old, unwittingly sitting on top of an anthill as I played outside. Abuelita, hanging laundry out to dry, heard my screams and rescued me from the swarm of ants that had collected at my feet and legs. She yanked off my overalls, hosed me down, and prayed silently over me while I recovered. Wide-eyed, I watched her lips rush through prayers, as if the speed of her "amens" could counter the speed of the poison. This was how I saw God.

During her visits, we shared a room. I would look over at her each night, trying to remain as still as possible while she prayed the rosary. She lit a small candle each morning and prayed. A statue of the Virgin Mary stared back at me from her place on my little desk every time I entered my room. Seeing the statue always made me quieter, solemn, when I entered the room. It was like I had entered sacred space that demanded certain behaviors from me. Those were the nights I prayed the hardest.

Several years ago, I had been anticipating the visit that we feared would be Abuelita's last. I arrived home to find her smaller than I remembered. She was shrinking, and I had grown. She slept in my bed, and I slept in the guest room. In the morning, when I entered my room to grab some clothes, I saw the familiar Virgin Mary. As I crossed myself with the holy water my grandmother had placed at the doorway, I came to understand that a lifetime of watching her living example of faith had informed, but not limited, the faith practice that I had grown into as an adult.

A lifetime of longing, of loving, of saying no, of considering yes, of seeing narrow roles for women, of defying those roles, of choosing reverence, of deciding that my prayers would only ask for strength or offer thanks—all of this had led to me a faith that would serve me well, because it was my truth. And this truth was from more than just what I had learned in First Communion, or during Confirmation, or by watching Abuelita pray the rosary across a dark bedroom.

Like many Latinas, I had conceived a faith practice that had room in it for all of my flaws and all of my possibilities.

four

Ay, Mami

Our earliest experiences revolve around the rules that are laid out for us, like a change of clothes, by our parents. These rules tell us what is right and what is wrong, putting expectations on us that sometimes don't take into consideration who we are.

The rules of any given Latino household reflect how the parents reinterpret (or don't reinterpret) their own past experiences through the lens of contemporary America. Especially when compounded with the push/pull of the different cultural experiences that come with being raised Latina, the adolescent years can be particularly difficult, for both the parents and the children.

Parents who lay out rules and expectations based on what they want for their children often find that their children don't see things the same way and are being influenced by another culture outside the home, one that doesn't promote those rules. Meanwhile, young Latinas grow up being hyperaware of the contrast between how their parents experience America and how they themselves experience it, and often find themselves negotiating things their parents don't understand, don't approve of, or will never know.

Dating is one of the places where young Latinas run up against the strictest rules. Without my parents having to say anything, I knew that I was not allowed to make out with boys. Other rules included what time I had to be home, what I could wear, and how much time my date needed to spend with my family. Other women talked about rules—spoken and unspoken—regarding whether they could travel with a partner, whether it was permissible to date people of the same sex, or whether they could date someone whose skin was a different shade.

When I looked around and saw the ways my non-Latina friends were dating with more freedom and less involvement from their parents, I was left with an overwhelming feeling of tension. By the time I reached college, the rules were so ingrained in me that I struggled with how to date, even when I started to fall for Christopher, a Latino whose history mirrored my own. Christopher seemed to have weathered his own personal identity storm a little better than I did—perhaps by virtue of being male, and therefore having to deal with fewer expectations and obligations.

I met Christopher within the first few weeks of school. He approached me one evening after a meeting. We shared a Puerto Rican heritage and Southern upbringing. On the exterior, he was tougher than most guys I knew. But he also had a deep tenderness that made him vulnerable and accessible. I was petrified by what I felt, acutely aware that falling for him would mean making decisions I wasn't ready to make about privacy, intimacy, and sexuality. So I pretended to care less for him than I really did.

One winter night I found myself alone with Christopher. Our attraction had reached a boiling point.

"Hey, girl," he moved toward me, and I looked at him shyly. My eyes tracked over him, taking in everything I was attracted to: his caramel-colored skin, his chocolate brown eyes, the mole on his

face. He slipped his fingers under my chin and tilted it toward him.
I closed my eyes, and we shared our first kiss.

"Come out with me," he said, and in that moment, our pattern
was born. I wanted nothing more than to be out with him, but it
terrified me too. Immobility gripped me, reminded me of the rules,
of what good girls do and what they don't do. I clung to the self-
image I'd cultivated—a sweet, innocent, impassionate girl—which
was central to my self-understanding.

"I can't," I whispered, placing my hand on his arm, and then
slowly backing away. My fingers touched the inside of his forearm
as long as they could before the distance became too much. That
moment changed everything. Christopher knew what he could and
could not expect from me. And though we circled around each other
for years, though we continued to battle our intense attraction—
sometimes succumbing with passionate kisses or weekend road
trips—I always had one foot firmly planted in the realm of immobility and the other in the realm of wanting. He shared with me
intimate details of his life, but I could rarely match his candor. I was
afraid of being direct, of telling him what I felt, of being vulnerable.

"Why are you so damn closed off?" he asked me once.

I couldn't answer him. I realized what I hadn't been willing to
admit to myself: *What if I opened myself to him, really let him have
my heart, and then couldn't ever get it back? And would I be the
woman he thought I was? Would I be good enough to have him
forever? Could he love both my gringa and Latina? Could I love
whatever woman I was in his company? And if it all fell tragically
apart, would it have been worth the risk?*

At that time, I was focused on the details about myself that I
found problematic: I looked different from the other girls on campus.

I didn't have the long blond hair and reed-thin body that were visible everywhere I looked. Instead, my body was curvy; I had full breasts that I struggled to hide so that they wouldn't draw the type of attention I was told wasn't okay. There was no flash, no flair, to me either. I wore no makeup and had an understated sense of fashion.

Because I was a hybrid, I was in a conundrum. My gringa and Latina hadn't yet learned how to live with each other in harmony. The easiest way for me to exist in college, therefore, was to just focus on being good. And so with Christopher, and others after him, I did just that.

I've since dated Latinos and non-Latinos. But the biggest hurdle for me was not about who I dated. It was about working through my defenses. I had some dating experiences that led me a step or two forward in my desire for integrity in intimacy, but then I would slide several steps back when those relationships came to a close.

These types of life lessons, these experiences, are not mine alone. But there's an intensity to them when your life is confounded by living between two cultures. Dating is difficult, especially when you're going out with someone who does not share your culture, or who *does* share your culture but has been acculturated differently. And there's a still different set of lessons you learn when the person you're dating shares both your culture and your acculturation. Dating is where so many of us cut our teeth, come into ourselves, separate from what our families want of us and for us. And for Latinas across America, dating really is an entire continent to puzzle over.

THE RULES: OBLIGATIONS AND DOUBLE STANDARDS

The biggest rule for many Latinas I spoke with had to do with whether or not they could date, and if so, when.

Carolina's parents divorced when she was very young. Her mother had a protective nature and a fear that her daughter's choices might limit her future, and this influenced Carolina's social life as a teenager. "I was not allowed to talk to boys on the phone. I couldn't date until I was in college. My mom was really stern," says the thirty-year-old Puerto Rican who grew up in New York City. "My job was to go to school and get good grades. My mom told me that I had to respect myself. I was very conscious of her words."

Lucia, who's thirty-eight and grew up in Texas, remembers being embarrassed by her Mexican parents' rules. "I was not allowed to date until I was seventeen. I was a senior in high school before I could start dating. It was embarrassing to tell someone that I wasn't allowed to date. If I did go out, I had to have an older sister chaperone," she recalls. "Sexuality was taboo. I remember asking my mom about sex, and she said, 'You don't do it until you are married.'"

Given the lack of information Lucia was given about sexuality, it's possible that what felt like overprotection ended up being helpful in the end. She knew very little about sex at a time when many kids were experimenting. By not being allowed to date, she realizes now that she probably avoided situations that would have exploited her vulnerability.

Marie Isabel—who's thirty-seven, Puerto Rican, and living in Pennsylvania—also had strict dating rules. "My date had to pick me up. My parents had to know who he was and who his parents were. If I was going to a movie, I had to be home within three hours," she recalls.

Laura, who's twenty-six and half Puerto Rican and half Panamanian, grew up in North Carolina and felt pressure from her family to fulfill a particular role—of nurturing, sacrificing girlfriend—once she started to date. "I could not date until I was sixteen, and even then it was really limited. I was expected to be a nurturer and the one who took care of others in my relationships."

When Gloria was younger, growing up in New Jersey, she resented the pressure that was exerted on her to play that role. But now, at the age of forty, this *puertorriqueña* has found peace with her parents' decisions. "There was no discussion about sexuality while I was growing up. We weren't allowed to have a boyfriend until we were eighteen, and then he came to the house for chaperoned visitations. I had a lot of resentment, but now I respect their decision and am okay with it. My dad only did what he knew, and my mom only did what she knew."

Thirty-seven-year-old Olivia, whose family hails from El Salvador and who grew up in New York City, ran into an awkward situation when she was in her mid-twenties and decided to take a vacation to Europe with a boyfriend, the man who's now her husband. "My mom began talking about the trip as if she were coming. I felt like I couldn't say she couldn't come, and so she came." In fact, Olivia, her boyfriend, and her mother shared hotel rooms on their trip. Olivia shared a bed with her mother. Olivia's sense of obligation to her mother ended up putting her in a situation that she didn't intend or want.

Many of the women I interviewed talked about how the messages they were receiving about love, dating, and sexuality were coming not just from inside the home, but from the larger culture as well.

"I got rules from the media and books—that I should get married, for instance. My parents played a role in that, but so did society and the media. My parents never spoke of homosexuality. It was expected that we'd be heterosexual," says Josette, who's of

Peruvian and Colombian descent, identifies as bisexual, and is currently married to a Latino.

Twenty-eight-year-old Paola of New York City, who's half Cuban and half Puerto Rican, still struggles with her family's standards when it comes to relationships. "I wasn't allowed to date growing up, and I am still not sure that I would be allowed to date," she says. Paola's life experiences have been greatly influenced by her parents' desire to emulate the life of their island homelands while still living in their New York neighborhood. It will take an act of courage for Paola to defy her parents' expectations and perhaps lead them to a change of perception. But before Paola's parents can change, she must loosen the grip that their expectations have on her. Paola and I spoke for some time, and as our conversation drew to a close, the resolve in her voice deepened, becoming both more clear and more audible. I don't doubt that Paola is just an affirmation away from feeling that it's okay to date for the first time.

The Growing Up Latina Survey revealed a range of starting ages for dating. While many women felt like they started dating later than their peers, 24% of the Latinas I surveyed started dating at sixteen, a common age for first dates in America. Another 18.5% started dating at age fifteen; 13% had their first date at fourteen; 9.7% first went out on a date at seventeen; and 9% started when they were eighteen. The youngest reported dating age was nine, and the oldest was twenty-five, and four respondents indicated that they had yet to go on a first date.

"KEEP THIS QUARTER BETWEEN YOUR KNEES" . . . AND OTHER SUGGESTIONS FOR STAYING CHASTE

Many women said there was no discussion of sexuality in their families growing up. In fact, in my interviews with more than eighty women, fewer than five said their parents had talked to them about sex. Most were left to their own devices when it came to learning what their parents hoped they would not experience until marriage.

Daria, who's thirty-three and grew up in New Mexico, recalls her sex education at home with her mom, who was an immigrant from Mexico. "My mom just told us to keep our legs closed and not get pregnant, because she wouldn't let us go to school and we'd be stuck in our hometown. She never talked about sex formally. She loved Donahue, and he would talk about scandalous things, and she would look at us and say, 'See?' She took the opportunity to portray what she didn't want us to be through visual images. She never sat down with us to talk about things. She used gossip to influence us."

My own sex education was a little more overt, but no more useful. After getting my mom to concede to that first date that I had begged, bargained, and pleaded my way into going on, my father presented himself in my doorway as I was getting ready. I thought he wanted to apologize for my mother's ceaseless grilling, but instead he sat on my bed and looked at my wall, a vivid collage of words and images I'd been working on for three years.

"We gotta talk, *nena*," he said without shifting his gaze.

Until then I'd been spared a sex talk from my parents, and I assumed that our devout Catholicism meant I wouldn't be subjected to any uncomfortable conversations on this topic. Certainly, there was nothing worse than hell, so why bother with warning me about STDs and teenage pregnancy? But eyeing my nervous father sitting on my bed, holding something cupped in his hand, I felt a sinking feeling in my stomach. His eyes left the wall, perhaps satisfied that there were no words related to sex plastered up there, and he opened his hand. In his palm he held a quarter.

"This quarter is for you to keep between your knees. Put it there tonight and do not let it drop until you are married. ¿Comprendes?"

I nodded, silent. It would be years before I could laugh at this incident, though it did become something of a family joke that even my father could participate in, poking fun at himself in the process. In that moment, though, I sat there stunned and silent. I already had clear intentions—convictions, even—to follow the rules of Catholicism when it came to sex. I had never disappointed my parents before, never acted in a way that would shame them, and I certainly did not want them pondering between themselves whether I was having sex. But that is what every kid probably wants—a free pass from talking about sex to their parents—and even though my lesson did not include the details of how the sperm meets the egg, their way of going about things was an attempt to let me know their expectations.

LET'S TALK ABOUT SEX

Some women bemoaned the double standards that existed in their homes when it came to their sexuality and the sexuality of their brothers. Cassandra is of Honduran descent and grew up in Miami. She's now twenty-eight years old and complains that "the guys could have girls over to spend the night, and my parents would say, 'Boys are different from girls.'"

Tamara, age thirty, who's Cuban American and grew up in Florida, recalls, "My sister and I were taught that sex was only for men's pleasure, and we should remain virgins. My brother could go around and have sex with every woman, though. My mom just didn't know how to handle the situation. She didn't want us to get pregnant, so she tried to scare us instead of educating us."

Respondents to the Growing Up Latina Survey have various frustrations when it came to stereotypes, most of all stereotypes that focus on Latina sexuality. When asked to list any stereotypes they feel exist about Latinas, the ten most common sex- and gender-related answers were the following: (1) we're promiscuous, (2) we get pregnant all the time, (3) we're oversexualized, (4) we're teen-age moms, (5) we are uneducated and let our men beat us, (6) we have no aspirations outside of getting married and having kids, (7) we are freaky in bed, (8) we all have big breasts and butts, (9) we wear too much makeup, our clothes are too tight, and our hair is too big, (10) we all have many children and are on welfare, trying to cheat the system.

One respondent opined that "the portrayal itself isn't nega-tive, it's the incessant perpetuation of it. One or two portrayals of a proud, beautiful, exotic Latina is great—but not everyone is like that. The stereotype that we are all very sexual makes our sexuality trite and common."

Sex, it seems, holds a great deal of tension for Latinas. And there's huge irony in the polarized messages Latinas receive from inside and outside the home. On the one hand, Latinas are taught by their faiths and families to preserve their virginity until mar-riage. Sex is often promoted as something that we're to provide for our husbands—for their pleasure, and to procreate. On the other hand, society holds Latinas up as the epitome of exoticism and sexuality. We see this aggressive sexual impulse in Gabrielle on *Desperate Housewives* and Rosario Dawson and Jessica Alba in *Sin City*.

It's no surprise that Latinas feel overwhelmed by the mixed messages and strong influences to behave one way or another when it comes to their sexuality. It seems that neither faction—neither family nor the media—is giving our young women exactly what they need. What would happen if the media became more diverse in their representation of Latinas, offering more roles and images beyond the stereotypical ones we're accustomed to seeing? How about more characters like the ones America Ferrera played in *Sisterhood of the Traveling Pants* and *Real Women Have Curves*? Or Judy Reyes's Carla on *Scrubs,* or Sara Ramirez's Dr. Callie Torres on *Grey's Anatomy*?

And what if young Latinas were also provided with more direct sex education by their parents? Giving girls the tools they need and educating them about sex doesn't mean that they'll run off and have sex. It simply means they will be informed enough to know how their bodies work and understand how sex works, so that they won't find themselves in a position of vulnerability when the time comes for them to make important choices. By keeping valuable information about sex from young Latinas, we put them in the position of relying on someone else for information—someone who may have selfish interests in mind, or someone who's equally naive about sex and intimacy. We marginalize young Latinas when we deny them information, making them more susceptible to the pleas of an adolescent partner who pretends to know more about sex and its implications than he really does. When we think about the disadvantaged, we often think about the poor or the uneducated in more traditional terms. But I would argue that the scope of disadvantage looms wider than that. Tell our girls nothing about their bodies, and they become more susceptible to the whims of others, a tendency that's difficult to escape once it's ingrained.

In fact, many sexologists believe that education is the best prevention against unwanted pregnancy. "Studies show that if you talk to your kids about sex and give them all the options, they are more likely to wait to be sexual than kids who get abstinence-only education or no sex education at all," says Dr. Charley Ferrer, a Latina sexologist based in New York City. "People say that if you talk to kids about sex, they are going to go out and do it, but if your kids listened to you that much, their rooms would be clean. What does happen if you talk to your kids is that they say, 'I am valuable enough to take care of myself' and, 'I don't have to go out and have a sexual relationship to learn what everyone is talking about, because I already know.'"

In terms of sexual activity, 42% of Latinas surveyed in the Growing Up Latina Survey became sexually active between the ages of sixteen and eighteen. Among those, 16% (the largest percentage) indicated eighteen as their starting age. The earliest reported age was thirteen; 4% of the participants answered with this age. The oldest age was thirty. Overall, 92.8% of the survey participants indicated that they had had sexual intercourse. The 7.2% who had not had intercourse ranged in age from eighteen to thirty-one, and 32% of those respondents indicated that they were waiting until marriage to have sex.

A March 2005 study in the *Archives of Pediatrics and Adolescent Medicine* published information about sexual intercourse habits among Hispanic and white teens. It revealed that the more acculturated the Hispanic youth, the more likely they were to have had sexual intercourse. They were also shown to be having sex earlier than white teens. Low acculturation in Hispanic teens emerged as a significant protective factor against the onset of sexual activity, since those teens were less likely to have initiated intercourse. The primary language spoken by the Hispanic respondents was used as a measure of their acculturation. Thus, their conclusion was that Hispanic English-speakers were more likely to have initiated inter-course, while Hispanic Spanish-speakers were less likely.[1]

The variation in Latina teen behavior exists for many reasons—and acculturation and whether or not one was born in the United States are both relevant factors. In a study published in the *Journal of Urban Health,* Alexandra Minnis and Nancy Padian found that U.S.-born Latinas exhibited very different sexual behaviors from foreign-born Latinas now living in the United States. According to the study, 58% of U.S.-born Latinas reported having their first vaginal intercourse experience at age fifteen or younger, compared to 22.9% of foreign-born Latinas. Also, 46% of U.S.-born Latinas reported having multiple sex partners in the six months prior to the study, compared to 16% of foreign-born Latinas. U.S.-born Latinas also had higher incidences of sexually transmitted infections. But the numbers were also troubling for foreign-born Latinas. While only 30.6% of U.S.-born Latinas reported a pregnancy (and 80% of those young women reported having an abortion), 66.7% of the foreign-born Latinas reported a pregnancy, with a 28.1% rate of abortion among them.[2] Sexually risky behavior among Latinas is indeed a legitimate concern.

Coming of age is awkward and challenging for any teen, but there are complicating factors when one grows up Latina. For Latinas, there are cultural, social, economic, and biological factors that impact our decisions, experiences, and health. In their report "State of Latina Adolescents' Health," Advocates for Youth note that while teen pregnancy rates have dropped in the last decade, the smallest decline was among Latinas. In 2000, Latinas had the high-est birthrate among all groups: ninety-four births per one-thousand women between the ages of fifteen and nineteen. When statistics were compiled in December 2001, young Latino men and women represented 20% of the AIDS cases reported among teens, although they only represented 12% of the population at the time. More distressing yet, Latina and African American women between the ages of thirteen and nineteen represented 84% of AIDS cases in that demographic, even though they only made up 26% of the population of women. In 2001, 44% of Latina high school students reported that they'd had sex, compared to 41% of white and 53% of African American teens. The report also showed that 57% of Latina teens who had sex did not use any method of contraception for their first experience.[3]

Sex education exists because it works. In fact, a study published in the *Journal of Adolescent Health* showed that when Latina mothers discussed sexuality—and their personal beliefs and values regarding sexuality—with their mid-adolescent teens, their children were more likely, a year later, to report abstaining from or delaying initiation of sex. An added bonus was that these teens also noted that they had a better-functioning relationship with their mothers.[4] Educating Latinas who are coming of age places them in a position to value their sexuality and shows them that there is a safe place to go with any questions or concerns they might have.

Zoe, who's twenty years old and was born in Colombia before moving to Georgia when she was three, shares her experience of having grown up with parents who were able to talk to her about sex and sexuality. "My parents always told me to be smart and to not be fooled by what a guy tells me. My mom told me to protect myself if I became sexually active. It wasn't expected that I would be a virgin until I was married. I feel like Hispanic parents expect that of their daughters. I want to [remain a virgin until marriage], but not because it was a rule."

Zoe exemplifies a new generation of Latinas who are coming of age today, and how they can become confident and clear about their choices and options on their way to womanhood.

DATING AND DIVERSITY

Dating in America provides an opportunity for diversity that Latinas certainly wouldn't have experienced had they been raised in their or their parents' home countries. This diversity, however, creates challenges—such as navigating the political, racial, social, cultural, socioeconomic, gender-related, and familial tensions that arise when Latinas opt to date someone who is not Latino, or who is Latino but doesn't share the same heritage or experience.

While 10.5% of respondents said that they would date only Latinos or Latinas, 36.3% felt pressure from their families to marry or partner with a Latino or Latina. Unfortunately, 29.2% of respondents indicated that they had downplayed their abilities or strengths to Latino men, perhaps due to a need to play a more traditional Latina role.

Interviewees, who were often dedicated to making progress in America while respecting their cultural heritage, shared complex feelings about dating Latinos. Some women felt that dating a Latino or Latina was a natural extension of who they were, and others felt as if it called for a sacrifice. No matter how they felt, there was no shortage of colorful commentary and consideration.

Alejandra moved to Charlotte, North Carolina, from Cuba when she was nine. Now twenty-two, she feels protective of her heritage and her family, and has an incredible pride in being Cuban.

"I feel so much more comfortable coming home with a guy who can speak Spanish and who is open about coming home to meet and spend time with my parents. I've always been very open with my parents about who I am dating, and they expect me to bring him over and stay for lunch, dinner, and to play dominoes. I do expect my boyfriend to spend time with my family, and I expect that because my parents do. When I've dated non-Latinos, they felt it was such a big deal to meet my parents. I didn't feel that I could talk to them about my family. Sometimes I felt embarrassed about the parts of my day when my family calls me for help, because I didn't want my boyfriends to think my parents were stupid or poor. My mom calls easily ten times a day, and some would say, 'Why does your mom call you ten times a day? That's weird.' That said, if I found a non-Latino I wanted to date, I would. These aren't things that make or break a relationship."

But for some women, this was a deal-breaker. Annabelle, a thirty-two-year-old Colombian American in New Jersey, cannot imagine being married to anyone who's not Latino. She's married to a Cuban. "When I dated non-Latinos, there was always difficulty for them to understand my culture and why my family was so important. I would always be very sensitive to them and their families," she explains.

But she's had difficulties with both types of relationships where her parents are concerned. "My parents weren't crazy about either type of relationship," she says. "The non-Latino was loved in the beginning and then not so much as the relationship went on. With my husband, there were class and education issues that my parents had a problem with, and immigration problems because I married him in Cuba."

Annabelle's relationship makes space for her feminist nature, and she's grateful for this freedom, because it was something she was seeking in a partnership. Maintaining her values as a feminist has not come without its outside pressures, however. "My mom raised me to be a feminist," she says. "I was always outspoken, and sometimes it backfired. In my relationship, we talk about feminism so much, but I don't consider him *machista* at all. In trying to be as equal as possible, we encounter other people's judgment of us. He is looked down upon."

For many Latinas, the idea of bridging the wide gap between two cultures seems too overwhelmingly difficult to even attempt.

"It is very difficult for me to date outside of my own culture because of the differences in language and behavior. I can't assimilate to anyone else's culture, so I can't expect anyone to assimilate to mine. It is not worth the trouble," reveals Marie Isabel, a thirty-seven-year-old Puerto Rican living in Pennsylvania.

Marie Isabel's view is informed by her desire to have her partner ably communicate with her parents and family members. She also wants any children she may have one day to be bilingual. But it's more than that, she tells me: "It's also the fact that most of my friends are Spanish dominant, and we speak Spanish most often. In fact, I would say that my day is eighty percent Spanish and twenty percent English. Even at work, Spanish is most often spoken. It would be difficult for my non–Spanish-speaking partner to be part of that circle."

Joselyn, who's twenty-three, of Mexican descent, and grew up in Brooklyn, currently lives with her Italian boyfriend. But her past relationships with Latinos played an influential role in how she looks at relationships today. "You feel like you have something more in common with Latinos—a culture, a language. You aren't this different thing to that person. They understand the type of food you eat." She says that her current boyfriend does embrace her family, which stems in part from the fact that he's also a foreigner, and so there are some similarities that feel comforting.

"I wish he could speak Spanish, but it's the respect, honesty, and appreciation that I get from him that I most like. He spends time with my family. Nothing is strange to him."

Miranda, a thirty-five-year-old Colombian American in New York, has dated outside of her ethnicity, although her parents do send the message that she should marry a Latino. She's dated Latinos and non-Latinos alike, and at this point in her life she's not opposed to her parents' expectation.

"There's just this understanding that we have as Latinos. I feel accepted and comfortable, and I can truly be myself with a Latino. I love that they understand my love for our culture, food, music, and literature," she explains. "With non-Latinos, I feel like there is something missing, and my family doesn't really speak English. Something is lost when my boyfriend can't communicate with my family," she concludes.

Carolina, who spoke earlier in this chapter, agrees. "I feel at home with Latino guys. They understand certain traditions and rituals, so they don't view them as unusual," she says.

Yvette, who was born in Peru and grew up in New York, is now twenty-six and grappling with these same pressures in a different way. At home, she was told to date Latino men. Now, because of her own sense of what's appropriate, and because of her own insecurities about branching out, she has only dated Latinos.

"My mother didn't think abortion was an option, even though she didn't want me," Yvette begins. "She never talked to me about relationships. I learned from books, TV, and school. I wasn't comfortable with intimacy and sex. I grew up in a difficult family, and in my mind, it seemed that being a woman was being weak. I have only dated Latino men because I feel comfortable with them. I was different from others when I was growing up, so dating Latinos was a safety issue."

Now she is working on being stronger and paying attention to what she doesn't want in her life, regardless of who she dates.

"Machismo was a major force in my life," she says. "The way I was brought up, women are the ones who let it happen. I had problems speaking up, saying what I wanted and what I liked. Now I am open, and I am very demanding."

Finding our voice strengthens our self-esteem and helps us become confident in the way we understand for ourselves what it means to be Latina, realizing that it doesn't have to be a troublesome either/or situation—it can be a comfortable also/and existence.

When Sonya, the thirty-two-year-old who's half Peruvian and queer identified, started dating an African American man (whom she later married), she found that dating a person of color was what resonated most with her, regardless of his ethnicity or race. "There are always certain elements in dating people of color that carry over—the sense of the importance of family, especially. With my husband and I, there's an understanding of the challenge and the conflict, the contradiction and the struggle, with ethnic identity and having been born here—the idea of not being ethnic enough."

I relate to Sonya's experience. I dated a Korean American for several years. While our cultures were different, we had a bond that was not just based on our attraction to each other. Our stories were similar, even though our ethnicities were different. We had similar challenges in our home lives and on campus. Our values and politics were similar. Our relationship helped me gain clarity about who I was and how I wanted to be in relationship to a partner, and it affirmed my life experiences in many ways. We came into each other's lives at just the right time, affirming the importance of who we were at our core, despite the differences we saw around us.

There are no easy, formulaic answers when it comes to dating. Women's experiences will vary, and the one truth across all grounds is that you owe it to yourself to take the time and energy to figure out what is right for you.

"BE A GOOD GIRL IN LIFE, A BAD GIRL IN BED" . . . AND OTHER IMPOSSIBLE DEMANDS

Many women I interviewed have had the pressure of Latina stereotypes influence their relationships, regardless of whom they dated or married.

Claudia is thirty-four and of Ecuadorian descent, and she grew up in New York City. She had her first boyfriend at nineteen and got pregnant when she was twenty-three. She recalls of that tumultuous time, "We were together for ten years but never got married. He was very old-fashioned Puerto Rican and thought that the woman's place was in the home. I went back to school, and that caused the end of our relationship. He didn't want me involved with anything. He wanted me home, taking care of the kids and the house. It was a constant fight. I fought with my parents too, because they would say things like, 'A good mother doesn't do that.' My mother never worked, and so she'd say, 'Why do you need to work?'"

Josette is twenty-nine years old. She is of Peruvian and Colombian descent and grew up in Queens. She is now married to a Chilean who is not traditional, but she went through some growing pains before she found herself in a relationship that felt authentic. She told me, "I dated an Argentinean who had old-school views on how women should behave—good girl in life, but bad girl in bed. I tried to be the perfect woman so he wouldn't go to another woman."

Josette's experience with this man had sexual consequences: "I had to fake orgasms a lot. I concentrated more on giving him pleasure and getting pleasure later. I think that came with the Latina expectation, and I think it's a female thing. It wasn't until I was with a Guatemalan guy who was open to new ideas that something started to spark in me. Then I dated some women, and that really opened me up to things. It wasn't until I was with my husband that I had my first orgasm, though."

But not all Latina women in America avoid the more traditional Latino. "I expect the man to pay in all situations. If they tell me to go dutch, then it's over for me. The man has to pick you up from the house," explains Serena, twenty-five, who was born in Nicaragua and lived there on and off for much of her youth. Serena, who now lives in Charlotte, North Carolina, also says that she wishes to marry in her native Nicaragua, in the Catholic cathedral of her family's hometown.

But there are also some ways in which Serena has been influenced by her American upbringing. "In my family, it was not allowed for a man to live with you before you married, but my boyfriend lives with me," she says in a conspiratorial tone.

Camille, the twenty-seven-year-old New Yorker who's of Colombian and Dominican descent, has similar traditional sentiments. "I have only dated Latinos. I went out on one date with an Italian guy, and the first thing he said was, 'I like to split everything,' and that just threw me off. My boyfriend likes me to cook

for him, because he came from that type of home. But I don't mind.
I really enjoy that. I like a traditional home," she says.

While Camille thinks it's important to bring her boyfriends
home to meet her family, she does not feel she needs to ask her
parents for permission about whom she can date.

I talked to several women who ran into experiences that mirrored Josette's with the Argentinean. Their response was to come
up with particular standards for dating Latino men. Marisa is a
thirty-three-year-old in Washington, D.C., who has her bachelor's
degree. She's of Puerto Rican and Colombian descent and has hard
rules regarding whom she will date. "I love my Latino men, but I
do have issues with some of them. I want them to be as educated
as I am. Educated Latino men tend to be more understanding of
modern Latina women."

Other women were absolute about not dating Latino men.
Cassandra, twenty-eight and of Honduran descent, was raised in
Charlotte, North Carolina, in a home where the boys were given
wide berth; she feels that this enabled them to become *machistas*.
Seeing it turned her off to Latino men. "I never dated any Latinos,"
she says frankly. "There weren't any in college. The ones I met
didn't have any aspirations."

Her comment reminds me of my work with young men in
gangs like the Crips, the Bloods, and La Raza while I was in college. During that time, what I came to understand from them was
this: It was exposure that made all the difference in their views of
what they could do with their lives. Offering them opportunities
they had never considered before was key. After all, how could
they envision going to college if no one they knew had ever gone
to college; if they had never seen a college campus? I couldn't help
but think that Cassandra's adamancy that the guys she dates be

educated might be more about their having a broad worldview and less about their having a degree.

Sandra, who's thirty-seven, Dominican American, and grew up in Queens, New York, wants equal footing in a relationship. Her experiences in past relationships with Latinos have made her skeptical about dating Latinos in general. "Latino men are more deep, very sensitive. They are not open to change. A little more macho. They are more passionate, more lovable in one way, but American men are more carefree. They don't put too much emphasis on arguments. They have a discussion and let it go, while Latino men hold on to it. Non-Latino men are easier to get along with. I find it much easier to date non-Latino men. American men don't get as jealous, and they hold true in their relationships."

Not every Latino man will cheat or be jealous, but Sandra has adopted an attitude and way of thinking that she feels will help her proceed more safely in relationships. And she is not the only woman I interviewed who gave up on dating Latino men after some negative experiences.

Sometimes it's a Latina's family that ends up having difficulty with the power balance in her relationship. Lucy, thirty-nine, is Puerto Rican and from the Bronx. She was married to a Latino and had a daughter with him. Now she is remarried to a white non-Latino man, and her father still sometimes struggles with the power dynamics in her new marriage. "If we're eating a sandwich or soup for a meal, my dad might come over and say to my husband, 'Is that a snack?' I constantly joke with my husband and say things like, 'I am the boss of you,' and my dad has a hard time with that—how we relate to each other. It is something completely new to him to see a man and woman relate to each other on an equal level," says Lucy.

"Latino men—and I won't speak for all of them, of course—conduct their lives in the machismo way that they were raised. For a strong, independent Latina woman, that is hard to deal with. My first husband was very jealous of me being away from him and presenting myself as independent."

Ironically, Lucy and her first husband made their peace with each other when she remarried. "My current husband and ex-husband get along really well. He was a lousy husband, but he's a very good dad. He's on good terms with my husband, because he sees the impact he's having on our daughter's life. My son [from my current marriage] calls my ex-husband 'Uncle.' I have two very secure kids because of the way we've all been able to come to terms with things."

Gloria, the forty-year-old Puerto Rican who grew up in New Jersey, also divorced her Latino husband, and it has influenced whom she is willing to date. "Not all Latino men are the same. My dad was one to cheat on my mother, and my ex-husband did the same thing—and that messes with your head. What bothered me more was that I couldn't leave the house, couldn't be with my friends. Since my divorce, I have dated Latinos, but in the back of my head, I know it won't go past friends. I know that is wrong, but I can't live with someone who has a *machista* mentality about women. I have Latino friends who have great relationships with other Latinos, but there are still a lot of men out there with that throwback way of thinking. I like to come and go as I please. I don't feel like I belong to anybody."

Ava, a twenty-four-year-old Dominican American who grew up in Rhode Island, is most satisfied dating African American men. "They treated me like gold. They see Latinas as a treasure," she says. Ava's comments reminded me of hip-hop and rap videos of the late 1990s, in which Latinas were featured prominently as objects of adulation. I felt the same general reaction when I worked in the inner city and mentioned my ethnicity, though I am a far cry from a video girl or Jennifer Lopez.

Clara is a twenty-nine-year-old Peruvian American who grew up in Jersey City, New Jersey and is now engaged to a Jewish man who is not of Latino descent. She candidly reflects on her experiences with dating Latinos. "Latinos have old-fashioned ideas about women. They say they want an independent woman, but they want what their mothers and grandmothers were. They say it is fine to have a job, but they don't truly want an independent woman. They want a woman to cook and clean and take care of the children."

Clara's family's reaction to her relationship with a non-Latino reveals the complexity—and what some might see as the incongruity—of the Latino sentiments surrounding relationships and ethnicity. "My parents are receptive to my fiancé, who happens to be white, because they think white is better."

WHEN COLOR COUNTS

Several interviewees, often embarrassed to be admitting it, revealed that interracial prejudices existed in their families. Colorism and racism are an undeniable part of the Latino experience in America. As white women are often projected as beautiful and valuable, it becomes almost second nature to value "brighter and whiter."

When I was teaching, I once offered a lesson designed to critique beauty and color standards among my minority students. On the walls around the classroom, I posted more than thirty pictures of non-white women (of various ethnicities) and asked my male and female students to use a sticker to vote for the ten women they found most beautiful. After the voting was done, I moved the photos of the highest vote-getters to my dry-erase board at the front of the room.

"What do these women have in common?" I asked.

There was silence for almost a minute—a painfully long time in a classroom.

"They're the whitest ones," someone finally whispered. This exercise is valuable, because it shows what is ingrained in us, how institutionalized racism can creep into us, even when we are minorities. It requires that we pay constant attention to what we think and how it plays out. This type of awareness will allow us to conquer the views that limit us.

Placer is of Dominican descent and grew up in Florida. Now twenty-four, she married an African American at age eighteen, and in doing so went against her mother's wishes.

"My mom always wanted us to date Hispanics or Caucasians. She was prejudiced against African Americans due to her past experiences. This turned me more toward them, which is probably why I ended up marrying one. I actually never dated a Latino. They had that macho attitude that I didn't want to be involved in. My mom didn't like my husband because he was African American. My brother is lighter than me, and he just recently had his first baby with a light-skinned Puerto Rican. My mom calls the baby Snow White, and she is more willing to take care of his babies than mine, who are darker."

Many of the women I interviewed either implied or said outright that these sentiments were generational in nature and would not move forward with the generations currently coming of age.

Blanca, who's twenty-eight, Dominican American, and grew up in Brooklyn, has dated men of various races and ethnicities but has not always kept her family in the loop about whom she is seeing.

"Latino men tend to be more controlling and possessive," she told me. "They are a whole lot more jealous and can expect a woman to serve them. White guys are, like, the complete opposite. They seem not to care. They are very easygoing—let you come and go—to the point where you think they don't care. African American men are in between white and Latino men but are more similar to Latinos."

"My family is okay with me dating non-Latinos, as long as they are white. If they are black, that is a big issue with my grandfather. I wouldn't introduce him to my grandfather unless he was the one. My mom is okay with it," says Blanca.

Angela, twenty-seven, was born in Puerto Rico and moved back and forth between there and the States for the first twelve years of her life before her family settled in New York City. She found that her parents were open about whom she dated as she came of age, but her grandmother wasn't.

"My parents didn't care much about ethnicity. They are pretty open-minded. My grandmother, however, was always like, *Don't date blacks, don't date this, don't date that.* By the time she was finished rattling off the list, there was no one left for me to date."

Sometimes the prejudice these women found in their families was exhibited against other Latinos. "My mom would say not to marry a 'wetback.' Her fear was that we would marry someone without a job. She wanted us to marry someone with economic stability, which I think meant 'white.' Subconsciously or consciously, that influenced who we married: We all married someone white," says thirty-three-year-old Daria, who grew up in Oregon and is of Mexican heritage.

Mariana's parents were Colombian, but Colombian men were precisely the ones her parents did not want her to date. "They wanted me to be with a white guy. My husband should have been whiter, lighter, and of some esteemed profession. They didn't want me to date a Colombian guy. 'You should marry up,' they'd tell me," says Mariana, who's twenty-seven years old and grew up in Dallas, Texas.

For Rosa, now forty, it was her father who expressed his concerns about her dating Latino men. Her family is Peruvian and she was raised in Chicago. She recalls what her father told her when she was younger: "Latino men have a wandering eye and a tendency to be unfaithful. With your type of character, you wouldn't last a long time with someone telling you what to do and acting *machista.*"

Dahlia, who's twenty-five, of Colombian and Cuban descent, and lives in New Jersey, has dated men and women, but her current relationship with a non-Latino is her first. "My parents think it's great," she says. "They had some skepticism about Latino men. They had all these bad stereotypes about them. They see me dating an American as a sign of progress."

Interestingly, Jesse's tension with her mother, who is of Mexican descent, results from her own closeness to her Latino heritage. Jesse, who's twenty-seven and lives in California, recounts, "My mom has stressed the importance of not dating Latino men. We have always had a conflict over how close I get to my culture. She sees being Latina as bittersweet. She sees a lot of pain in being Latina because of the racism she has experienced. She doesn't want me to end up married to a Mexican man who beats me or leaves me for another woman."

Enid and her sisters, who are of Puerto Rican and Colombian descent and grew up in Miami, received one consistent message. "My mom really pushed us to marry white guys, because she had this image of *Americanos* being good husbands. We could pass as white, but I wanted to marry a Latino. They focused on us dating people who were less traditionally Latino and *machista,"* says Enid, who's thirty-four. She and her siblings, however, had a searing critique of their parents' relationship. "We always said that if marriage is like what Mami and Papi have, then we didn't want to get married."

There is so much fear and protectiveness among Latino families who are living in America. Some parents fear prejudice, and they encourage their children to date a group that is not typically the brunt of other people's prejudices—namely whites of non-Latino descent. Others fear economic disparity because they have already experienced it at some point in their life, and they encourage their children to marry for stability, often equating financial security with white non-Latinos. And, finally, there are parents whose greatest fear is that their children will lose their culture. These are the families that often influence their children to marry Latinos.

Though many of the women I spoke to struggled with influences and critiques from their families, there are women who have had to deal with pressures from their friends as well. Penelope, the twenty-six-year-old Mexican American who grew up in Texas, is in her first serious relationship, which has lasted almost a year. She is a proud Latina who works on immigration issues and other political movements. Her friends are mostly Latina, and her boyfriend is white. The two have encountered the most criticism over their relationship from her friends.

"It was an issue among my friends that the man I'm dating is not Latino. I was definitely challenged on it. My mom actually likes and appreciates the fact that I'm dating someone who's not Latino. My mom has had a lot of problems with Latino men." Friends can be as influential as parents—and their judgments and opinions are sometimes more important, because they are of the same generation and going through the same experiences.

Joselyn, who's twenty-three and of Mexican descent, finds that her parents are open to her relationship with a man of Italian descent. "My parents trust me and my decisions. They just want me to be happy. They really like my current boyfriend." When she reflects on her parents' openness, several things stand out for her.

"Both my parents are from Mexico City, but I was born and raised in a mostly white, non-Latino area. I went to private Catholic school, and most of the kids were non-Latino white, so the friends I made were non-Latino. There were a few Mexican families where I lived, and our families knew each other, but I always had two sets of friends and basically two sets of lives: the white friends and culture, and the Mexican friends and culture. Because my parents were exposed to my friends, and then later the boys that I dated, they grew accustomed to the fact that I was just going to be friends with the people I clicked with. It's also true that there was a slight gang problem in the area we lived in, and many young Latinos were into that kind of lifestyle. So, in a way, I think my parents preferred that I dated a non-Latino [over] someone going down the wrong path. My mother always said I should be proud of the two cultures I grew up in—the Mexican culture and the 'Anglo-Saxon' culture, as she says. My parents had a sense that I was getting the best of two worlds, and saw the good in each."

KISSING JESSICA . . . OR MARIA

Some women have dated across various racial and ethnic backgrounds and sexualities, because they wanted to find the experience that makes them feel most at home and passionate.

Twenty-six-year-old Laura, who's half Puerto Rican and half Panamanian, thinks it's most important to date the person who brings out the best in her.

"When I was in relationships with Latinos, I had a very secondary role, in terms of the fact that I was expected to go along and just be there for the ride. At the same time, I felt honored and respected. In my relationships with white men, I felt very secondary and a little exoticized. The power dynamic was less equal. I didn't maintain my own power. I came after the man. My needs were never put first. When I dated an African American, I had less freedom to go where I wanted to go, when I wanted to go. All three types of men were possessive over my time and interactions with others," she recalls.

"Right now, I am dating a woman. I have more personal power within the relationship that I am in now. It is more of an equal partnership. My goals and aspirations are just as important to her as they are to me."

In the Growing Up Latina Survey, 89.5% of the respondents indicated that they were heterosexual, 4.3% indicated that they were lesbian, and 6.2% listed their sexual orientation as "Other."

Jesse, the twenty-seven-year-old woman of Mexican and European heritage who lives in California, realized that she was a lesbian while she was in college. "I was a real tomboy, and I wasn't really into the same things that other girls were into. I was into sports and playing cars. Middle school happened and it wasn't okay to be a tomboy, and so I femmed it up. I was with a great boyfriend in college, but he wasn't doing it for me. A good friend confessed that she was bisexual, and then all of a sudden it became an option for me. I didn't act on it until I graduated and moved three thousand miles away—to New York. That was necessary. I couldn't be a lesbian so close to home."

Jesse has yet to tell her mother about her sexuality. "The message was to marry one man and stay with him the rest of your life. Being gay or lesbian was completely inappropriate and could result in being excommunicated, so I am not out to my mom."

Sarah, who's now thirty and living in California, came out as a lesbian to her family when she was twenty-five. Looking back now, with the awareness that she is actually bisexual, she says she might have executed it differently. But she is proud of how her family—one parent is Colombian and one is Cuban—handled the information.

"I was in college and very 'sex proud,'" she explains about her sexual awakening. "There was a workshop on sexuality, and I thought, *This is going to be like* Cosmo. *I am going to go learn about sex*. The woman who headed it up was a lesbian, and I became very fascinated by it, but it still took me forever before I hooked up with a woman. I came out to my mother at twenty-five, and it was not very well planned. All I managed to get out of my mouth was that I hadn't been dating men for a while because I had been dating women. Now I'm at a point where I realize how hard the coming-out part was. I had a friend once tell me not to come out to my family, because I might end up with a boy. But it was important for me to identify as queer, and her advice was so Latina: 'Preserve the family unit.' But I feel like I have so many privileges. A friend asked me recently what made it possible for me to come out, and I realized that it was because I felt very adored and cherished. I didn't doubt my mother's love. I lost only one auntie in the process. I still feel a huge amount of privilege in being able to have these conversations."

When Jenny, thirty-eight, came out to her parents, their reaction surprised her. She is part Mexican and moved around a lot when she was growing up. Ultimately, she was confronted by her sister about her sexuality. When Jenny confided that she was in fact attracted to women, her sister asked Jenny if she wanted her to tell their mother. Jenny consented.

"She told them, and then there were two nights in a row of my mom wanting to talk to me. I didn't feel any negativity from her. In fact, I kept trying to substitute pronouns while I was talking, and my mom would say, 'Don't you mean *she?*'" Jenny's voice lifts at the memory of her mother correcting her, that one pronoun proving her parents' willingness to accept her.

After a visit home with the woman she was dating, Jenny was surprised to hear from her girlfriend that her parents had wanted to talk to her and cornered her. "My parents apparently had this conversation with her that went, 'We don't have to worry about Jenny anymore, because you will be taking care of her.'" Perhaps Jenny's coming out went relatively smoothly because her sister had prepared her parents; it's possible that her family was not tied in to any traditional vestiges, such as a church, that might have had held a predetermined point of view with regard to homosexuality. Interestingly, they regarded her relationship with a woman much in the same way they would have regarded one with a man: Jenny should have someone to look after her.

IT'S NOT JUST *YOUR* BIOLOGICAL CLOCK THAT'S TICKING

Sometimes the tension between parents and their lesbian or bisexual daughters has to do with the parents' desire to have grandchildren.

"My parents want me to be in a heterosexual relationship, and I'm not. My mom wants a grandchild—and I have to have at least one. They want me to get married and have kids," says Liza, a twenty-seven-year-old Puerto Rican living in San Francisco. For now, Liza is finishing law school, and while she does hope to one day have children, she says it will be with a female partner.

Parents' desire for grandchildren is indeed a point of tension in some Latino families. Some parents feel their children can't have them soon enough; others guard vigilantly against their daughters having them too young. While only 49.1% of survey respondents felt that it was important for a woman to marry, 58.6% felt it was important for a woman to be a mother. Across the board, they believed that their families' opinions about marriage and motherhood are even more traditional: 77.1% of the respondents felt like their families expected them to marry, and 78.5% felt like their families expected them to become mothers.

"In the beginning, I received lots of pressure from people wondering when I was going to have children. After a while, people stopped asking. It is a personal choice to have kids or not, or maybe a couple can't," says Rosa, the Peruvian who grew up in Chicago, who at forty is married but does not have children.

Evelyn, who's now thirty-four, was twenty-eight when she had her first child, and she did everything she could to create the family environment she thought would be best for her unborn child and future children. Puerto Rican and from the Bronx, she recounts the saga of her relationship with the father:

"As soon as we found out that I was expecting, we planned for our wedding. A week before our nuptials, my fiancé confided to me that he didn't love me and didn't want to be a father. I had to go through the humiliation of canceling the wedding and then telling my family that I was expecting. When I was five months pregnant, he apologized and said he was confused. Stupid me and my family principles—I decided to give him a second chance. Five months after our son was born, he left again. I got myself situated, regained my confidence, lost the baby weight, and was back to the independent woman that apparently drew him to me in the first place. I let him back in yet again. We had one night together, and our daughter was conceived. He told me to abort, and I agreed. I told him I had gone through with it, even though I had decided to keep the baby. Shortly thereafter, he moved to Florida to be with another woman.

"The next time I saw him, I was [visibly] pregnant, and I confessed that the baby was his. He was upset and said that he should have gone with me to the clinic, but he knew that family was very important to me and that all I ever wanted was to have a tight family. When my daughter was one month old, he played on that and proposed for the second time. To be honest, I didn't trust him or love him when we married. I figured I could fall back in love with him as my trust grew. I did get that trust back, and we had our third child, and then two years later, he had enough of me and the family life and asked for a divorce."

Now Evelyn looks back on her situation with frustration. She put her pride and common sense aside, she says, to have the family she wanted. But to celebrate lessons learned and her newly found independence, Evelyn went to a tattoo parlor and got the tattoo her husband had always been dead set against—a tribal butterfly that symbolizes her new life. Evelyn is a woman with a new voice and a new confidence that was hard earned through difficult times. We all make decisions that are against our better instincts because we feel pressure or because we think we want or should want something that is presented to us.

Mayra is thirty years old, of Puerto Rican and Mexican descent, and grew up in Chicago. Her situation started off just as tumultuously, but it had a different end result. "I was twenty-two years old when I found out I was pregnant. My boyfriend broke up with me the day before I found out. I went to a women's center, and the counselor there was very understanding and compassionate. We discussed what my plans would be if I was pregnant, and I told her that I would keep it. She said that no matter what the result was, I was going to be okay. We looked at my test together, and she told me I was pregnant. I had mixed emotions. I was happy I was going to be a mom, but scared because I would have to tell my parents, and sad because I would not be raising this child with a father."

Two weeks later, Mayra told her mom the news. "She was upset, more so because she felt sorry for me and worried about what my father would say and do. I finally told my father, and his reaction was that of pity. He felt bad because I would be a single mother, but he took it a lot better than I had expected. He didn't yell or scream. He said not to worry, that everything would be okay."

Mayra's ex-boyfriend had a different reaction. "I told him the day I found out. His exact words were, 'What? You're pregnant? I can't talk right now. I'm busy.'"

It would seem, after that conversation, that Mayra would indeed be raising her child alone, but on the day the baby was born, her boyfriend begged for another chance. Eight years and two more kids later, they are a happily married couple with a thriving family.

Claudia is thirty-four and grew up in New York City. She made the decision to stay single when she found out she was pregnant at twenty-three, although it initially made things very difficult for her with her Ecuadorian family. "It was my first real relationship. I was nineteen, so I was a bit naive. I thought if we were careful enough, I wouldn't get pregnant. I did use birth control for the first couple of years, but after that we didn't think we needed it. We thought, *Oh well, if it happens it was meant to be.* We were young and naive and thought we would be together forever," she recalls.

"We were going through some rough times when I found out I was pregnant. I was in shock, and then I thought, *Oh my God. What are my parents going to say?* I had confided in my cousin, and she told my aunt, and from there it got to my mother. She called me at school and said, 'I heard about your situation, and it's okay. We will plan a wedding, we will pay for it, and you'll say you got pregnant during the honeymoon.' I didn't say anything at first, and then weeks passed by and I told my parents I didn't want to get married; that I was going to wait to see what happened. They were like, *What?*"

When Claudia told her partner about the pregnancy, she was nervous because of the mixed emotions she had about him and their relationship. "I waited a week and then told him. By then I knew I wanted to have my child, but I didn't want to marry him. He was very supportive. He wanted to support me and help me with the baby, but at the same time, he wanted me to give up my dreams and goals to take care of the family. He told me I was going to be a mother and needed to forget about my goals; that the only goal I should think about was being a good mother and wife to him. We lived apart for a while, but eventually we moved in together. He did everything to make me feel at home and show me a comfortable lifestyle. But I was never truly happy, because he wanted me to stay home and not work or go to school. He had the typical *machista* mentality. I tried to conform for the sake of my family, but eventually I ended up despising him for trying to hold me back. I went from taking orders from my dad to taking orders from him. So, not too long after that, I moved out, got my own apartment, and lived on my terms. It felt good to have my own space, to buy things on my own with my own money. It was a financial freedom as well as an emotional one. I knew what I wanted in life and knew that I really needed to succeed for the sake of my child. I wanted to be able to give this child the world without anyone's help. I didn't want to be on public assistance or still living at home. I struggled, because I was going to school and working, but I was blessed, because my family supported me and guided me, even though they kept insisting that I get married."

Today, Claudia's family accepts her decision to not marry the father of her first child. "Now they compliment me for the decision I made to stay single and work out my life."

Although Claudia turned her situation into a positive, life-affirming experience, she cautions young women coming of age today. "It was hard, and young women should try to do it the right way. Make sure you are in love, and that you respect and admire the person. Most important, achieve as a person. Education is the key. Establish yourself, so that you don't need to depend on a man or have to stay with someone because you have no other choice. Once you've established that, then you'll have so many more options, and you can achieve much more."

PLEASURE OVER PRACTICALITY

Intimacy is a significant part of all romantic relationships, and the Latinas who shared their experiences for this book were quite candid: 90.8% of the respondents said that they were familiar with their bodies, 91.5% of them said that they had experienced an orgasm, and 73.2% described themselves as sexually adventurous. Prioritizing both pleasure and performance when intimate was important to 55.4%, while 34.3% said that their only priority was pleasure. These statistics illuminate trends that Dr. Ferrer (mentioned earlier in this chapter) has noticed in her work.

"Latinas are really getting out there, getting more experience. It is our sexual awakening—not a revolution. We are starting to want more. We want much more than Mami had. The younger generation—the ones in their twenties—are much more open to making their desires known than the women in their forties and fifties—those in my generation."

Elsa is a thirty-three-year-old adult-novelty-toy saleswoman who grew up in Chicago. She's Mexican American and has witnessed the sexual awakening taking place among younger Latinas by virtue of her profession. "Older Latinas go more for the creams, massage oils. They do more of a lovey-dovey thing. Nothing too bold like a bedroom toy. They are intimidated to bring it home. They wonder how it will make their husbands feel. They always focus on the men—something that won't make him feel uncomfortable, or like he has no purpose or is not good enough for them. Of my Latina clients who are in their forties to sixties, I would say that ten percent end up buying a toy. Of the Latinas in the eighteen-to-thirty age group, however, about sixty percent of them buy toys. They are more open minded and want to introduce toys in the bedroom. When I host sex-toy parties, these women say that they've told their partners [about the event], and [the partners] often even provide them with money to spend at the party."

Dr. Ferrer commented on sexual awareness among older Latino men. "Of the callers on a web chat I did for Univision, seventy percent were men, and they were asking questions like, 'Is it true that I will go blind if I masturbate? Is it true that I can't climax with my girlfriend if I masturbate? Is it okay if I say I don't want sex one night, even though I am Latino?' There is a lot of misinformation out there. A lot of the problem is that machismo says that our men are supposed to know it already. That is one of the major problems in our culture. We say, 'You are supposed to protect us. Give us the information.' The men are in a catch-22, because they don't know the information—but they're supposed to, so they don't feel like they can research it."

Also, in Dr. Ferrer's experience, many Latinas still rely on their partners to keep them safe. They will allow their partners to guide whether they need to use a condom to protect against STDs or pregnancy, and this can be problematic.

While some of the statistics in the survey were encouraging, others were not: 16.2% revealed they have had a sexually transmitted infection, which suggests a greater need for education and communication.

"We have a major HIV issue in the Latino community, but no one is talking about it—not even the clergy, when it should be their duty to protect their flock. We make up less than sixteen percent of the population of New York, and we have over twenty-five percent of all new HIV cases being reported. Of that twenty-five percent, fifty-seven percent of them are women," says Dr. Ferrer.

"In our culture, women aren't supposed to protect [themselves]. We protect everyone else, and our family comes first. When I do my seminars, I always let women know that we have been brought up to believe that we are nothing without our men or families, and yet without us, our men and families wouldn't exist." According to Dr. Ferrer, many start a new sexual relationship without getting tested first. "I try to bring that [issue] into my workshop. Why don't you make that part of your commitment to each other? The piece that I see about our culture is that women are supposed to keep the honor of our family—be quiet; what happens in the family stays in the family—but it is that same honor that's killing us, putting us in situations where we are raped, abused, or suffer STDs. The way that you honor your family is that you speak up," says Dr. Ferrer.

Among the women who responded to the survey, 49.2% revealed that they had been physically or emotionally threatened by a partner, and 38.4% revealed that they had been abused, illustrating a continued need to provide services to our men and women, as well as more avenues for discourse, education, and counseling. Regardless of whom we partner with, we as a people need to be vigilant—to educate our young men and women about how to be in a relationship with another person, about what boundaries are important, and about how to correctly express frustration or disappointment.

Overall, the respondents to the Growing Up Latina Survey long for positive, productive relationships that reflect the women they are today—and not just what their parents may have hoped or expected for them. The women revealed that they most of all wanted their partners to offer love and affection, followed by companionship and sexual intimacy. They listed respect, emotional satisfaction, intimacy, and equality as priorities in their relationships. They may not be headed into marriages that emulate their parents', but they are applying the principles of multiple cultures in ways that allow them to get what they most desire out of love and life.

five

The Latina Mystique

*L*atina. It's an identity that's often burdened by other people's expectations. The women who shared their stories for this book seemed to be relieved to have the opportunity to voice their experiences about dealing with these expectations.

We mine words to label our experiences, and yet sometimes those words become too much, morphing into ideas that convey something larger than what we mean. "Being Latina" doesn't mean for me what it might mean to another woman, just as my experience of being raised in America surely differs from others', even my own sister's. Over and over again, I was struck by the various ways in which we articulate our experiences as Latinas—many of which are based on the words that are put upon us, the identities that others give us in an attempt to define for us who we are. In my conversations with Latinas from around the country, I found how loaded the concept of "being Latina" is for so many of us; how such concepts sometimes set us up for disappointment, failure, and dissatisfaction; and how they are often based on things that we don't even understand.

The notion of the "Latina mystique" is one of the most prevailing stereotypes in American culture, and yet there are several other stereotypes about Latinas. Confronting how we're perceived can be an awakening. By acknowledging these images as stereotypes, we are more able to see why they're invalid, and how important it is to live our lives as examples of the multidimensional Latina experience.

When I was in my mid-twenties, the Latina in me was frustrated. She stayed up late into the night and contemplated marriage and feminism. My friends were starting to marry and have kids, and my Latin mother was dropping hints about marrying the man I described as her "Great White Hope." Meanwhile, the gringa in me tried to ignore what she perceived as unfair expectations. Mamacita had been praying for a husband for me for far too long. She lit candles and recited rosaries for her *hijita soltera*.

"Don't ask for an *esposo* in my name," I would implore over the phone line, agitated.

"*¿Y si no, qué?*" she replied, implying that she would always do what she damn well pleased.

"Pray for starving children. That's the type of prayer you call on God for." My head hurt from having this conversation with my mother yet again. I was twenty-four and absorbed in a teaching career that I loved. I wasn't ready to get married and have children. I already had two hundred kids whom I worked with every day. I just wanted to give my everything to the kids who showed up in my classroom or on the soccer field without having to worry about a husband. I felt like I had a lifetime ahead of me—and plenty of time to get married if I chose. But I was also just fine with the idea of not getting married.

My mom had gotten married in her mid-twenties, unusually late in her day, especially for Puerto Rico. I always thought her experience would make her more laid back about her children's decisions around marriage. What I was coming to realize, however, was that once we got married, she would have less stress about our lives and well-being. If she could turn over her worries to our husbands, well, then, she could feel better about our futures. I cringed at how she thought husbands would save my sister and me. I wanted her to know that one of the joys of growing up American was that I believed that I could save myself. But she wasn't hearing it.

"Oh *sí?*" she challenged, and I could see that I had done nothing to alter her agenda—except perhaps given her fodder for a prayer's postscript to make this *hijita* less "spitfire" and more *feminina*.

My own thinking went something more like this: I—the multi-ethnic child of Latino parents and an American upbringing—should be able to take from my culture what I needed and then add anything else as I went. A little bit of MTV here, some pizza there, football on Thanksgiving, no forced events where I'd have to wear dresses or makeup, dating without either party facing parental inquisition. Then I'd throw that all in with the Taína in me: loud music, spicy foods, long embraces, energetic dancing, decibel-shattering conversations in Spanish, and an extended family tree.

This sort of "I can just pick and choose" mentality was nice and neat and convenient. And yet, if there's one thing I've learned, there isn't much that's nice and neat and convenient.

Mamacita imagined us married, and tried to will my sister and me down the aisle long before we were even looking that way. As we aged, her commentary grew focused and loud. We ignored this habit, as if it might somehow seem less apparent the more we downplayed it. Mamacita only got more vocal, evoking in me a tendency to completely disengage—or, worse, a tendency to provoke an argument. I saw the way her eyes gleamed with the idea that marriage would be my salvation. Marriage, and then quickly, immediately, children. Yes, this was an assurance, even insurance, that I would become the Latina I had never fully been in her eyes. I'd always been too independent, too willful, too American. I tried to ignore her disappointment in my casual appearance, my autonomy, my dismissal of the importance of men, marriage, and children.

The idea that there was just one way to be a Latina—and a stereotypical way at that—rendered me silent, frozen on the borderlands between my Latina and my gringa. The pressure of the Latina mystique chilled me. I was coming into my own at a time when Latinas were figuring more prominently in hip-hop videos and mainstream media. *Selena* had just come out, and the Fly Girls on *In Living Color* were giving Latinas like Jennifer Lopez real airtime. And there I was, a twentysomething who favored long skirts and baggy sweaters. I didn't look the part of those Latinas, and I certainly couldn't compete with the more commonplace images I saw all around me in the South: the pretty blond cheerleaders, the fair-skinned, highlight-streaked athletes.

As I got older and traveled, I experienced a different sort of frustration. I began to encounter boys and men in my hometown and around the country who found me sexy and seductive, as well as "free game"—not because I was those things, but because I was ethnic, a girl from the Island, a Latina who would surely be able to titillate them in whole new ways. Suddenly, my Latina had to deal with the pressure to be the curvy J.Lo type, while my gringa was dealing with Barbie-doll pressure. And for who I was—a girl with a casual, girl-next-door vibe—I couldn't muster up a good impersonation of *either* of those two extreme stereotypes.

But soon I got to the point where I truly grasped the idea that nobody, not even J.Lo, is so incredibly one-dimensional. The expectations being placed on me and other Latinas were part and parcel

of the stereotypes we have to live with and move beyond—not realities. I didn't perceive myself as sexy and exotic. After all, I was
struggling with two identities. I wasn't wholly identified with the
idea of being so different that men would pay me attention simply
for my look. And yet clearly, I'd felt different enough all my life
that I yearned for connection, for that elusive friend who came from
where I did. So there I was: I couldn't be a white girl, and I couldn't
totally embrace being just a Puerto Rican. Why? Because life can't
be boiled down that simply. The Latina mystique, the Barbie mystique, mystique *period,* is based in mystery, not reality.

For years, I never really knew how to perceive myself, because
I was waiting for the answers to come from someone else. I was
waiting for someone to tell me how much of a Latina I was, or
how much of a gringa. I let other people's judgment of me determine whether I was pretty or plain, alluring or unappealing, excit-
ing or mundane.

I wanted something to resonate in me, to know that something
was right because I *felt* it; but I was grasping, because I was still
also, somehow, waiting for the confirmation to come from the outside. Ultimately, I realized that the only way I could make peace
with myself and find a consistent view that reflected the woman
I was becoming was to search for the confirmation I was seeking
on the inside. I needed to inform others about how to interpret
me, rather than the other way around. That was something that
required coming to terms with my Latina and my gringa, and then
owning both parts of who I was. The most important issue was not
how other people defined what they saw when they looked at me,
but how I defined what I felt, and how I melded my parts.

Very similar struggles, I would come to learn, were experienced
by countless other Latinas who came of age in the United States.

PERCEPTION IS EVERYTHING

"I felt a bit invisible growing up," explains Olivia, now thirty-seven and living in New York City, who has fair skin and red hair and struggled to affirm her El Salvadoran identity while "not looking the part."

"There was a stereotype of Latinas being hot, and I always thought, *Is this a joke or something?* Iris Chacón [a Puerto Rican singer and actress who became famous for her well-endowed figure and flashy performances] didn't feel right. That seemed very exhibitionist and objectified. I learned [from my family] that women are demure; women are followers; women are relationship driven."

Further complicating Olivia's discomfort were her experiences at school. "I went to a predominantly white school, and the images there were very conflicting [with] what I got at home. The message at school was that beautiful women are thin. It was good to have curves in my community, but not in my high school. Within the home, the messages were very conservative, proper. In my high school environment, there was a liberal attitude toward sexuality that was very different from home."

Thirty-year-old Carolina, who's Puerto Rican and grew up in Massachusetts, also felt pressure around the sex appeal that's stereotypically attributed to Latinas. Because of Hollywood, Carolina theorizes, " . . . a lot of guys think that we are bombshells—perfect and golden and gorgeous. That is not reality. Latinas are portrayed as sexpots, there to satisfy men's desires. We are ordinary women. We get headaches. We don't feel like having sex all the time. You never see a more wholesome side of ethnic women in the media."

Frustration tinges her voice as she considers Latino standards of beauty. "Latinos think that you have to have curves, an ass, some shape, nice long hair, nice complexion. We have to be a woman who takes care of herself—that's why we spend so much time and money in the salon."

MIXED MESSAGES

Carolina also expressed frustration over the impossible female body type that was expected by Latino men in the States, who, she says, " . . . expect more of the American ideal of beauty. You have to be skinny, which is a hard standard to meet. There are certain things you can't change about body type."

Sarah, who's thirty and part Colombian and part Cuban, got the skinny message in school growing up in New Jersey. "Be very skinny. Be blond. Be tan. That was such a challenging time for me. Act proper. Act dainty. It was a real jolt in those teen years, because I was from a working-class background, where I saw women really get in people's faces. But then my school was more middle class. I read *Cosmo* and *Glamour* religiously. It was the '80s, and I had hair up to the sky. I loved Bon Jovi and all those video hos. The message was: Be dainty, but be the video ho—but then no one will want you later."

Thirty-six-year-old Eva, who's Puerto Rican and grew up in Spanish Harlem, was used to being seen but not heard. She says, "The message was: Never let a boy kiss you below the neck. Always be completely matronly and saintly. I had an altar in my room. You had to transcend the flesh. You had to be very reserved with your body. The woman was supposed to cook, serve, and clean. It was a woman's role to be the domestic provider and fulfilling wife. You needed to treat the man like he was a king. Children sat separate from adults at meals. You didn't have an opinion as a child. There were adult conversations, and you had no place in them."

Eva's collegiate experience—several states away and in a small town—was surprising to her. "Everyone was like, *What do you think, Eva?* about this or that. I remember being flabbergasted that someone asked me my opinion in college. In New York City, the fact that I was Latina was commonplace. So in a small college town, I became somewhat exotic and special. Relationship-wise, it seemed like I was bringing a certain amount of baggage from my family, because white girls, guys told me, didn't need the type of attention I was demanding. I was expected to be very sexual. A lot of people projected sexual attraction on me because I was Latina, and that was such a contrast to what I grew up with and what was expected of me by my mother."

Even now, Eva struggles with that perception. "There is still a stereotype that I am going to be hot in bed, that I must be this sexual machine. I am also struggling with the whole maternal thing—and I struggle with people assuming that I have kids, that it would be unnatural if I didn't, that I have a responsibility to do so."

For Jesse, the mixed-heritage woman from California, most of the conflicting messages about what her body should look like came from home. (As a reminder, she's the woman who hasn't felt comfortable sharing her bisexuality with her family, and yet her relationship with her mother is better today than it's been in the past.) She told me, "On the one hand, my mom is really proud of having curves and a full figure, but at the same time she is hyperconscious of my body size. It is stereotypical in Latino culture to be hyperaware of the body, and my family comments on it in a way that white families don't—in a way that is shameless and unapologetic. The message was very confusing: Be thin, because you want a man to be attracted to you. Be proud of your curves, but don't get too big. Growing up with pop culture and the media just complicates it more, because you don't see variations of Latina images."

WEIGHTY MATTERS

In my interviews, I noted an increased awareness of the prevalence of Latinas in the media among eighteen- to twenty-five-year-olds. This younger subset of women feels that the beauty spectrum in the United States is somewhat broadening to include Latinas. They see Eva Mendes and Salma Hayek in makeup ads; they watch Eva Longoria on prime time TV. And, of course, these women are very beautiful, but there was a time when Latina women never even came close to being cover models.

This focus on beautiful Latinas can feel like a relief, but it does not come without pressure. Red-carpet commentary often focuses on Salma Hayek's and Jennifer Lopez's curves. And sure, they have curves compared to women like Calista Flockhart, Kate Bosworth, and Nicole Richie. But Hayek's and Lopez's figures are, for many Latinas, as unattainable as Paris Hilton's. It's almost patronizing to have a big deal made out of those curves when the average Latina is looking in the mirror at curves that look a lot more like America Ferrera's in *Real Women Have Curves*. It's the depiction of women like Ferrera that can empower Latinas to finally feel a part of the beauty standard in America. But then we need to be mindful about the impact of throwing braces on Ferrera's teeth and calling her "Ugly Betty" on an ABC prime time *telenovela*.

Most often, when Latinas struggle with their size and weight, their struggle is exacerbated by white, non-Latino American standards. And since we want to fit in, there are inevitably going to be times we wish we could just beat our flesh into submission. Other times, it seems as if we've conquered our own demons, only to find that our mothers and aunts have grabbed on to that North American standard of slimness, feeding us the same messages that lead to feelings of inadequacy.

"My mother was always trying to put me on diets or give me diet pills," says Lola, a Mexican American from San Antonio, Texas. At age thirty-four, she still grapples with her own beauty perception. "When I was twenty pounds lighter, I was more social, more flirtatious. I was confident enough to ask guys out," she says.

Like Jesse and Lola, I, too, have a mother who will say whatever is on her mind about her daughters' looks and appearance. My sister and I often call each other to commiserate after a barb has been delivered. A common reply to each other is, "Geez, I can't believe we didn't develop an eating disorder." The irony is that our mom believes that in making observations about our weight and appearance, she is being helpful. In fact, she believes that her comments are necessary for her to do her job as a mother. Fortunately, Sonia and I have found a way to negotiate these conversations with our mother and have each other to confide in and support. Otherwise, the pressure would become too much.

Jesse, Lola, Sonia, and I aren't the only ones who deal with intrafamilial tension regarding perceptions of what's an acceptable female body size. I talked to two women, each one half of a La Gordita and La Flaca sister duo, and regardless of which half of that equation the interviewee was, she felt self-conscious about it. My mother called some of my friends La Gordita when she asked about them. I would fight her about it rather than answer, always getting her response that it was an innocent designation. Indeed, back on the Island, it may have been an innocent way of referring to someone, because "soft," "chubby," or even "fat" weren't considered bad words or insults; they were just observations. But in the United States, where every bite of food is loaded with guilt or critique, being called La Gordita feels like a social death sentence.

Certainly, weight matters, and being overweight can put a woman at risk for various chronic health problems like high blood pressure, Type II diabetes, coronary heart disease, hypertension, and arthritis. Even children and young women can contract these problems.

Recently, the Girl Scouts Institute compiled statistics on Latina girls and their weight in their study "The New Normal? What Girls Say About Healthy Living." Their revelations include facts like the following: Latina girls are the second-most overweight group of children in the United States, with Mexican American adolescents between the ages of twelve and nineteen exhibiting the greatest likelihood of being overweight. Obesity among Puerto Rican and Mexican American children starts between the ages of six and seven. Acculturation seems to increase the risk of being overweight among Latina girls, as it can have a negative effect on one's food consumption, eating habits, and body image. Some of the examples cited by the study include the fact that acculturated Latinos eat less fruit but more fast food; 59% of Latina girls use the vending machines on their school campuses for lunch. Latinas born in the United States to immigrant parents are more than twice as likely to be overweight compared to foreign-born Latinas who later move to the United States. First-generation Latinas are less likely to be overweight than their second- and third-generation peers.

Findings also revealed that Latinas were less active than their peers. In 2002, only 36% of Latina sophomores played interscholastic sports, as compared to 52% of non-Hispanic sophomore girls. Also, 33% of Latina girls who don't participate in sports listed a lack of energy as the main reason. The trend continues when we grow up. Nearly 60% of Latina adults are described as physically inactive.[1]

So how do we address the issue of weight without making it all that matters? Emphasizing healthy foods and activities without negative statements like, "I can't believe you're eating that" are important. Moreover, adult Latinas need to serve as positive role models for our girls and teens. We should encourage them to be active: join a cause, take up a sport, learn how to play music, embrace the arts. We can encourage them to make sound choices while banishing negative language. What I observed in some of my conversations with successful Latinas was that all of them found something in their early years that became part of their identity and affirmed them when times were hard. The Girl Scouts study noted that girls with active mothers are more likely to be active, and that girls whose mothers struggle with a negative body image are more likely to struggle with their own bodies, regardless of what they weigh.[2]

Only 57.4% of the participants in the Growing Up Latina Survey observed that their mothers were emotionally confident while they were growing up; 62.3% described their mothers as physically confident (confident in their skin, comfortable with the way they looked) while they were coming of age.

Iris is a twenty-four-year-old Colombian American who lives in New Jersey. She's self-confident, but this confidence is not without its complexities and pressures. "I am very confident about the way that I look. In my head, I always have to feel like I am the best with the way I dress and the way that I look," she says. As I talk to her I can't help but wonder whether the pop culture representation of Latinas for Iris's generation has created some of this pressure.

While I may have been starved for Latina images when I was growing up, there wasn't a standard being created for me. But several of my conversations with women under the age of twenty-five made me aware that while they are more confident on the surface than their older counterparts might have been at that age, they also feel pressure and an expectation to look like women such as Jennifer Lopez and Salma Hayek.

MEDIA MADNESS

Twenty-one-year-old Alyssa, who's Puerto Rican and Cuban and grew up in North Carolina, had negative feelings about herself during her teenage years. "I didn't look like the girls in magazines, which is how I wanted to look. People were having sex by freshman year. For me, it was not something that I was raised to talk about, so it was definitely a culture shock."

Her feelings of isolation were complicated by what she saw in the media. Despite her intentions, she compared herself to the non-Latina actresses she saw on television and in the movies. "You look at someone and think, *I like that stomach*, or *I would like to have those arms*. There are two kinds of Latinas. You're either a sexy, nice-body-with-a-big-butt-and-big-boobs Latina, or a big girl who likes to cook and is a bossy sister. It is hard to find good role models for Latinas, because Hollywood definitely goes for the sexy, spicy Latina."

Off the top of my head, I cannot think of a well-known Latina whose television role is the equivalent of a "plain Jane," or even a girl-next-door type. There are few Latinas who play a character rather than an essence: no one like Chloe from the TV show *24*, Libby from *Lost*, or Eames from *Law and Order: Criminal Intent*. The way a Latina looks—positive and negative—is always a part of the storyline. Michelle Rodriguez of *Lost* is a hot-tempered yet smoldering force. Rosario on *Will and Grace* is a caricature of a

Latina maid (to be fair, everything on *Will and Grace* is a caricature, but Rosario's role certainly doesn't help matters). Catalina on
My Name Is Earl is stereotypically beautiful, and she's a maid with
no papers.

What if the portrayal of Latinas were broadened? What if they
actually gave characters more substance? What if there were as
many depictions of smart Latinas as there are of Latinas who confirm the stereotypes? What if the struggle and sacrifice and even
the roots of each character were revealed? What if we actually saw
the everywoman Latina on the small and big screen? What if there
were room for bisexual and lesbian Latinas onscreen? By the looks
of things, the American adaptation of the Latin American *telenovela* is about to explode. Will U.S. consumers respond to something that's not reflective of contemporary America? The product,
depending on how the producers choose to depict the characters
and market the shows, could go either way, making a caricature
of the Latino experience or educating Latinos and others about the
Latino experience.

Some of the Latinas I spoke to are not put out by the stereotypical image used to portray Latinas. Even though Natalia, thirty-
eight, quips that Latinos like their women "scantily clad, in skin-
tight clothing with very high heels—the vixen look," she is also
flattered by Hollywood's portrayal of Latinas. Natalia is Puerto
Rican and grew up in South Carolina. She says, "I have never been
offended by how Latinas have been portrayed. They are always
portrayed as the girl who will steal your husband, but I almost see
it as a compliment that my culture is so charismatic—that if you
aren't careful, watch out."

While Natalia feels empowered by media images of Latinas,
Alyssa has found her power in spite of those images. Even though

she's only twenty-one, Alyssa has done the hard work of becoming comfortable with herself. When asked if she was secure in her appearance, she surprised herself with her answer. "I think so, yes. That is amazing to say after years of not feeling that way. I looked at myself for a long time and just brainwashed myself with 'I am beautiful.' In the last two or three years, I actually feel more sexually appealing."

Alyssa's voice registers a tone of relief and gratitude. But I wonder about her choice of words and their implications. Have we gone so far in dictating what is beautiful that women feel the need to brainwash themselves? There must be a better way.

Yvonne, the thirty-three-year-old Puerto Rican who lives in Charlotte, North Carolina, is trying to instill confidence in her daughters at an early age so that they never have those internal negative feelings about looking different from their peers. "Sexiness is about confidence. You portray yourself in such a way that you attract people," she reflects. When it comes to her children, she says, "I compliment them for their internal traits. I say, 'That was so thoughtful of you. You are so compassionate.' Only one time have we talked about whether or not one of them was pretty, and that was because she asked, and so I told her that she was, but that it was most important to make sure that all of her internal beauty showed."

It's not surprising that though Yvonne de-emphasized the importance of physical attributes, her daughter still needed to know if she was pretty. This situation shows the pervasiveness and power of the beauty culture, and how it impacts girls from a very young age. Yvonne's daughter's awareness of beauty reminds us that messages come from everywhere to influence each one of us—not just from our families.

When asked what she perceives as beautiful, Thalia, who's twenty-seven and of Mexican descent, says, "It's a sense of knowing who you are, because then you walk it, live it, exude it. You truly live the life you imagined, and you shine."

When asked if she is happy with her appearance, Thalia laughs. "Oh yeah. I'm one of those people who believes I look better than I do."

Wouldn't it be nice if we all believed so confidently in ourselves and our possibilities, and if those things were what resonated with us as beautiful? You don't have to be a model to be beautiful. What's clear in every interview I conducted is that "beautiful" is about our sense of self, our sense of purpose, our desire to live and be and grow. Master that, and you trump any catwalk.

LOVING OURSELVES

Some women revealed that their level of confidence varies based on where they are. Unlike places such as South Beach in Miami, a city like Washington, D.C., features so much visual diversity that it's harder for people to feel like there is just one model for beauty.

Moving to New York from Texas was a great experience for twenty-nine-year-old Delia, a Mexican American. "Being in New York, I have learned to love my body and embrace it. I feel the sexiest I've ever felt, because other Latinas are around me, and the perceptions around body image here are different. In Texas, there's an image of beauty that's all about being thin and not too dark. In high school, I felt like if I was thin, then people would like me. I have really grown into my skin here. In New York, I feel like men appreciate a different type of body. It's the culture. Island culture [referring to the large concentration of Puerto Ricans and Dominicans in New

York] is a lot different than the culture where I grew up. Now I really embrace my 'hybridity,' and I embrace Island culture."

Frances, thirty-five and of Colombian descent, was born in New York City and lived there until recently, when she took a personal and professional sabbatical to Florida. Like so many of the women I interviewed, she received one message from her mom and other messages at school. "My mom has always said, 'You're not going to be young forever,' so she's always celebrated going out and placed an emphasis on looking our best. She would say, 'A woman is like a flower. You have it right now on loan; celebrate it.' There was a stage where I really did feel like I had to be skinny. That came from magazines. But all those girls were white and skinny. I was in junior high school and dieting and purposely not going out in the sun so I could be as white as possible."

Later, Frances rebelled against the models that were presented for her to emulate. "The one thing I see in Latin culture is that there is something really beautiful and celebrated about something feminine being expressed. Looking like a woman is really celebrated. Into my twenties, I fought the stereotype of what it meant to be female. I saw my mom, who had five kids very young, and I felt like she had sacrificed a lot. I didn't want to be traditional and depend on a man. I built my identity around rebelling against that stereotype."

Later, in her twenties and early thirties, Frances began to redefine her understanding of the feminine. She says, "Now it has been about constructing a new way to be feminine, because I see what that rebellion against femininity has cost me. It cost me a lot of intimacy. I am discovering the beauty of things that have traditionally been defined as feminine."

But her hard-won comfort with the feminine has not been seam-less. She continues, "I have never had a weight issue, and women friends who are bigger always say something about my size. It really bothers me, because I don't comment on a woman's body, because every woman has body-image issues. Just because I am slender doesn't mean my body is up for grabs."

This is a good point. Many of us have self-image issues, and body size isn't the half of it. American culture places importance not only on the perfect body, but on good skin, hair, style, and more. But we don't have to give in to that pressure and present ourselves in ways that confirm those very notions. We can set an example to young Latinas that they are more than the sum of their physical parts. We have the opportunity to change lives and change self-perceptions by choosing to focus on the things that feed the soul, rather than that which feeds the image-focused media machine.

While Frances has worked to create a definition of beauty that does not focus on her size, she says that living in Miami can be distracting. "I notice women who . . . have that full expression of spirit, who have a connection to who they authentically are. Women with that wild spirit inside of them are the women who capture my eye."

I asked her if she feels secure in her appearance having said that, and the light in her voice dims a bit. "Some days yes, and some days no. I felt more secure in New York, but in South Beach, it's all about big breasts and feeling like I'm not going to be sexu-ally desirable."

Elsa, the twenty-one-year-old of Venezuelan descent, moved from Miami to North Carolina and has come into her own in her new environment. "I was definitely a tomboy, and my father would say, 'You need to dress nice—and like a girl.' As far as body image, both of my parents were cautious about my weight. I am not as thin as everyone in Miami. Growing up, there was a message that I needed to be feminine and fit in. At school, you had to dress in the latest fashion, dress a certain way to be attractive, fit a certain model so that people would look at you. I chose not to do that, and so I was overlooked."

Moving to North Carolina changed things for Elsa. "Now that I'm not around my family, I have picked up the whole feminine thing for myself. Messages I receive in North Carolina are positive. I have darker skin, and people are recently telling me how beautiful it is. I get compliments on my curves. My friends here make me feel like it doesn't matter that I am not as thin as everyone else. It matters how I project myself, too. The way you present yourself changes how other people perceive you."

Since moving to North Carolina, Elsa has been able to surround herself with people of her choosing, unlike in high school. "The thing that's had the biggest effect on how I feel is who I am around. I am still a work in progress, but I am so much better than before. I feel more comfortable being in a place where not only one body size is the standard. I am not that influenced by the media anymore. I rebel against the trends they try to feed me. They don't have the authority to decide who is beautiful. You can't teach someone to be beautiful. You can't just say, 'Suck this in and reshape that.'"

How a woman sees beauty is a choice. She can see it the way *she* wants to see it, or she can see it the way the world hands it to her. Many women are beginning to see beauty in the former way, and I wish that someday soon every woman will have the ability to do so.

For Mia, a thirty-two-year-old Puerto Rican who grew up in Brooklyn, the experiences she had growing up have made her want to positively influence her niece and sisters. She remembers how difficult the mixed messages were for her as a teen: "Girls tried to reveal as much as they could outside the home. That was their idea of expressing their sexuality. Boys disrespected those girls, though, because that was the example that was being set for them by other Latino males. You were looked at as a piece of meat when you left your house. It was unpleasant. My mother dressed very provocatively, and she was very confident in her appearance. She wanted me to express the same confidence in my appearance."

I witnessed my own version of what Mia observed when I taught high school and watched how the girls who dressed in a revealing way were treated by the boys. My female students who wore outfits that were seemingly chosen to attract attention often turned caustic when they were met with catcalling and gawking. At school, Mia learned that she did not want to be treated poorly, and so she chose not to dress suggestively, even though her mother was advocating it. Today she remembers how hard that was for her.

"People said I should straighten my hair. I wasn't tall enough. I was too thin. I've been told that I am a stick with bumps. When I was younger, I felt there was too much emphasis on my breasts, since they were so big. I was objectified."

Now Mia is confident about what she thinks, and she speaks up. "I tell my young niece to be proud of who she is, and to stop trying to straighten her hair. Her natural beauty is what her beauty is. When I was growing up, you had good hair or bad hair, and curly was bad because it was difficult to manage. I don't agree with all of that."

Twenty-year-old Lisette, who's Puerto Rican and grew up in New York City, received the message to straighten her hair from her peers. "My mom and dad were always positive about my body image, whereas my peers were very mean to me, telling me that I should straighten my hair because it was ugly. My parents were against that. They always told me, 'You are beautiful the way that you were made.'"

Many women expressed that Latinos in general seem to appreciate a curvier body, but that also presents its own set of problems. "It is a very unrealistic body type," says twenty-four-year-old Magdalena, who is of El Salvadoran descent and grew up in an Italian neighborhood in New York City. "Not everyone can have a very curvy body with a small waist. I sometimes feel inadequate because I have big breasts; my sister has the big butt. We each have the missing parts that the other doesn't have."

When I think about my own experience, it seemed for a while that *la isla* was barreling down on my American upbringing as if it might be the end. *Get a diamond ring on her finger,* my mother must have been thinking, *and she'll come back to our team.* But I was not the standard gringa, nor was I ever the traditional Latina. It wasn't until I started teaching and realized that it was my calling that I began to feel confident and unite my soul with my perceptions—something that finally gave me the sense of satisfaction I'd been craving.

Maybe at the root of my resistance to my mother's pressure to get married was the fear that I'd be forced into a box of understanding that I'd never experienced. I was a shape-shifter, transcendental, a mirage. And I'd fallen in love with the not belonging, the mystery, the freedom from place. I was afraid that getting married meant making a choice to conform, that it wouldn't allow me to be who I wanted to be. Dealing with dual pressures, from the outside and from within, made me feel like I was going to have to make a sacrifice somewhere.

I imagine that all of this was why my Latina was awake way past midnight most nights, while my gringa waited for me to figure out how much of her I could actually embrace. My Latina—cut from a different mold than the one Mamacita wanted for me, different from the one some of my teenage students imagined—was keeping vigil for the moment I would figure out how to integrate the other part of who I was. Once I was able to do this, I was able to find peace with who I am—based on my heritage, my two cultures, and my upbringing.

After all, we are all the union of our parts. The truth is that every woman can be saccharine and salt, beauty and brawn, gentle and razor sharp. We, the multiethnic children of Latino parents and American upbringing, are able to take from our culture what we need and integrate our parts to become our best selves.

six

How Latina Are You?

In the book *The Joy of Doing Things Badly,* Veronica Chambers, whose mother is Panamanian, wrote that she hated playing How Latin Are You?—a game she describes as "measuring fluency and accents against birthplace and birthrights."[1]

Many of us know exactly how she feels. As if not speaking fluent Spanish indicates that you don't know what it means to have "Wetback!" or "Spic!" screamed at you when all you're trying to do is cross the road. As if not visiting your familial homeland means you don't know some of its soul. We've all experienced the desire to document someone else's authenticity, and yet what happens when the measures of authenticity vary from person to person? The issue of why people do this brings up some questions. Could it be that what we're after is our own search for affirmation, the chance to label ourselves rather than have someone else label us?

Each Latina wants to be allowed to be Latina as *she* understands it, as *she* has experienced it, as *she* knows how. We don't want to follow someone else's rules—whether that someone else is Latina or gringa. We don't want to fit into some box of understanding that isn't our own. And we certainly don't want to become Anglo without all the rights and privileges that come with it. This was my first awakening to my Latinidad—having to stand up for it myself, because others weren't willing to acknowledge it.

I have often faltered in conversation, struggled with what I wanted to say and what I could not say. My frame of reference—first-generation Puerto Rican girl in the American South—never found company for reflection. At home I did not have the words in Spanish to explain to my parents what it meant to be seen as un-American, that my citizenship was just as valid as the citizenship of the blond boy sitting next to me in social studies (though it didn't always feel that way). He spat at me once, phlegm and hatred wrapped in one. I confronted him, calmly but forcefully enough, but I kept the horror of the incident, the way it spliced my soul, to myself. I was embarrassed, and I didn't think anyone would understand the depth of the pain, the way it felt like a direct attack on who I was.

I didn't have the language to process the experience with my parents. I had learned English in school and Spanish at home, and there was no way for me to explain how this experience was racist when my parents had never mentioned the word "racist" in conversation. Likewise, how could I explain how it felt to be treated this way to my friends who weren't Latina? What if it made them feel like they had to choose allegiances? What if it made me seem like more trouble than I was worth?

Not until my preteen years did I begin to understand that because of my skin tone, I might be categorized and defined without my consent. In the dark and musty hallway of my sixth-grade building, I fumbled with my locker. My olive skin was darker than usual from the tan that always crept over me in the summer. My black hair hung over my eyes as I wound the lock back and forth. A girl with a long, wild rattail opened the locker next to

mine and candidly asked, "Are you mixed?" I struggled to understand what she meant, how she might see me as "mixed." She
reworded her question and then finally just blurted out, "Is your
daddy black and your momma white?" In South Carolina in the
mid-1980s, heritage mattered as much in friendship as kindness
and decency.

I told her I was from Puerto Rico, an island in the Caribbean.
She stared at me, vacant and dissatisfied.

"You gotta be one or the other, white or black. I'm just gonna
call you white, 'cause you're smart."

That was that. She closed her locker and walked off
contentedly—and later even asked me if I wanted to come over to
spend the night at her house. The exchange was complete for her,
and yet numbing for me. I had no desire to be white in her eyes, or
anyone else's. I wanted my own definition; I wanted to be seen in
the way that I saw myself: a first-generation Puerto Rican trying to
find her own way.

We moved to the States when I was two, my sister, Sonia, eight,
and our brother, Tito, ten. Though we resemble each other (especially because there were no other Latinos around), we've always
been very different. Sure, siblings turn out differently all the time,
but when I look at the three of us, I can't help but consider some
of the outstanding factors that made our experience unique from
other families'. Looking at us now, as grown adults, I often think
about our own continuum of Latinness (which isn't an idea I am
completely sure about yet, but is one that's presented all the time
by Latinos and non-Latinos alike). Tito is now Bert, a preppy man
who coaches collegiate soccer, drives an SUV, and listens to alternative music—and whom I have not heard speak Spanish since I was
out of elementary school, even though that's the language the rest

of us speak at home. When my parents go to Puerto Rico to see family, Bert tells his friends that his parents "are vacationing in the Caribbean." (I've always laughed at that way of phrasing it, as if they withdrew their extra thousands and took off for a bender in the Cayman Islands.)

But I don't fault "my Tito," the nickname I took to calling him when I was little to differentiate between him and all the other Titos we visited in Puerto Rico. I've considered that his behavior has been his own coping mechanism, and we all manifest these mechanisms in different ways, so I let go of the frustration I felt years ago. In fact, if I am going to be fair about letting people define themselves, then I have to give him the room to do just that and not hammer *la isla* down his throat.

In keeping with the whole continuum idea, Sonia is the most Latina of us. She speaks beautiful Spanish, writes it so well that I use her as my spell-checker when I write a letter to my grandmother. She wants nothing more than for a good Puerto Rican dish to be served for dinner. She is darker than I am, but her features and hair are more European, like our mother's. I am paler, but you can see the Indian and African roots in my face, body, and hair. And I've often thought that Sonia is more Latina than me, simply because she's more traditional.

I speak Spanish freely, but not always easily. There are words my parents didn't teach me and some I still don't know. I write it relatively well, but with little attention paid to grammar. I can read a Spanish-language newspaper and figure out difficult words based on context. I am a proponent of Latino rights in the United States, and I struggle with whether to greet someone in Spanish when I suspect they're Latino, or whether to always go with English first. After all, I'm startled when someone greets me in Spanish, but just as surprised when someone assumes I'm white. I'm a Latina conundrum in some ways, but aren't we all?

People often ask me about my ethnicity, and I explain that I am Puerto Rican (yes, both my parents are Puerto Rican), and that I came to the States when I was two. But answering the question "Where are you from?"—for me and almost every Latina I know—is confusing business.

"Do you speak Spanish?" Yep.

"So you moved here from Puerto Rico?" These questions are meant to assign me a grade of Latinnness. By answering yes, I become more Latina, more authentic.

"No, actually, we moved here from Germany. I was born in Germany." This tidbit of information often throws the asker into a state of total confusion, so much so that I almost never bring it up, even if it means that someone misunderstands my history.

When I've insisted on telling the whole story, that my father was in the military and we moved around a lot, "Are you German?" is still the most common response. And then, often, as if to set the record straight in the mind of the asker: "Oh, so you never actually lived in Puerto Rico, then?" Thus begins the whitewashing.

BLENDING VOICES

Self-definition is a powerful thing. It's an empowering thing. Listening to the women interviewed for this book talk about what they loved about being Latina and how they handled questions like, "Are you a real Latina?" or, "Are you mixed?" was amusing, empowering, mortifying, and eye opening all at once. After all, when all is said and done, no matter what our gender, skin color, ethnicity, religion, socioeconomic group, or sexual orientation, we all just want to wake up in the morning and be who we intend to be (or at least think we are) without rerouting, redefining, and reorienting to someone else's expectations.

Thirty-eight-year-old Natalia is Puerto Rican and grew up in South Carolina. "Being Latina is something that has always had a pretty big influence in my life. There's no part of me that I would consider the non-Latina Natalia and the Latina Natalia. It's just one Natalia," she says with authority and experience. "I have my own uniqueness without having to go find what it is. It was built in already. Some non-Latina women sometimes don't have a sense of uniqueness that tells them who they are."

When asked to address the challenge of being a Latina in America, she responds thoughtfully. "It can be a challenge when I meet someone who has an unopen mind about where I am from or about my culture. Sometimes having to explain who I am to someone can be a challenge."

The struggle of voicing one's experience while wanting to embrace one's ethnicity was echoed by many women. "I can't check being a Latina at the door in any situation," says Eva, the thirty-six-year-old Puerto Rican from New York City. "What it fills me with is so essential to who I am, even when I'm not around other Latinas, it's like my skin. I love the way we are with family. I love our music, our sense of passion. I love having a language."

Then Eva tells another story that reminds me of that time in New York City when my Latina was called out ("Hey, Boricua, over here!") and identified—and all that man had recognized was how I moved down the street, not my khaki shorts, Reef sandals, and Henley T-shirt.

"Once, I was waiting on the corner, waiting for a *pon* [ride]," Eva recounts, "and someone drove by and screamed '*¡Nuyorican!*'" She shares with me that she loved that recognition, which was something reflected by many Latinas I've spoken to who have, perhaps, too often passed as white or black and have appreciated a moment of being noticed for what they are. Even though most women I know don't appreciate being yelled or whistled at, there are times when an experience like that makes one feel seen and recognized, despite its relative negativity on a lot of other levels. My own experience left me with a sense of satisfaction about being recognized, spotted, and appreciated for my identity, perhaps because it had been something that had been untended to for so long.

Eva takes a break in her story before continuing in a less ebullient voice. "It's a double-edged sword, because language also hurts me," she says. Eva is an artist, and the depth of her expression reveals itself as she continues. "I sometimes show myself with two tongues coming out of my mouth in self-portraits. When I am in Puerto Rico, I never feel like I am doing the language justice, and when I am here, I lose the fluidity. Sometimes people here who don't know that I'm Latina will say, 'I had no idea that you spoke Spanish, because you speak English perfectly.' Even my cousins who live here in the States have told me that I speak like a white girl. They say, 'You say *awesome*. Only white girls say *awesome*.'"

Mia is thirty-two and Puerto Rican. She lives in New York City, and her experience is similar to Eva's. She vents, "I have been told by other Latinas that I talk like a white girl, because I enunciate and speak clear English, without an accent and without the Ebonics."

Many Latinas are criticized for acting too white, sounding too white, for being, somehow, too influenced or sucked into mainstream American culture. Being called a gringa, or American, by a Latino is never meant as a compliment. It's code for "sellout." But can you really sell out when you are inextricably part of two cultures?

In *The Maria Paradox,* Rosa Maria Gil and Carmen Inoa Vazquez write, "If you do feel trapped between North American and Hispanic cultures, it's because you're looking at the situation in the wrong way. . . . A healthy adjustment is not an either/or process. On the contrary, it consists of gradually 'retraining' and 'restraining' yourself to blend two distinctly different cultural styles. . . . We have all at one time or another found ourselves consciously behaving in contradiction to our Hispanic self and felt that by 'going American,' we were betraying our ethnic identity. This is a textbook example of the either/or fallacy. What's crucial to successful acculturation is looking beyond either/or, assessing the particular cultural situation and determining what behavior would be most appropriate in the North American context in which we find ourselves."[2]

REPRESENTING

Twenty-nine-year-old Clara, who's of Peruvian descent and living in New York City, says, "Every time I go to Peru, I feel like I'm in some alternate culture where I am not Peruvian but I am not American. You start to question your own identity and where you belong."

Growing up in Houston, Delia, who is twenty-nine and Chicana, developed her own voice as a poet and actress and came to feel a responsibility for projecting that voice to assist other Latinas. "I represent the Southwest. I consider that my responsibility as a writer and as someone who's privileged. It is my responsibility to speak those experiences. It has definitely been a staple in who I am and building up my character to this point."

Being a Latina is such an inherent part of who Delia is that she was surprised by how different Latino culture was when she moved to New York City. "It really was a culture shock for me. There is definitely a difference between Chicanos and *Mexicanos*. Since moving here, I have gotten to be a part of a big Mexican community, but I will always be seen as different because I'm Chicana. Even though we share food, icons, et cetera, I'm still seen as privileged."

She continues, telling me about an incident at work. "My boss once directed my attention to a new coworker and said, 'Can you help Sarah out a little bit? You know, she is from Mexico City.'" Delia's boss didn't intend for Delia to feel a kinship toward Sarah. He was saying it so that Delia would understand why Sarah might need help. To him, Delia was as non-Latino as he was, but she just happened to speak Spanish—a bonus in this situation with Sarah. Delia explained that she was Chicana, wanting him to understand that about her and feeling like it was the perfect chance to bring it to light. But her boss just shook it off.

Jessica, twenty-two, is a student in Chicago of El Salvadoran descent. Chicago has made her appreciative of the differences in culture—especially within the Latino culture, which is so often lumped into one category. Unlike New York City (where there is a disproportionate number of Dominicans and Puerto Ricans), or Texas (where you most often run into people of Mexican descent), or Miami (where Cubans are the majority of the Latino population), her Chicago was not dominated by one ethnic group over another, nor was her Latino experience dominated by just one culture of Latinos.

But the cultural sensitivity that Chicago fostered in her was not necessarily shared by her peers at her all-girls Catholic high school, where Jessica was in the minority. "Before high school I had no notion of what a stereotype was. In my neighborhood, if you weren't

Hispanic, you were black. So going to a private high school was a culture shock. People thought I was Greek or Italian, and then they realized that I was hanging out with the brown kids. That was the first racism I faced. People would ask me, 'Why are you hanging out with the brown girls? If you're white, why do you deny it?'"

Jessica, who describes herself as light-skinned, recalls this experience with some degree of frustration. "I find it offensive, because white people are never approached with these questions," she continues. "I try to make the person who asks me stuff like this as uncomfortable as possible by letting them know how uncomfortable their questions make me feel. It's especially offensive to me when questions like that come from another minority, especially a Hispanic person. It shows how they are not aware of the fact that Latinas come in all different shades."

Race labels are often a conundrum among Latinos. Since Latinos' skin color can be any shade—from a pale white, like my mother's family, to a dark brown or black, it's nearly impossible to identify a Latina just by sight. I am reminded of the opening stanza of "A Week in the Life of the Ethnically Indeterminate," a poem by Elena Georgiou.

MONDAY

Sitting in MacDonald's on 103rd and 3rd
I notice a couple staring at me
and hear them say Indian.
They walk towards me.
The woman has white skin,
blond hair, blue eyes.
The man has ebony skin,
black hair, brown eyes.
Excuse me, says the woman,

we were wondering
where you were from.
Yeah, says the man,
because you look like
our people.
I look at the whiteness
and the blackness,
wondering who their people are.
We're Puerto Rican, they say
and walk away.[3]

Some Latinos easily self-identify as white or black—as their race—and then give a nod to their homeland by identifying their ethnicity, whether they're Afro-Cuban or white Puerto Rican. But others find the race label inaccurate, noting that their heritage is a blending of multiple cultures, and that everyone's heritage is a mix, as opposed to white or black.

KNOWLEDGE IS POWER

Lucia, thirty-eight, grew up in the 1980s in Texas with a group of girls who weren't too invested in going to college. In fact, most of them disregarded the idea of Latinas even going to college. She remembers a conversation she had as a seventh-grader with friends who shared her Mexican heritage.

"I said I wanted to go to college, and they looked at me like I had the biggest alien head on my shoulders. They told me that I was trying to be white, and that I didn't fit in with them anymore." For Lucia, this experience did change whom she hung out with. She made new friends, most of whom were non-Latina.

Daria is a thirty-three-year-old Mexican American from New Mexico who also encountered tension around the issue of college. "The Latinos in my town just weren't going for education. They didn't see that as part of their track. I remember a friend asking why I was smart, and I said, 'Because I read.' But I had such a big chip on my shoulder about being too good for that town. The Latinos there didn't see themselves as having much of an option. The counselors pushed to send the white students to college, and my Latino friends were never talked to. The only reason I met with a counselor about college was because my mom went and talked to one of them about it."

Some women found that college actually altered their experience with their culture. Gloria was born in Puerto Rico and moved to New Jersey when she was five. Now forty, she recalls how college impacted her. "I had an opportunity to be raised in two different cultures. In my house, we were brought up with our customs and traditions, and when I went outside, it was different. I had to struggle to keep an identity that I wasn't proud of and later realized that I should be proud of. I wanted to fit in with all my friends who were not Hispanic, and then when I went to college I realized that being different was okay. That was when I decided to learn the language and go to Puerto Rico and learn about my culture."

As a teacher, I told my college-bound high school students that they would change as much from age eighteen to twenty-two as they did from age thirteen to eighteen, because of the way college exposes you to so much and challenges your way of thinking. I promoted the idea of college because I knew it would leave my students with a wider repertoire of ideas and tools to use in their decision-making processes. Then, when I became a college administrator, I told my college students that they would change as much between the ages of twenty-two and twenty-six as they did between eighteen and twenty-two. I had a few high school students who ended up attending the college where I worked, and they reminded me that I had made similar claims before. They wondered if those claims could hold true for different points of life. But I insisted that they were true. I am a firm believer that experience provokes awakenings, and that awakenings encourage growth and healthy change. An awakening can happen for anyone at any time, but it's illuminated in a different way when it's an ethnic awakening. The pressure of expectations changes when your world changes, and suddenly you can see what's significant and positive about what makes you different. The experiences that make you unique become the core to who you are, rather than worries or concerns.

These types of cultural awakenings often lead to a newer phenomenon that's called "retro-acculturation." If "enculturation" is the term used to describe learning our native culture, and "assimilation" is when we adapt to our new country, perhaps at the expense of our native country, then "acculturation" is when we adopt some of the rules and norms of our new culture, which can coexist with what we deem important from our native culture.

Building on these ideas, retro-acculturation happens when we've assimilated to our new culture but then begin to search for elements of our ethnic identity to incorporate into our new concept of ourselves. This process might entail embracing traditions we've never had, or learning to speak a native tongue at an older age. These types of awakenings often happen when a fairly assimilated Latina starts her own family and yearns to pass on her heritage to her children.

Research has shown that U.S.-born Latino teens begin the process of culturally defining themselves around the age of sixteen.[4] For many, this begins a process of retro-acculturation. Recently, researchers have found that retro-acculturation is starting at an even earlier age. This tendency is attributed to a demographic awakening among Latino preteens and teens as they become aware of the Latino community surrounding them, and because there's more tolerance in the wider society around being ethnic, or multiethnic. In fact, in many parts of the country, it's becoming trendy.

Shaking up the narrow expectation some have for Latinas has been the mission of many of the women I interviewed. Gianira, forty-seven, is a college Spanish professor who heads her department. She was raised in Puerto Rico and moved to the United States in her twenties to pursue her intellectual and professional interests. Her professional role has come with joys and limitations in regard to her Puerto Rican ethnicity. "I have added a new role model for students and other Latinos in the community. We can be successful professionals. That is something I am proud of accomplishing. There is a large concentration of Puerto Ricans here, and most of these students come from blue-collar workers and didn't know you could be a professional. I am introducing them to Puerto Rican writers, and they had no idea about the rich culture."

Listening to Gianira relate her experiences reminds me of my work with young gang members. Exposure to the possibility of getting out of the life they expected for themselves makes all the difference. The smaller a kid's world, the shorter his list of prospects. Having a sense of potential for one's life comes from having acquired information that can, in turn, become new opportunities. Gianira gives her students that information just by standing in front of them.

Though Gianira's experience has been rich and rewarding, there is a counterpoint: "I am not taken seriously. It cost me a job one time. They wouldn't look at my record as a teacher and a scholar because they couldn't get past who they thought I was." Since then, Gianira has learned to curb some parts of her personality that she felt were leading people to alter their perceptions of her. "I have learned to play down my character and ebullience. I am more cautious. I had to change the way I dress. In Latin America, you dress in brilliant colors and tight clothing. Here, people told me that I dressed like a black lady. I was like, *What is that?* When I go back to Puerto Rico, I am reminded how much I miss dressing however I want."

The way people perceived Gianira reveals a problem in this country's racial psyche. Businesses want the minorities they hire to be ethnic enough, but if you're "too ethnic" it's a threat. "Too ethnic" challenges the status quo and makes someone who's never been the minority feel uncomfortable. "Too ethnic" can put you in an awkward place, giving you an even bigger battle to fight in your quest for respect and appreciation.

Gianira's experience of having to change her appearance in order to be more acceptable reminded me of an interview I once conducted with an image consultant for a profile I was writing on her as a successful businesswoman. She said that professionally, a lot of times you have to wear the uniform. But listening to Gianira, I consider how much that uniform is defined by the mainstream ethnicity right now, by American culture. We hear that corporate America is diversifying, and indeed, many firms are paying big dollars to recruit minorities. But are they only recruiting minorities who look and sound like them, as reflected in Gianira's experiences, as well as those of many of the other women I interviewed? It remains to be seen whether America can actually embrace real diversity enough so that Latinas and other minorities don't feel like they have to check parts of their essence at the door.

STANDARDS FOR LATINIDAD

Enid is thirty-four and of Puerto Rican and Colombian descent. She talks about how non-Latinos often encourage toning it down. "I feel like I can't be loud, and that I need to be more reserved. I feel myself being more mellow."

I know exactly how she feels. My non-Latino husband has a habit of putting a hand on my thigh if he thinks I'm talking too loudly at a restaurant. In turn, I've taken to gently pushing his hand away the first time as a warning, and glaring at him the second time. I've told him time and again that it feels as if he's trying to suppress who I am, my natural enthusiasm. I'm convinced he's the only one who's conscious of the volume of my voice. No one ever turns our way when I'm talking.

Enid grew up in Miami, and she admits that her own understanding of being a Latina broadened as she matured and experienced the world on a grander scale. "I have had white women tell me that I am not really a Latina. I take it as an opportunity to educate people. I ask, 'What does that mean?' I grew up believing that you weren't a Latina if you didn't know Spanish. Then I went to college and realized that some people's parents deliberately didn't teach them Spanish because of fear of discrimination."

Of the interviewees, many of the women who did not grow up speaking Spanish expressed regret at not being able to speak it, which is certainly something to consider for those who feel that speaking Spanish is one of the qualifying factors of being an authentic Latina.

Dahlia, at age twenty-five, is still figuring out her own standards of being Latina. She's Colombian and Cuban and grew up in New Jersey. She ponders, "I am not a great salsa dancer, and some people ask 'Why don't you know how to dance? Don't you people grow up dancing?' And I want to say, 'No, we don't all grow up dancing.' I do recognize that if I didn't speak the language, I wouldn't feel authentic. But I am also to blame in perpetuating this idea around authenticity. When I see someone who doesn't really look Latina, I think they aren't really Latina. Or if they don't speak Spanish, they don't really count. The language is a big part of it."

Thirty-two-year-old Annabelle, who lives in New Jersey and is of Colombian descent, recalls how her black friends always said she was black, and her white friends always said she was white. "It just never made sense to me. I really don't have patience for people who ask me questions about my ethnicity. If I have to fill out a form that asks for ethnicity and Latino isn't listed, I check black, white, and Native American."

Victoria, twenty-five, who's a working actress in New York, speaks about how her ethnicity has been a limiting factor for her. "I had one casting agent tell me that I shouldn't say I was Puerto Rican on a casting call, because it would make people look down on me." The presumptions people in the business have about her make it difficult for Victoria to get the roles she wants. People make assumptions about her based on her ethnicity before getting to know her, or before they even see her. They assume she will be ghetto, married, and with children. She has witnessed these stereotypes firsthand on a number of casting calls.

"When a Latina looks Latina—has the black hair and the brown skin that go along with the more typical look—she is portrayed as the girl with the baby, or the crackhead, whore, or prostitute. But if she looks more European, or looks like an already famous Latina, then she is allowed to pull other roles off and can be more legit."

These casting decisions might seem casual for the person making them, but the implications for thousands of girls across the country are dramatic. Always portray the prostitute or maid as a Latina, and the stereotype is fueled.

In the June/July 2006 issue of *Latina* magazine, Mia Maestro, an Argentine actress, spoke about the Latina in Hollywood. "Right now it's a very good moment, because there are so many more roles for Latinos, especially for women. There is just so much to discover about us, as well as so many things to break away from, such as the cliché of what everyone thinks a Latin woman is. The Dominican woman is not the same as a Cuban woman or a Mexican women or an Argentine woman. Yes, we do have the same language, but we also have so many differences—and I don't think that's yet been discovered in Hollywood."[5]

Differences do exist among the various Latin American and Latino cultures. Friends used to always ask me what the difference was between tacos, burritos, enchiladas, chimichangas, and other Mexican foods. "I don't know," I would have to answer, and together we'd compare the ingredients listed to figure it out. Many are surprised that we don't all share the same political views, but if you look at the political range of our home countries, it's rather telling. From the United States Commonwealth of Puerto Rico to communist Cuba, the political views of Latin American countries are diverse and disparate, influencing their countrymen and women in very different ways. You can't assume that a Latino is a pro-life Democrat or a Catholic. Cuban Americans are often seen as Republican, but what do you make of the fact that Cuba's abortion rate is the ninth highest in the world?[6]

Magdalena is twenty-four. Her family hails from El Salvador, and she grew up in an Italian neighborhood in New York City. At first, she didn't mind the blending in or denial of her ethnicity. It was so much work trying to figure out what to say about her ethnicity that she sometimes stifled her true self in the company of non-Latinas. "I didn't have many Latina peers, so I did that to fit in. I had to be more like them. As a young child in an all-white elementary school, I feared experiencing racism," recalls Magdalena. Since then, she's become sensitive to the way that Latinos can be either all lumped together or reclassified into different races or ethnic groups.

"People say that I act different than other Latinas because of the way I talk," explains Magdalena, who is often mistaken for Native American or Hawaiian. "I try to defend myself by saying, 'Yes, I am Latina, and I don't know how the way I talk has anything to do with being Latina.' So many white people tell me, 'You're more white,' or, 'You pass as white.' I get really pissed off, like, *What the hell does that mean?*"

Latinas often think there is some elusive image that we should be living up to, a prototype within our generation to monitor and emulate. Generation X and Y have limited options when it comes to role models in the media. Most are, in fact, more like poster girls: J.Lo, Salma, Shakira, Michelle, or Eva. What about other young, vibrant Latinas who diversify our options? Soledad O'Brien is one. Zoe Saldana, Rosario Dawson, America Ferrera, and Alisa Valdes-Rodriguez are others, but we need more. We need our understanding of what it means to be Latina in America to become more complicated, diversified, and deepened. We need to engage in the propagation of an understanding that broadens what we think being Latina looks like, sounds like, reads like, feels like, is.

MIXING IT UP

Nadia is a twenty-one-year-old student in Minnesota whose mother is white and whose father is from Paraguay. Nadia feels pride for Paraguay but has yet to feel completely comfortable in her own identity.

"I love having such a rich history, and that my family is always there. I feel like I am part of another world," she explains, before touching on the challenges she faces as a Latina. "It is a challenge to hold my own as a Latina, because I'm part white. I am less Latina than most, because I'm mixed, and because I don't speak Spanish fluently. I don't fit into any specific mold of what [being] Latina should mean."

Nadia sees that her struggle might be partially born of her dad's own fight for assimilation. "My dad was so focused on assimilating his children that he never spoke Spanish in the house, and no huge effort was made to maintain culture. I have a lot of resentment toward him for that."

She is starting to reconcile the idea of merging her two identities. "In my adolescence, I would say that I was mixed. Now I take a lot more pride in my Latina heritage. I feel comfortable saying I am a Latina without feeling like I'm somehow disregarding my white background."

But her newfound peace isn't enough to make Nadia feel like she is Latina without any qualifiers. "In college, a lot of Latinos are really into socialist movements. I have a different kind of disconnection from them, because I have a different political background and belief. For that, I feel judged."

Nadia grew up in a predominately white, non-Latino environment. Now that she's in a more diverse environment, she's especially sensitive to the political differences she sees among her Latino peers. Regardless, Nadia is pressing forward and working toward a place where she can feel truly comfortable with who she is. "It's important to acknowledge your roots and then acknowledge the constant struggles of what it is to be a Latina and a minority in this country—taking pride in your culture, but also taking pride in being an American."

Jenny, thirty-eight, is half white and half Mexican and feels a special kinship to her Mexican family, although few see her as Mexican. "My ethnic identity is a double-edged sword, and I feel insecure asserting one over the other. I am biracial but I am light-skinned, and I look like a typical Anglo. I wish that people could recognize my Latin heritage, but they don't. I love my mom's family and their passion for life—and even how screwed up they are. I like the energy. There's a warmness. There is a comfort zone I have in being around Latinas. Within the Mexican American family, the women are always the strongest, or at least that is what I have seen, and I like that."

When I was a kid, my siblings and I always knew that getting our mother on board with some idea was the fastest way to make sure it would happen. Mamacita was the deciding force in our house, and that was not unique to our situation. My hope for future generations of Latinas—and current generations of Latinas, for that matter—is that this power will be spread to other parts of our lives.

Some Latinas have negotiated a way to always feel both Latina and American. Brenda, fifty-four, comes from a Mexican family and grew up in Texas. She says, "There have been times that some Latinas have perceived me as not Mexican enough due to my not speaking Spanish correctly. I don't listen much to Mexican music, or watch Spanish TV, or speak Spanish at home. But I have also lost many non-Latina friends due to my discomfort at having to hide or not share too much of my Latina self. When I am in a group where I am the only Latina, I always have a strong sense of not belonging, and of having to disguise my Latina traits, so as not to scare or offend these other women."

Brenda, however, feels that she's found a solution to her situation. "I have had to seek out other Latinas who are equally lacking in their degree of Mexican cultural practices in their own lives. There are many of us out there, hungering to find one another in order to create our own groups where we will feel more like we fit in or belong."

Sarah, the thirty-year-old half Colombian and half Cuban from New Jersey, struggled when she was younger to find friends who could relate to her experience. "I had two best friends. One was Filipina, and the other was Chilean. I cornered the Chilean one in the bathroom one day and asked, 'Do you speak Spanish?' After that, we talked in Spanish like it was our secret code," she recalls, and we both laugh at her memory.

"I did really well in school, and I have a dominant personality, so it was easy for me to feel comfortable asserting myself. It got more challenging when I went to high school, because it was so much bigger. There I made my posse all Latinas. They were my peeps all through high school, but they were never in my classes. So for me, the fun people were the Latinas, and then I went with the dorks to class," she laughs, acknowledging that yes, in some ways she thought of herself as a dork, too.

NEGOTIATING TENSIONS

Raquel is a nineteen-year-old college student who grew up in Baltimore, Maryland. Her heritage is Guatemalan, and her roommate is Puerto Rican. "I feel like we can be called 'not Latina enough' because we don't reflect the tough, urban, accented, *West Side Story* Puerto Rican," says Raquel. The fact that their families haven't struggled the way that other Latino families have has created tension for both of them. Their families' financial status has made them sometimes feel excluded by other Latinos.

Twenty-six-year-old Yvette is tired of people being surprised that she's Peruvian and not Puerto Rican or Mexican. She moved to Queens, New York, from Lima, Peru, when she was seven. "It was hard coming here, especially being from Peru. Everyone thought that if you were Latina, you were Puerto Rican or Mexican. I had to constantly explain why I looked different. We have straight black hair and different features. I felt like I couldn't identify myself with [any other Latinos], even though we were all Spanish-speakers, because of the vast differences in culture," she recalls.

"When I was younger," Yvette continues, "I had to get a map and show people where I am from. Most stereotypes come from within the Hispanic community. We can be racists, one group toward another. You have to look a certain way, depending on what you are. I am darker. I hated my skin color, because I was one of the darkest in my family. They called me Negrita. It was a constant reminder that I was darker."

Cassandra, twenty-eight, was born in Honduras. She moved to Miami at the age of four, and then to Charlotte, North Carolina, when she was twelve. "I learned to accept people at a very young age. I was curious and not judgmental. I remember coming to Charlotte at twelve and seeing racism and discrimination. The black girls thought I was half black and half white. I was shocked that there wasn't more curiosity about those who were different," says Cassandra.

Elsa received mixed messages within her home that also conflicted with her own developing sense of self. "My father is very racist against his own culture and other cultures. He wants to be white. He wants me to marry a white guy and to be an upper-class American. My mom is very open minded. She just cares that someone is a good person. It has been difficult to know what is okay and when I'm crossing the line. I remember there was a point at school when it wasn't cool to speak Spanish. In Venezuela, they call me La Americana, even though here I am obviously viewed as Hispanic. In Hispanic culture, everything you do is everybody's business, but I had a strong feminist sense, and that is something that is not very acceptable in Venezuela. If you are not married, you are not valid in Venezuela. My mother thinks I should try to find someone, and yet my dad always told me that I wasn't allowed to date anyone until I was twenty-one." Elsa is now twenty-one, and negotiating these mixed messages will be a significant part of her growth. Her acculturation has involved developing a significant sense of her self and her dreams, and her execution of these desires may require having to separate her own needs from those of her parents.

Language is a slippery slope for many Latinas and has been part of what they negotiate in their two worlds. Penelope, a twenty-six-year-old Chicana, grew up in Texas before relocating to California as an adult. She spoke Spanish until age six, when her parents forbade her or her siblings to speak it any more. Now, she says, "I am a perfect English-speaker, but at the loss of my Spanish." You can hear the grief in Penelope's voice when she speaks about her language in this way. But her feelings of loss are complicated. "In Los Angeles," she says, "it's considered offensive if I don't respond to someone in Spanish, but it is equally offensive to me that they expect me to speak Spanish and don't understand the difficulty it took for me to learn English."

Twenty-one-year-old Alyssa walks a tightrope every day and is witness to the way that she pleases different groups based on her language or her looks. She's of Puerto Rican and Cuban descent and notes, "If I didn't speak Spanish the way that I do, I would definitely be looked at as not a real Latina. I look American enough to please the Americans, but I speak Spanish well enough to please the Latinos."

Liza, who's a mix of white, Filipino, and Puerto Rican ancestry, also feels like she's in a position of conforming to whatever expectation people have of her. Twenty-seven and living in San Francisco, she can relate to Alyssa's feeling of walking that tightrope. "I can pass for Latina, but I can also pass for white, so I get criticized by both sides. White people don't want to see things that are culturally different; they ignore it. White people see me as a fake Latina sometimes, because I'm conveniently light for them. They expect me to ignore my ethnicity, but I never do and I never will. On the flip side, Latinos don't know whether they can trust me."

Another common experience women face is people confronting them with being "less than" Latina because they don't have an accent when they speak English. Twenty-seven-year-old Angela grew up in San Antonio, Texas, and articulates this experience and her frustrations with it. "The most irritating statement is when people say 'You are Puerto Rican? You don't sound like it,'" she fumes, exasperated that some people think an ethnicity always has to have a sound.

Esme's experience was more solitary. She's Puerto Rican but did not grow up with Latino friends or extended family. Because of that isolation, she does not feel Latina. Now twenty-three, she tells me, "I don't have a strong attachment to being Puerto Rican. I don't speak Spanish. I'm not around other Puerto Ricans ever." Her family's religious experience was not in a predominantly Latino congregation, nor did they live in a community with many other Latinos. Soon, it became easy to acquiesce to the world around them.

One thing that is very painful for many Latinas is when other Latinas challenge their authenticity. "I have gotten flack from people because I'm pale and I lead a privileged life. That's hurtful," says Marie Isabel, a thirty-seven-year-old Puerto Rican from Pennsylvania.

Carolina, the thirty-year-old from Massachusetts, has had the painful experience of watching a friend erase her Latino culture from her identity in order to make things easier for herself. "She refuses to speak Spanish. She is ashamed that she has that blood in her. I hate that. If you have a strong foundation and family, you should feel like you can be who you are." Although Carolina says this, she's also able to empathize with her friend's feelings, noting that it can be really difficult to embrace the fullness of Latino culture when all the messages are encouraging us to tone it down. "When I go back to the Island, I never feel authentic," she says of her native Puerto Rico. Meanwhile, she has had to learn how to answer the questions she fields stateside. "People want to put you in a box, and we don't all fit neatly into boxes. I usually have to say, 'I am not Spanish. I was not born in Europe.'"

One survey respondent spoke of the frustration she feels as an academic. "As a scholar, and earlier as an aspiring scholar, I did not feel comfortable performing highly visible identities. I saw the resistance that my older cousins encountered by dressing, speaking, and carrying themselves in a way that was viewed as Mexican, and I saw it as a barrier. Ironically, now I feel pressure to perform some of these same identities in the academy, in some ways to demonstrate my authenticity."

Joselyn, who's twenty-three and of Mexican descent, now lives in New York but grew up in a small town in Illinois. "At least once a week, I am asked where I am from. If I don't think the person has any interest in me, I say I am from Illinois and force them to ask the question that they really want to ask. I would like to look Mexican and have people say that I look Mexican. Most people just see what they want to see. I just don't understand why they feel like they need to let me know that I don't fit into their mold. There is a lot of internal discrimination that goes on within the Latino community—if you don't speak Spanish, if you don't dance to the right music. That is more hurtful than anything—to get it from your own ethnic group. I grew up with two cultures, on the cusp of two cultures. I am a combination of both things. At times it's been a source of frustration to me, but my parents have always shown me that I am very lucky to have two cultures and two languages."

LETTING GO

Many Latinas in the United States are juggling their multiple cultures to create a world that they can fully and joyfully inhabit. Sometimes this means letting go of things they view as negative within their Latino culture.

One survey respondent produced a passionate list when asked what aspects of Latino culture would not be included in her life as she moved forward. "Machismo," she wrote at the top of the list. "I will not allow my son to treat women like dirt." Double standards were another one. "I need both of my children to be held accountable for all their decisions in life, regardless of gender," she continued. "Latinas as Spitfires: While I embrace and indulge my sexual appeal, I will not be looked at as only a sexual conquest. Especially for men who are not Latino. Prejudice: I encountered a lot of comments from family members who did not like people of African American or Dominican descent in particular. I've never closed the door on anyone based on origin. In fact, some of my dearest friends are African American and Dominican. I really do see us as all the same. We struggle and come from the same kinds of experiences."

Another survey respondent wrote, "Attention to the physical is a cultural tradition that I renounce. The first thing I do when I see my younger cousins is ask about school, their goals, and their passions—not about their boyfriends or whether they look fatter or thinner."

The majority of the women who responded to the Growing Up Latina Survey felt that the spiritual and the pious are significant parts of their upbringing. Of the total respondents, 96% were raised in a faith tradition, but only 32.7% participate in a faith community today. So, it's no surprise that some of the respondents were sensitive to how they were moving forward in their lives with regard to faith, since it seemed to be a defining principle of their youth.

Many respondents wrote about the way that they approach faith and spirituality differently from the way their parents' or grandparents' generation did. "I am not very pious," wrote one respondent. "I rarely go to church and am not a devout Catholic. I don't believe in marriage. I see marriage as an exclusive agreement within institutions (church, state) that ostracize certain individuals—queer communities, individuals who cannot afford to get married, et cetera—and advocate certain gender roles."

Another woman expressed that " . . . while culturally I feel close to Catholicism, I can't see myself practicing many of the things that my grandmother would. Though I find La Guadalupe beautiful symbolically, it wouldn't be sincere to have her in my home and hold a vigil to her. I think religious differences are what separate many modern Latinas from their moms and grandmothers."

Other respondents worried about the way women are viewed by some within the Latino culture and protested against the stereotype-based limitations they felt.

One woman included the following statement on the list of things not to be replicated in her own life that she saw in previous generations: "Being forced to choose between education, career, motherhood, and/or family, or postponing your desires and dreams to start a family on your own."

Another wrote, "I will not allow racist, sexist, or homophobic traditions to continue in my home. I will not expect men to be seated before women at special dinners. I will not encourage or demand a wedding ceremony of my partner. I will be open to an alternative celebration of love and partnership. I will not demand a *quinceañera* for my children (if I have any), but I will be open to their desires for one."

Another wrote, "The dependence on looks to be a determining factor for Latinas. I grew up knowing that I was pretty to the eye, but my real power was in my brain. Being pretty was a bonus—not my ticket in. Seeing how Latinas are portrayed for their bodies and not for their intelligence. I will not pass this on to my two girls."

HOLDING ON

Other values and traditions, many felt, are crucial to Latinas' understanding of themselves, as well as their sense of heritage and tradition. One woman wrote, "I'd like to maintain not only the stuff I grew up with—food, holiday traditions—but also incorporate other Latino and multicultural traditions. We incorporate many Dominican customs, such as the tradition of the godfather throwing coins to the child when she is baptized, because my husband is Dominican. I teach my daughter about other traditions, like Diwali,

Ramadan, Saint Lucia's Day. Since we live in New York, I would say our cultural influence is so diverse that our parents' heritage is just one piece of the mosaic."

Many respondents mentioned food. One wrote, "A lot of my family life has revolved around food. Family parties, Christmas, Thanksgiving, even Sundays were about eating. Not just eating, but the preparation of the food as a way of bonding and bringing women together. Christmas to me is always about *pernil* and rice with *frijoles negros* on my mom's Cuban side. On my dad's Puerto Rican side, my aunts make *pasteles* during the holidays. Food is what brings us together, and I will always look forward to those holidays as an opportunity to eat together."

Some women were very philosophical in considering what traditions would move forward with them in life. One respondent wrote, "My family taught me to be proud of my Puerto Rican heritage to the fullest. Everything that is Boricua style fits into my lifestyle. I make sure of that. I enjoy sharing my culture with others. It makes me proud that I'm not one to disown my heritage because of ignorant minds, or temporarily claim it when it can be to my advantage. I am proud of who I am and where I come from, so my lifestyle strongly reflects that on all fronts."

Another explained, "Upon reaching adulthood, I learned to preserve all ceremonies, holiday foods, and traditions. Growing up in the States, you tend to drift away from these traditions in order to blend with the American culture. However, once I discovered the meaning of these traditions, I feel I was able to identify myself more with Latino cultures versus the Anglo."

Several interviewees were intent on holding on to parts of their native culture and found ways to incorporate unique details into their weddings. Eva's bridesmaids wore orange and deep-pink sarongs to reflect tropical colors and Puerto Rican styles. Her menu had classic Puerto Rican fare like *arroz con gandules* and *pernil*. Their music was a mix of English and Latino staples, and Eva danced a swansong at the end—a traditional flamenco dance.

Other women just had simple catchphrases to explain their approach to tradition and holding on to their heritage.

"The older I get, the more Puerto Rican I become," wrote one.

"Speak English. Live Latin," another shared.

One interviewee also had streamlined advice. "You have to learn to create a balance," says Placer, the twenty-four-year-old Dominican American from Florida. "You can't totally leave one culture. Rather, learn how to balance both lifestyles."

Some of these practices are small things, but no matter the size, the intention serves to keep us all connected to our identity. These practices validate where we came from and honor who we are becoming, regardless of anyone else's interpretation of our experience.

We are molded at a very young age to believe in choosing sides, in aligning ourselves with a particular belief, and picking what we like best. "What is your favorite color?" we are asked as children. "What is your favorite food?" We live in a society that cannot function without categorization. The forms we fill out in childhood give us just a few options for what we can be according to race, omitting the reality that the greatest understanding people have of themselves is their connection to all of the parts that make them who they are.

Growing up in America as a Latina means heading into the world ripe with two influences (oftentimes more). Though that can be complicated, we are doing it with more and more skill. We are starting to clarify people's understanding of us. We are learning to appreciate the richness of our experience. We are becoming sensitive to the fact that our Latinidad is not determined by our language or our looks; it is determined by our hearts. We know that we have the power to define *ourselves* and tell the world just what that definition is.

Finally—because of the work women who've come before us have done, and the work that we are doing—we are not inventing our way as we go. We have the capacity to join with our sisters in support of all the ways in which we choose to be Latina—no matter where we exist on that invisible continuum. We are all authentic, because of what we have lived, and that is what we should recognize most when we look into one of the faces of our *comadres*.

Seven

María de la Barbie

What does it mean to be beautiful in America? The answer to this question brings up all kinds of clichés. Reality shows, magazines, sitcoms, movies, and music videos propagate a certain image—tall, thin, and blond—that's unattainable for most women. But pop culture isn't the only place where beauty matters. Female news anchors, executives, and CEOs, even high-power board members, find that beauty plays a role in breaking through the glass ceiling. Beauty is so valued, it's become a commodity.

The question that comes up for me when I think about the power beauty has over our lives and experiences is this: What happens to girls whose self-image is shaped by other people's beauty standards, and whose own features aren't reflected back to them in the everyday images the media promotes? For today's young Latinas, there are some Latina role models, but most of those role models represent yet another unattainable beauty standard. Many Latinas live with a feeling of not being accepted because of how they look. For those of us who have dark skin, raven hair, and a short stature, there isn't much external validation. The average woman of any ethnicity is different from what's celebrated on television, in magazines, and in life. But often, in Latin culture, these

differences are exacerbated by the fact that the families' input offers such a distinct point of view—one that's often at odds with the
larger culture.

Thus, as Latinas we can be caught in between two standards of
beauty—not feeling beautiful in either culture, or feeling beautiful
in one but not the other. No matter where we stand, we're on the
precipice of judgment, with one set of values that informs our lives
shaped by American pop culture and another set shaped by our
families' culture and traditions.

Oftentimes there's another perspective as well—our own: a
perspective that takes into account the impact of the first two and
how they push and pull at our self-image and feelings of who we
are. This last perspective is the place where we can find peace in
ourselves, which is what ultimately leads us to our real beauty.

I have memories from childhood that indicate just how much
American pop culture influenced my worldview. In one memory,
I'm sitting in front of the TV, lamenting the size of my nose compared to the girls' noses on-screen. I can remember my mother telling me that I could pinch my nostrils and pull my nose outward to
change its shape. And I followed that advice. Pinch, pull, pinch,
pull. But my nose never budged.

As early as third grade, my best friend, Jenny, and I used to lament our weight in comparison to other girls'. I remember walking
to her house one day as we schemed about the perfect plan to rid
ourselves of those extra pounds.

"We could just pinch our fat off and put it on somebody else
without her knowing it," we laughed. As an adult with some extra
pounds to spare, I look empathetically back at my third-grade self,
wondering how it was possible that I thought I was fat. We were
just eight, and wiry. When Jenny and I remember it now, we are

both dumbfounded by the fact that popular culture was sending us the message that we needed to be smaller.

I also remember watching *The Dukes of Hazzard* on Friday nights, and how much we loved that show, and how Daisy Duke would strut her stuff in those oh-so-short shorts. There are plenty of times when I might have learned that being skinny was how you should look, and that showing off your body is how to get attention.

One summer when I was a preteen, one of my cousins from Puerto Rico came to visit for a couple weeks. We spent our days playing a game we called Model. We did our hair, tried on various outfits, and posed awkwardly next to plants or on the edge of a bed with one hand under our chin while snapping photos of each other with my Kodak 110 camera. I still have those pictures. We both had thick black hair that was unmanageable, despite our attempts to iron it (this was before the availability of flatirons). We were emulating the white girls we saw in *Seventeen* and *YM,* even though we were a far cry from them.

Later I became so absorbed in other things that beauty was not my primary—or even secondary—obsession. As a middle-schooler, I ran for seventh-grade president in an effort to keep my family from moving. Either it worked or they decided they didn't want to move, because I won and we stayed.

I was involved in student government and community service throughout middle and high school. During that time, I wasn't at all stylish. Each morning, I woke up fifteen minutes before my ride came. I arrived at school with my tumble of curls sopping down my back, a Pop-Tart in hand. I wore jeans and T-shirts. And the first major blow to my self-confidence didn't come until ninth grade, when my football-star boyfriend, a junior, dumped me for a cheerleader I had introduced him to at the homecoming dance (because I thought I was too short to dance with him). She was 5'7" to his 6'4", a much better match than my 5'1". The cheerleader was almost my antithesis: Tall and thin, she had porcelain-white skin with pretty black hair and light eyes. I pined and I pitied myself, but I managed to rebound.

By the next fall, Wade and I were serious, and it was a relationship that would last until the spring of eleventh grade. My junior year, I threw myself into school and started losing weight. Still, I wasn't thinking too much about my looks. I wore no makeup, dressed casually, hung out with boys that were friends rather than potential flames. By my senior year, I was dating someone from another high school, and even though I sometimes looked around at my peers and felt not feminine enough, it wasn't enough to change my behavior.

The real shock to my worldview came in college, where the diversity of my high school no longer shielded me from seeing how different I was. At a school where the tuition was high and where less than one-third of the students were on financial aid (I being one of them), I was not just an ethnic minority. I was a socioeconomic minority, and both of those differences felt compounded in my daily life. It was then and there that I began to wonder whether my beauty and body were inadequate. It was then and there that I started to feel isolated, alone, unrecognizable—where I realized that I would have to reconcile my gringa and my Latina.

THE SCENE MAY BE BROWNER, BUT . . .

When J.Lo hit the scene, it seemed that Hollywood suddenly up and took notice of Latinas in a different way. As a Fly Girl on *In Living Color,* her dark, curly hair and strong body reflected her roots.

Jenny from the Block was sturdy, not starved. Then, when she played Selena, the slain Chicana singer who was the number-one Latina star in the United States and Mexico before she died, she was introduced to a much broader audience because of the number and diversity of Latinas who flocked to see her on the silver screen.

Soon Jennifer Lopez had caught our collective imagination. She exemplified the modern Latina, but it wouldn't be long before her urban Bronx edge was traded in for a more sophisticated image that turned her into a national—not just Latina—beauty icon. Still, the attention she was getting affirmed Latinas all over the country. Suddenly there was someone who looked a lot more like one of us than the standard blond beauties of the 1980s and most of the '90s. She became the poster girl for Latina beauty: olive skin, full butt, feminine curves. It wasn't long before other Latinas entered the scene: Eva Mendes, Michelle Rodriguez, Zoe Saldana, Eva Longoria.

In the Growing Up Latina Survey, respondents were asked to list in rank order up to five well-known women of any ethnicity whom they considered beautiful. Eleven of the fifteen top choices reflected women of color. Only two were blonds, which reflects the fact that Hollywood does have many more minority and women-of-color role models than it did fifteen or even ten years ago. The top fifteen women from the survey, in order, were: Salma Hayek, Halle Berry, Angelina Jolie, Jennifer Lopez, Eva Mendes, Catherine Zeta-Jones, Eva Longoria, Beyoncé Knowles, Talisa Soto, Charlize Theron, Jessica Alba, Penélope Cruz, Scarlett Johannson, Adriana Lima, and Tyra Banks.

More and more, women of color, and Latinas specifically, are gracing the covers of magazines, acting as spokeswomen for beauty products, and starring in major motion pictures and television dramas. Beauty in the new millennium, it seems, is diversifying, and the women interviewed for this book have certainly noticed the change.

"Being a Latina has become more mainstream and acceptable, so we're popular right now," says thirty-two-year-old Mia, a Puerto Rican who lives in New York City. "In the media there is more exposure for Latinas, because we're becoming a fad in American mainstream culture. You certainly see more Latinas than when I was growing up."

Thirty-four-year-old Claudia, who's of Ecuadorian descent and lives in New York, says she felt better as soon as J.Lo entered the public scene. "I grew up with a complex about my body, because I was pretty thick. I always considered myself fat based on what I saw as the perfect American girl. Watching TV and looking at magazines, you see these skinny girls. I used to wear baggy clothes because I felt fat. But once people like J.Lo came out, I started to feel better about my body."

Camille, a twenty-seven-year-old New Yorker who's of mixed Colombian and Dominican descent, agrees with this sentiment. "I just never saw many women like me on the TV when I was growing up. Now I am seeing more women who look like me, and I am making a connection. But when I was growing up, I wanted light eyes and a different body type."

Still, the diversification of the type of women being represented in pop culture and by the media has not completely alleviated the pressure that many Latinas feel about their bodies and looks.

"The media has had a huge, huge impact on what I see as 'pretty.' I am okay with myself, but when I am around other college girls, and they all look like what the media shows, I am uncomfortable," says eighteen-year-old Nora, who's *puertorriqueña,* grew up in Charlotte, North Carolina, and feels pressured by American pop culture to have big breasts and a small stomach. "It is all about the body. You don't even have to have a pretty face as long as you have the body."

You would think that the greater representation of Latinas on the small screen and the silver screen would reinvigorate the confidence of Latinas across the country. It's not that easy. Some protest how these women are presented and the implications those portrayals have on the women who are out in mainstream society on a daily basis.

Twenty-five-year-old Gabriela is of Colombian and Cuban descent and is from Houston, Texas. "On the one hand, they portray [Latinas] as hoochies, but on the other hand, they are the fiery and sexy characters who bring a *boom!* to the screen. You have your Salma Hayeks and J.Los, but they are thinner and different from other Latinas," she says.

I agree with Gabriela's observation. I have always marveled at how the mainstream media praise Latina actresses like Salma Hayek and J.Lo for embracing their curves—but compared to many, these are relatively petite women. Salma and J.Lo may have curves, but their bodies are far closer to the bodies of Hollywood's other "It" women than to the average girl on the street in middle America.

Many of the women I interviewed lamented the lack of diversity among the Latinas in Hollywood. "Hollywood doesn't have enough diversity of Latinas. I haven't seen a Latina with cocoa-brown skin and black hair," observed Yvonne, thirty-three, who's Puerto Rican and now lives in Charlotte, North Carolina.

There are Afro-Latina actresses, but many play black characters rather than Latina characters, like Zoe Saldana in the movie *Guess Who?* and Gina Torres of the *Matrix* movies. However, there is an

exception: Gina did land a part playing a Cuban, her true national-
ity, when she fast-talked the directors of *Alias* into giving her a role
they had intended for a Russian or Czech character. Thus, Anna
Espinosa was born, showing prime time television audiences that
Latinas come in more than one shade.

While J.Lo is often praised by the media for staying true to
her roots, others would argue that she's been altering herself little by little—her hair, her look, her attitude—since her days as a
Fly Girl.

"Everything you see on TV, it's not who we are. The Latinas are
very thin, and they all look similar. J.Lo keeps getting lighter. Her
hair keeps getting straighter," says thirty-three-year-old Mariselle,
who's Puerto Rican and Dominican and grew up in Brooklyn.

In the fall of 2006, Jennifer Lopez darkened her hair just
before the Toronto Film Festival. The following day, before-and-
after photos appeared on People.com with the write-up: "Jennifer
Lopez unveiled a radical new look at the Toronto Film Festival
last night—her hair is now a deep espresso brown! We haven't
seen J.Lo with hair this dark since her Fly Girl days. Was she inspired by all the other stars going dark? We're so used to seeing her
with her perfectly highlighted honey-colored locks, we're a little
in shock! But we give it a big thumbs up."[1] It's fascinating that
despite the increase of women-of-color actresses, it's still breaking
news when one woman of color returns to a shade resembling her
natural hair color.

People then asked its readers to voice their opinions on her
new shade. Responses varied from comments that it better suited
her skin tone and made her look younger, to one person who wrote
in saying that when Latinas go lighter than their natural hair color,
they just look fake.[2] The reaction to J.Lo's hair color says something

positive to me: that the diversification within the United States and its media is having an affirmative effect on what people see as viable beauty options. And this is good news for everyone. If mainstream media began embracing women of various sizes and statures, perhaps it would not be long before those images also influenced what we consider to be beautiful in regard to body shape and size.

Clara lives in New York City, and she offers another analysis of Hollywood and J.Lo. She's twenty-nine and part Peruvian, and she opines, "I don't think we even had a voice until J.Lo's butt came along, and suddenly we're getting some recognition that Latina women have butts because white women don't. But J.Lo really made a name for herself with her body, and I think that's sad, because Salma sometimes gets overlooked—and she's an amazing actress."

Reactions to Lopez's acting have alternated between praise for her performance in movies like *Selena* and *Out of Sight* and criticism for films like *Anaconda* and *Gigli*. Yet reviews have consistently called her ravishing and beautiful, and her looks are rarely overlooked in a critique of her performance. The way Latina actresses are scrutinized for their appearance is telling about what critics value and what they believe Latinas are bringing to the screen.

It's not just stereotypes about looks that critics play into. Stereotypes about the "Latina character" are featured, too. In 2006, in a review of the play *Torches,* which ran in Charlotte, North Carolina, a male reviewer wrote of a Latina actress: "After years of mostly forgettable performances in and around Charlotte, [she] seems to be tapping into her inner Latina. In quick succession, she has sizzled in two hot-blooded roles."[3] Seriously?

One survey respondent wrote that she felt that Latina actresses were still viewed in a marginalized way. "Famous Latinas are not celebrated on the same level as other actresses. They are just considered beautiful for their slender and exotic looks."

Other survey participants worried about the implications of how Latinas are portrayed. One respondent wrote, "Most of these women are portrayed in sexual roles. The most famous Latinas in America are movie stars, which may cause Americans to think that we do not have any Latina women who are famous for other successes, such as politics, writing, social movements, for being community leaders, et cetera. I do feel that some of these women, like Salma Hayek, have done a great job at being educated about societal problems, and not just for being pretty faces."

"It's somewhat sad," says Jessica, a twenty-two-year-old Chicago student of El Salvadoran descent, describing the way Hollywood portrays Latinas. "We are rowdy, rambunctious women—uneducated, speak with a slight accent, with big butts—who dance merengue. The Latinas who've made it are from specific backgrounds, like Mexico and Puerto Rico, and they're closing the public's eye to all the differences of Latinos and Latino culture."

Pop culture movements are dramatically affecting young Latinas in the United States. One such movement is Reggaetón, a musical craze that's a hybrid of different music and cultures.

"Young people are desperate for identity. I see this a lot in the girls that I advise," says Gloria, age forty and born in Puerto Rico. She now mentors young Latinas in New Jersey. "They have this whole thing in trying to identify with the image that Reggaetón promotes. It is the big charms, the big pants, the slang. This doesn't make you Puerto Rican. I think it's really sad where things are heading. Latinos have a lot more representation on TV, but there is a stereotype going around because of Reggaetón and movies and videos that show Latinos as streetwise. This is what the young kids identify as being Latino."

As Latinas, we're inevitably shaped by the images we see, but we can choose whether and how we internalize these values. In my research, women's opinions ranged widely. Some felt that American culture has truly made progress based on the mere fact that there are so many more Latinas in the mainstream media than there were five years ago. Others felt that we are still marginalized, and the very notion of lifting up these few women is equivalent to treating them like tokens, or poster girls, for Latinas as a whole.

Me? I fall somewhere in between: I'm thrilled to see the diversity that exists in the world begin to take root in American media, but sometimes I'm mortified by things like the choice of title for the ABC *telenovela Ugly Betty*. I know it's meant to be sarcastic and ironic, since Betty is the most together, well-intentioned, and good-humored character on the show. It might even be a clarion call for us about how we see beauty. But there is still a poignancy about calling her ugly, naming an anxiety that's so acute. To me, it seems to speak to the fact that plenty of people don't flinch at calling women ugly, fat, and many other descriptors that are direct attacks on our physical appearances. What are we saying to young girls when we identify someone as ugly just because she has bad hair, braces, and glasses?

I know that not having Latina role models when I was growing up was difficult, but sometimes I wonder whether it's even harder for Latinas growing up today, because the Latina role models on display are really in a league of their own. For a while it seemed as though Latina role models were far underrepresented compared to the range of female African American role models who were becoming more visible: Black girls had Queen Latifah, Aisha Tyler, Halle

Berry, Beyoncé, Kerry Washington, and Janet Jackson long before any real Latina presence could be seen in the media. Fortunately, women like America Ferrera are showing us a more representative view of Latina women. Her work in *Real Women Have Curves* and *The Sisterhood of the Traveling Pants* revealed the depth of the Latina experience.

Sara Ramirez's role as Dr. Callie Torres on *Grey's Anatomy* portrays a strong, smart, beautiful, and average-size Latina. And it works, except for the occasional script misstep, such as the scene where another doctor describes her as so sexy that she is "dirty sexy." Why does the Latina doctor have to be the one who's *dirty* sexy?

WHAT ARE YOU LOOKING AT?

The media—fickle and constantly changing as it is—embraces beauty because of its emphasis on everything visual. American mainstream or pop culture ideals are often propagated by the way they're interpreted. As viewers and consumers, we are largely responsible for the very things that bother many of us.

Lisette—who is twenty, of Puerto Rican and Italian descent, and from Manhattan—says, "American media is telling women that they need to have big boobs, perfect teeth, little noses, be skinny and tan, have straight hair. White women are always talking about changing themselves—especially aging women."

Josette, who's twenty-eight and living in San Francisco, talked about her opinion of plastic surgery as a characteristic of the American ideal. "It's very plastic, fake, fantasy, unreal—so perfect that it looks ugly," she says. Twenty-seven-year-old Thalia of San Antonio, Texas, describes the U.S. ideal as "thin—and not even thin with shape. Pencil thin. Androgynous."

Mariana, who's of Colombian descent and grew up in Dallas, Texas, says, "In America, the faker the look, the better." When I ask her about it, she admits that this perception has greatly affected her happiness and confidence. "I am never secure in my appearance," she tells me. "When I was growing up, the fact that I wasn't considered pretty and no boys were ever attracted to me affected me a lot. When I was little, my wish was to be pretty one day. I was always the smart girl or the nice girl. I feel like my looks are not reliable enough. If another pretty girl comes around me, I get very insecure. Being around a lot of white people when I was younger kind of messed up my confidence. Now I'm twenty-seven, a size six, and on Weight Watchers. I'm scared that I'm going to get fat."

Marie Isabel has a quick response to the idea of beauty in American mainstream culture. "You are supposed to be thin, tall, and Susie Homemaker," answers the thirty-seven-year-old *puertorriqueña*. "I'm a size eight, and by white American standards, I am fat."

Angela is a twenty-seven-year-old Puerto Rican from San Antonio who echoes Marie Isabel and Thalia. "Women need to be size two, skinny, and blond with blue eyes. It's the two-by-four look: a straight line with no curves. It's what you see in so many magazines or actresses. They almost look androgynous. It is so unrealistic for most everyone."

Forty-year-old Rosa, who's Peruvian and grew up in Chicago, also balks at this unattainable ideal. "I think, especially in American culture, that being thin is everything. But as we all know, the majority of Americans are not thin. We are expected to conform to that image, and yet clearly we don't. We are made up of all sorts of shapes and sizes. The media has a lot to do with promoting that thin, Caucasian beauty."

Mia describes the trends she sees as harmful to young women in general. The thirty-two-year-old Puerto Rican living in New York City says, "There's a ridiculous drive for perfection: how thin you are, the labels you wear, following the trends. It's dangerous, because it has a potential to distort young women's perceptions about their bodies."

"Nowadays, the media makes it seem like if you aren't thin or skinny—if you don't look a certain way—you aren't going to be completely accepted by society. Even when you are beautiful, they still try to find other things that are wrong with us. There are all these shows about wanting to look like other people. People automatically assume that you can look better," adds Marisa, thirty-three, who's of Puerto Rican and Colombian descent.

It would seem that if we could change the way the media promotes its images, we might be able to curb some of the disturbing trends that lead young women to feel bad about themselves. However, a study by Dr. Naomi Mandel and Dr. Dirk Smeesters titled "Positive and Negative Media Image Effects," in the *Journal of Consumer Research,* offers an interesting point. I interviewed Dr. Mandel to get a better understanding of their work.

"Previous research has found that women often feel bad about themselves after viewing thin models in advertisements. We wanted to see if there were any exceptions to these previous findings. In fact, we discovered that there were two moderating factors to prior findings: (1) the extremity of the model's thinness (or heaviness); and (2) how the researchers measure women's self-esteem. We also found that women's responses to the ads depended on whether or not they saw similarities between themselves and the models," Mandel told me in the interview.

The researchers measured self-esteem using two scales. The first test asked women to use a seven-point system that ranged from highly unattractive to highly attractive to describe a model and themselves. With this scale, the women rated themselves lower after viewing a thin model. The second test measured self-esteem using a free-response system, and an interesting thing happened then.[4]

"Women reported their self-esteem as lower after looking at an extremely thin model than after looking at an extremely heavy model, but they reported their self-esteem as higher after looking at a moderately thin model than after looking at a moderately heavy model. When viewing a moderate model (thin or heavy), women see the similarities between themselves and the model, and thus see themselves as thinner when looking at thin models than when looking at heavy models. When viewing an extreme model (thin or heavy), women see the differences between themselves and the model, and thus see themselves as heavier when looking at thin models than when looking at heavy models."

When I asked Dr. Mandel about the implications of this research, her answer flew directly in the face of the notion that just changing the media could end the problem. "Our findings suggest that ads such as the Dove Real Women ads may not be effective. Not only do they not raise women's self-esteem, contrary to Dove's claims, but they are unlikely to increase sales of beauty-related products. My intuition is that in order to sell beauty-enhancing products, one must make the consumer feel insecure about her appearance, and then offer a plausible solution to her problem. This is what we are currently studying," says Dr. Mandel.

So if changing the media isn't the solution, perhaps changing the way we react to the media is. If we buy in to the images that we're fed and hold them to be true, then our time and resources are certain to be disproportionately invested in our appearances. Our appearance can't change the world. Our appearance doesn't invest in our community, doesn't raise children, doesn't cure cancer, doesn't provide microloans to small-business owners around the world. Women everywhere are an invaluable part of the fabric of community. We save lives and create great things. So why waste our valuable talents by allowing the media to dictate what's important in our lives? We have better things to do than spend all of our time concerning ourselves with what the media thinks is essential. Let's define what's important for ourselves.

A WIDER BERTH

The weight of the media and beauty perception in the lives of women is severe. Respondents to the Growing Up Latina Survey were asked whether they thought American society expects women to do whatever they can to be more attractive, and 94.4% of the women said yes. Also, 87% believe that attractive women are move valued in our society, and 70.3% believe that attractive women face fewer obstacles on a daily basis.

These perceptions significantly impact the lives of Latinas. They perpetuate feelings of otherness and create standards that seem unattainable; as a result, some women feel as if they are second rate because of their appearance.

Latinas' feelings about beauty within their own communities varied greatly. Most women felt much more accepted within the familial Latino community, noting that there is more acceptance of a range of beauty and body types.

"I don't think there is a set type, a 'this is how a Latina should look' mentality. I think Latino men are very accepting of the differences Latinas have. It's about having confidence in yourself," says Jessica, the twenty-two-year-old of El Salvadoran heritage.

Raquel is nineteen, and her family is Guatemalan. She agrees that Latino culture leaves more room for women to be real women: "I think our culture allows us to be more comfortable with our bodies. They embrace women as they should be—curvy, or in any shape or form. My white peers have to deal with a more media-obsessed culture, so they tend to follow what the media is telling them at the moment," she says.

Some of the data from the Growing Up Latina Survey support the notion that the wider berth many Latinas feel they have within their culture's beauty standards positively shapes their self-image. When asked if they were satisfied with their looks, 16.6% of the women strongly agreed, and 64.9% agreed. When asked if they were satisfied with their body shape, the numbers went down but were still mostly positive: 7.1% strongly agreed and 54.7% agreed. Overall, Latinas were more confident about their facial attractiveness than their physical attractiveness: 59.9% said they were satisfied with their facial attractiveness, and 25.3% said they were very satisfied. With regard to physical attractiveness, 62% reported being satisfied, and 10.9% were very satisfied.

The women I interviewed touched upon the idea that there are distinct preferences around appearance that vary even among Latino cultures. When asked what she believes Latinos find beautiful, Diana, who's twenty-one and Puerto Rican, spoke to her own experience of what she feels people from Caribbean Latin American countries find most beautiful. Now living in Marietta, Georgia, she speaks about her experience of Puerto Rico. "Where I am from, the islanders like a Coke-bottle shape. Natural beauty is what is big in Puerto Rico." She tells me that she physically developed at a young age, and so the body image she felt Puerto Ricans valued was one that she always felt she had.

But the Latino standards of beauty are by no means simple. "Caribbean women are different from South American women. South American women are less curvy, don't have the big hips or big boobs. They have straighter hair," says Yvette, who's twenty-six years old; she was born in Lima, Peru, and moved to New York when she was seven. "The images I got from TV were those of curvaceous women—and not all of us Latinas fit that profile. Not all of us are sexy and sensual. I believe most of the images are from a Caribbean perspective, which leaves others out. I am slim and petite. Where do I fit?"

An important point to make is that there is no typical anything. Just like there is not one typical white, Asian, or black girl, there is no typical Latino—and no typical Puerto Rican, Colombian, or Mexican either. Having just one image of Latinos—when there are twenty-plus countries and immeasurable amounts of cultural mixing—is impossible.

Thirty-year-old Sarah, who's part Colombian and part Cuban, laments the messages she received from her family that reinforced what she read in magazines. "The overwhelming message was that you have to focus on one thing, one asset that you have. My aunt told me that for her, it was her tits. 'I have beautiful tits,' she would say. She is one of the sexiest women I know. She would sit me down and say, 'Why don't you focus on your eyes and lips? You have bold, beautiful lips.' So at fifteen, I was in the hospital with broken bones and putting on lip gloss to meet the doctor, and my aunt was saying, 'You are going to be such a catch for some man, because you have such good lips.' I have pretty severe acne and a lot of skin conditions, and my aunts had me go through so many different products with the goal of getting clearer, lighter skin. The message was that I had to suffer to be beautiful. Then you grow up and find out that it's not true. Dating women helped me a lot in terms of security. A lot of the self-esteem I have now came from dating women."

Sarah's experience in the hospital is not unusual. I've listened to plenty of Latinas lament how their mothers insisted that they look their best at the most inopportune times, like when they are lying in a hospital bed after giving birth. Sarah's liberation came when she realized that surface beauty isn't what signifies your worth. It's your own sense of self that's the most valuable component of beauty.

Although the great majority (84.1%) of the women who responded to the Growing Up Latina Survey felt that women today are held to a higher beauty standard than women were twenty years ago, they personally weren't spending to keep up with that ideal: 75.2% of them spent less than $50 a month on beauty products and procedures, with another 20.7% spending less than $100. Though it's true that we might be held to a higher beauty standard, I think it's also true that there's more critiquing and distrust of the media. We are becoming more and more aware of the number the media is doing on our minds, and we are becoming more vigilant about differentiating between real pressures and unrealistic ones. Though some women will be driven to surgeries or spending thousands on upkeep, there are also women who have found their own inner sense of security and self-confidence in spite of the media. The media, though powerful, don't have to get the final word on determining how we feel about ourselves.

THE FIRST CUT IS THE DEEPEST

I've been interviewing Mariana, the twenty-seven-year-old from Dallas, Texas, for over an hour, and I already feel as if she is an old friend. Then I ask her this question: "Have you ever considered or had plastic surgery?"

Her answer reminds me that this isn't just a regular conversation between friends. Our exchange is part of a quest to better understand beauty and body image among my Latina *comadres*.

"I had a nose job when I was sixteen," she says. "I had a little bit of a bump on the bridge, and I didn't like my nose. My mom said she didn't like it either, so she told me to get a nose job before my Sweet Sixteen so I wouldn't hate the pictures."

I recalled my own quest to pull my nose longer when I was young, and I wondered what I would have done if my mother had told me that she didn't like my nose and encouraged me to get a nose job.

Mariana continues with her story. "Then, when I was in my early twenties, I still didn't like the way my nose looked, so I had another nose job."

Her first surgery was in New York. Her doctor had reassured her that she would recover quickly, but that wasn't the case. The recovery was difficult—complete with vomiting, pain, and bruising. She had her second surgery in Bogotá, Colombia, while she was visiting family. They were the ones who encouraged her to try again. The procedure and recovery went far more smoothly, but still, she looks back at both experiences now as unnecessary.

"I don't recommend surgery for anyone unless you have a serious defect. And my nose is not really that much different at all. Beauty goes beyond the nose," she says.

Interestingly, her American doctor had insisted that he would keep the ethnic appeal of her nose and just remove the bump that so dismayed her. It was important to him that she keep the look that honored her Colombian roots. In Colombia years later, on a visit to see family, it was the fact that Mariana's nose still held her Colombian heritage that led her family members to urge her to alter it once again. It's strange how each doctor admired and catered to the outside culture's look.

The results of the Growing Up Latina Survey loosely parallel the overall rates of plastic surgery in the United States. Almost 5% of the survey respondents reported having had plastic surgery (and another 42.5% have considered it). Latinos in the United States lead all minority groups in cosmetic surgery, comprising 6% of the 9.2 million cosmetic surgery procedures performed in the United States in 2004 (and 8.5% of cosmetic procedures in general, including noninvasive procedures). According to the American Society of Plastic Surgeons, more than half a million procedures were performed on Latinos in 2004, which represents nearly double the number of procedures performed on Latinos in 2000.[5] In 2005, those numbers jumped by another 921,000 procedures, an increase of 67% from the previous year. The most popular surgical procedures for Latinas were nose reshaping, breast augmentation, and liposuction.[6] And these surgeries, as you can imagine, don't come cheap. In 2004, the average cost of an augmentation was $3,437; liposuction averaged $2,704, and rhinoplasty averaged $4,047.[7]

Internationally, the United States leads the world in plastic surgery. Mexico ranks second; Brazil ranks third; Argentina, eighth; Ecuador, seventeenth; and Colombia, twenty-third.[8] But these numbers are misleading because of the population of these countries. In terms of number of procedures per capita, Mexico ranks ninth; Argentina ranks eleventh; Ecuador, twelfth; the United States, nineteenth; Brazil, twenty-third; and Colombia, thirtieth.[9]

I had always heard that Argentinean and Brazilian women were among the most beautiful in the world. The rates of plastic surgery in those countries, however, made me wonder about these women and their reputation for beauty. At what cost had that beauty come—both physically and financially? Has the pressure to uphold the standard that's been placed upon them become so strong that plastic surgery is a relatively common thing in those cultures?

The number of Latinos in the United States who have procedures also raises another question. Is the increase in surgery among Latinos representative only of the rise in plastic surgery in the United States in general, or is there a beauty standard among Latinos that makes them susceptible to increased plastic surgery?

To gain some perspective, I spoke to Dr. Henry Vasconez, Professor of Surgery and Chief of the Division of Plastic and Reconstructive Surgery at the University of Kentucky. Originally from Ecuador, he has seen an increase in the number of Latina patients in his practice in Lexington, Kentucky. When asked what cosmetic-surgery requests Latina patients were making, he listed rhinoplasty, facial rejuvenation, and body contouring—which can include breast reduction, breast augmentation, and liposuction.

"My Brazilian, Argentinian, and Mexican colleagues are very busy with cosmetic surgeries. That leads me to think that Latinas look at beauty and self-image as very important," says Dr. Vasconez. Citing the historic and cultural pressure for Latinas to always look their best when out in public, which has not always been an American priority, Dr. Vasconez believes this pressure influences the ease with which some Latinas seek out plastic surgery once they have overcome any economic limits to it.

"The sense that they want to look good—and that in order to do that they're willing to allow change to occur—is a more prevalent idea or concept for Latinas," he says.

The women interviewed for this book give faces to the numbers behind Latinas having plastic surgery in America. Maritza, a thirty-year-old Mexican American who lives in Texas, had plastic surgery done when she was twenty-eight. She traveled to Mexico to get the nose job her family had been encouraging her to get since she was seventeen. While Maritza acknowledges that she feels more comfortable when people look at her, and she no longer minds having her picture taken, she is not completely satisfied.

"I wish I had done it smaller," she says, which made me wonder how many women are ever completely satisfied after cosmetic surgery. In fact, her family also believes she should have gone smaller. Still, she cautions others to be careful with their choices. "Do it because you want to, and try to keep it natural. Do not overdo it."

Amelia, nineteen, is of Argentinean descent, and she too had rhinoplasty, at age seventeen in her home state of Maryland. "I had a very crooked nose. It was hard to breathe, especially when I played soccer, and it was just disgusting to look at. I wasn't happy with how I looked, and it didn't make me feel confident."

Amelia's mom approached her about the surgery and was supportive of her getting it done. "My mom helped me prepare for the fact that people would be talking about it in school if I went through with it. . . . She told me, 'Who cares? As long as you are happy.' She told me not to make a big deal about it and not to lie about it. She told me to just say, 'Yeah, I got plastic surgery. Don't I look great?' And then people wouldn't care."

Insurance covered a significant portion of Amelia's surgery, and today she is happy with the results. "I am one hundred percent more confident than I ever was before surgery. I get compliments all the time, and when I tell people I got surgery, they can't believe it. In this age where plastic surgery is so common, I think it really wasn't a big deal, and my family was extremely supportive and turned it into something really insignificant, so I didn't make it a big deal, either. I would do it all over again, one thousand times over."

Forty-year-old Gloria, a Puerto Rican mentor to young students in New Jersey, recently treated herself to breast augmentation when she started seeing that the positive results she was getting from working out at the gym weren't affecting her bustline. "No matter how much time I spend in the gym, I wasn't going to get these babies unless I paid for them. I went from an A to a full C. It has absolutely been positive. It was something that I really wanted to do, and I decided, *Why not?* I work hard at the gym, and I deserve them. I work hard at feeling good about the way I look. I don't feel like physical things are everything, but your looks play into your confidence, which you carry with you everywhere. I am more confident now than I have ever been in the last ten years."

Because she was raised in a household that promoted both modesty and conformity, Gloria's decision to have surgery wasn't just a decision to get the chest she had never had. It was claiming her ability to make her own decisions; for her, it was about being the woman she wanted to be after years of following her parents' firm expectations.

SIZE MATTERS

I received the following email from Penelope:

> I recently turned twenty-six and celebrated another 'milestone' in my life: For ten years, I have been bulimic. The topic of eating disorders among women of color is only now garnering needed investigation. I have never disclosed the facts of my disorder to anyone—not family, not friends. Part of the reason for my secrecy has been that eating disorders are historically the province of white, middle- to upper-class women (or so the stereotype goes). I recently had to have back-to-back root canals, plus seven fillings. It never occurred to my Latino dentist to ask why. The women in my life are all successful, well-educated, professional Latina women—all of whom, like me, came from low-income backgrounds. All of them grapple with their weight but still have healthy self-images and revel in their mockery of women with eating disorders. I have long wanted to write about my experiences but have never been content with the venues from which to do so. It has been equally difficult to seek help. Most therapists and support groups are *not* in Latino neighborhoods.

Penelope's email broke my heart, and when we set up a time to talk a couple months later, I was the still the only person she had ever spoken with about her disorder. We spoke for hours, and she shared her background of having grown up in a tough home with a critical mother. She had always been determined to succeed, which led her to both an Ivy League education and an eating disorder.

Penelope grew up in Texas with Mexican parents. "I was raised around ultrafemininity and glamour," she says. "My mother really put an importance and emphasis on beauty. When I go back home, we have to get our nails done, our hair done, our makeup right. My mother takes it very seriously. She resents stereotypes about

Mexican women—the idea that we don't have good taste or style. My sister and I weren't allowed to wear T-shirts growing up, or chew gum. There is a certain grace that I learned from being around my mother that I appreciate now."

But the ways that her mother influenced her are also part of the problem. "I am naturally small and thin, but from the time I was very young, dieting and weight have been a huge factor. My mother was constantly on a diet when I was little. It was very hard, though, because she would still make Mexican meals, and there was this torture to eating it, because we knew it wasn't healthy. She constantly tells me that I am getting *gordita,* or that I look great because I have lost weight. I recently lost twenty-five pounds and visited with my grandmother, and she told me I looked great over and over again, which is difficult for someone with an eating disorder. I don't know that I will ever be too thin for them."

Penelope's bulimia grew worse with the pressures of her Ivy League school. Now it's been several years since she graduated, but she has yet to feel comfortable enough with herself that she believes others' comments about her appearance—that she looks thin—are true.

"Most people say when you hit your twenties, you become comfortable with your femininity. The way that I look is not the way that I want to be. I buy every single magazine, and it is difficult, because I don't look like the women in the magazine. I have been told by a lot of people that I am beautiful, but I have no concept of that. I think I look hideous, because I am not as thin as I want to be, or as tall as I want to be."

I am reminded of something Eve Ensler wrote as she reflected on writing her play and book *The Good Body.* After demonizing her own stomach for its inability to lie flat, she speculated about how much women could accomplish if they could just get over themselves—get over their eyebrows, noses, cellulite, gray hairs, shortness, and small breasts. In her introduction to the book, she writes, "This play is my prayer, my attempt to analyze the mechanisms of our imprisonment, to break free so that we may spend more time running the world than running away from it, so that we may be consumed by the sorrow of the world rather than consuming to avoid that sorrow and suffering."[10]

My conversation with Penelope made me wonder about what we as Latinas, as sisters with a common goal, can do to heal ourselves. The best way to get our collective minds around the idea that there is no perfect prototype is to show women the range of possibilities among us. As Ensler says, diversifying the visual images we offer is a good start. Latinas need to see that we do not all need to look like Hollywood's Latina trendsetters to be compelling and influential.

Penelope went through a recent period without purging. She is in her first relationship and was in between jobs when she decided to devote herself to a healthier lifestyle by resisting her urges to binge and purge and by adding exercise to her daily routine. In a follow-up phone call, she tells me that she did it the right way, working out with a trainer and on her own.

She's by no means done with her struggle. As we talk she complains about feeling heavy. She tells me, "I feel like American culture places its emphasis on beauty that is effortless, and that's a real distinction between Mexican and American cultures. Americans go to the tanning salon, get their teeth whitened. It's perceived that the beauty is effortless, but really, it is not. Latinos understand that there is an effort to it."

When I thank Penelope for her willingness to speak truthfully about her experience, even as she is still dealing with her pain, she speaks of her reason for doing so. "Historically speaking, weight consciousness is not the province of sexy, bold Latinas. But we exist. We are out there. But I have never met another Latina who admitted to having bulimia. For years, I have wanted to tell my friends. I have told them everything about me except for this, because it's not something that is discussed, because it's a 'white girl thing.'"

Penelope is not alone. I have talked to other Latinas who struggle with anorexia and bulimia. But unfortunately, national statistics on Latinas with eating disorders are not available, since as a group we are not the focus of large-scale research studies on the issue. This indicates a pervasive but inaccurate belief that Latinas do not suffer from eating disorders.

But it's clear that Latinas do have a problem with body dissatisfaction. The National Eating Disorder Association found in one study that among the leanest 25% of sixth- and seventh-grade girls, Asians and Latinas reported significantly more body dissatisfaction than did white girls. In another study of Asian, black, Hispanic, Caucasian, and Native American adolescents, Latinas were the second-highest group trying to lose weight—at 36.1%, after Native American girls.[11]

Twenty-eight-year-old Paola, who's Cuban and Puerto Rican and lives in Queens, is another young Latina who struggled in silence with her eating disorder. "I battled with an eating disorder for many years, and I was so ashamed, because I don't think the Hispanic culture understands mental illness or eating disorders. Food is a source of love among the Hispanic culture. In the day programs and in-patient hospitals I went to during my treatment, I was the only Hispanic female. Eating disorders are still largely seen as a disease of white, middle-class females. My family didn't understand me. The doctors didn't understand my family. It was a lonely fight. Only now have I begun to meet more and more Hispanic women who struggled with identity and standards of beauty. I think it's a topic that has been unspoken or overlooked for way too long."

I agree with Paola that, with food being central to Latino celebrations and an integral way in which we show care and affection for one another, many of us find it hard to believe that any of our people would regard food with anything but gusto. But eating disorders know no boundaries; they exist in every culture.

Paola wants to be a source of inspiration for other women to share their internal struggles. She tells me, "I was an English major for a few years, and for me, words are very powerful. The act of writing is a form of empowerment. I think that I want to be interviewed, because I want to be a part of something powerful that may help other women. I think it would be a form of healing for me as well. My family grew up proud to be Hispanic but wanted to prove to people that we were different from the stereotypes. There weren't a lot of Latinos where I went to school, but my parents wanted me to not give up my roots while trying to be accepted, so it was a mixed message," she says.

Paola worked at creating her own identity, finding a way to merge her three cultures into something that would serve her well. But there was a feeling that could not escape her. "I have never been happy with my appearance. I don't like the way I look. It's not like I can say if I got my nose done, I would like the way that I look. It's the feeling that I don't look like other people look. I had that feeling before I went to college, but it got worse there."

Soon, the conflicting role that food had played in her life—"I want it, but I don't want it"—began to overshadow her experience.

College exacerbated Paola's tendency to not eat. "Maybe I wasn't capable of giving myself that care or nurturing. Sophomore year of college, I was placed on a medical leave because of my weight. I went into a day program and I got really depressed. This was the first time that my family was finding out that I had a problem, and they weren't supportive, because they didn't understand it. In their minds, this is what happened when they let their daughter go to college."

The cultural gulf between Paola's reality, her doctor's language, and her parents' reality proved difficult in the healing process. "I was in and out of day programs for the next four or five years. The doctors always said that I was not typical of the girls who get eating disorders because of my ethnicity and my behavior patterns. I didn't exercise as much as others. I didn't have an obsession with the media. I didn't have sneaky or ritualistic behaviors. They were telling me I didn't fit in, and that just made me more frustrated, because I didn't fit in with Latinos and I didn't fit in there. My family was frustrated because they hadn't heard of anorexia. They didn't get it. And so their approach was, 'We need to cook the foods that she likes, and she needs to come home.' My family felt like I was doing this *to them*. They didn't trust the doctors. The doctors were telling them to let go of me—and there is no letting go in Latino culture. That is seen as not being a good parent. They were personally hurt by that advice. You don't air your dirty laundry; you don't talk to people about your problems. Insurance doesn't pay for a lot of these treatments. Even now, they don't let me forget that it cost them a lot of money."

Today, Paola is healthy and feels that she has so many things to live for. "You have to be patient," she says. "It takes a while to get where you are going. It's tough for young women, because often we don't know who we are yet. Especially when you grow up half this and half that, and people want to know if you speak Spanish or English, but you speak both in the same conversation."

Paola and Penelope are not anomalies. In an article for *Daughters,* a newsletter for parents, Laura Donnelly noted that recent research from *SCAN's Pulse*—a journal for sports, cardiovascular, and wellness nutritionists—showed that Hispanic girls have an equal or higher risk of disorder eating compared to white girls. In a Minnesota study of eighty-one thousand high schools, Hispanic girls reported the highest incidence of disordered eating habits (including skipping meals, binging, purging, or using laxatives or cigarettes to lose weight or suppress appetite).[12]

Some researchers attribute the rise in eating disorders to acculturation among Latinas. As Latinas become more ingrained in the culture of the United States, its mainstream values—perhaps thinness especially—influence young Latinas.[13]

In the Growing Up Latina Survey, 50.8% of the women said that they were unsatisfied to very unsatisfied with their weight; 74.2% of them had dieted at some point in their lives. Almost 20% were on a diet four or more times a year; 15.6% of them reported having an eating disorder at some time in their life. Only 42% said they rarely or never felt guilt about eating, and 53.2% of the women said they felt uncomfortable describing their looks in a positive way.

Soon, waiflike role models may no longer be the ideal. A recent backlash against the emaciated bodies that strut up and down the catwalks of the world's most celebrated fashion shows emerged in 2006, when the Madrid Fashion Show banned overly thin models. They set a minimum weight requirement of 125 pounds for a 5'9" model. India, Great Britain, and Italy have followed suit, though experts have speculated that American consumers will have to demand models with fuller figures in order for the market to change.[14]

Part of the problem is the fame, visibility, and near-goddess status we have given models and other celebrities. And fame breeds copycats. We need to be vigilant.

ON BEING "JUST RIGHT"

During my freshman year of college, I went to the Florida Keys with my friends. Within days, my skin had turned from a pale olive to a dark brown. On our way back to school, my friends and I stopped in my hometown to have dinner with my family. One look from my mom forced me to seek exile in the living room as she hollered about my desecrating God's temple with my tan. Skin color can be an ugly benchmark among Latinos. There is too light, too dark, and, like in *Goldilocks and the Three Bears*, there is just right.

While only 3.8% of the women in the Growing Up Latina Survey said they were dissatisfied with their skin color, many had stories to tell about other people's dissatisfaction with their skin color or other features that might reflect their ethnicity.

Mariselle, the thirty-three-year-old from Brooklyn, shares, "I am very light, and that makes people question what I am. People tell me, 'You don't look Puerto Rican. You look white.' My hair is wavy and brownish and not that curly. There are a lot of instances where people speak about me in Spanish not knowing that I am Hispanic."

Twenty-three-year-old Joselyn's skin color was also an issue in her home. She's of Mexican descent and says, "My mother is dark skinned, and so I was always taught to protect my face and not get sunburned."

Sonya is of Peruvian descent. She's thirty-two and grew up in Boston. She was also challenged by features she felt betrayed her ethnicity. "I am short and thick. I am not voluptuous. People make comments that outright refer to it being a shame that I stopped growing. I have an Indian nose. My grandmother offered to pay for a nose job for me when I was sixteen. I got mixed messages from my mom. She would tell me I was cute and then tell me my ass and thighs were too big. People have always been very confused by my appearance and have wanted to be able to identify me. In the Latino community, I get different reactions. Because of my skin color, I am sometimes sought after because I'm the pretty white girl. It was challenging to feel like I fit into the Latino community. I had to wear my identity on my sleeve. I had to fit in to the conversation that I was Latina. I used to have fantasies when I was young that I could make my skin darker or make my eyes brown or my hair darker."

Alejandra, who's twenty-two and Cuban, is comfortable with her hair and skin but finds she has to encourage others to feel the same way. "I have really curly hair. African Americans tell me I have good hair. Latinos ask me why I don't straighten my hair. I'm Afro-Latina, so a lot of people ask me if I'm white, black, or mixed. I just answer that I'm Cuban, and that everyone in my family is a shade of this color. From Latinos and non-Latinos alike, I've gotten the message that you have to be small, but if I lose five pounds, my parents would freak out, while Americans would tell me how great I look."

Esme's hair is tightly curled, and it makes her feel incredibly self-conscious. The twenty-three-year-old Puerto Rican says, "I have a negative feeling about my hair, because it was always out of control. I remember my brother saying he loved straight hair, and when I heard that, I started thinking my hair was ugly. My hair is relaxed now, and most of the time, I wear it straight. I like myself better with straight hair."

I understand some of Esme's conflict. My curls are also out of control, in a stick-your-finger-in-a-light-socket sort of way. My hair made me feel unprofessional when I started my career, and I started straightening it. These days I rarely straighten my hair, since, as a writer based out of my home, it seems irrelevant for me to look polished each day.

But whether hair is straight or curly is not an issue for every Latina. Many of the respondents, 69.1%, said that they wear their hair naturally—whether it's straight or curly.

Hair color is another matter. One respondent was very self-conscious of her hair color. "I highlighted my hair when everyone was doing it. I didn't want to be the only one with dark black hair. I like to do whatever's in." More than one interviewee mentioned the ever-lightening of J.Lo's hair (until her recent return to dark brown, that is). Almost 49% of the women surveyed said they highlighted or dyed their hair, with 41.8% of them dying it lighter and 40.5% opting for a lighter shade in the summer and a darker shade in the winter.

It's easy to be worried about the media's influence on our lives. But there is a need for us to also simply be kind to ourselves, to be kind to our bodies. Not just because we deserve more respect and more self-care, but also because the world deserves more of our attention, and we just can't give it out if it's diverted to obsessing over our thighs. Among the women surveyed, 51.1% said that their own personal experiences influenced their perception of feminine beauty; of the remaining women, 16.8% were influenced by television and film; 12.5% by their family; 9.2% by print media; 5.9% by the viewpoints of men; and 4.6% by the viewpoints of their friends.

That 51.1% whose perception of beauty is not defined by the media and other outside influences is encouraging. We are halfway there. Now we must begin the final fight to liberate the minds and souls of the other 48.9%—a group that sometimes, I must admit, includes me.

Asked to list three words that most accurately described them, the top adjectives chosen by the survey respondents were: natural (65.1%), attractive (42.9%), feminine (34%), cute (32.7%), pretty (30.1%), and sexy (26.3%). The most common answers to the question of what made them feel beautiful (they chose just one descriptor) were: having a sense of confidence (18.6%), feeling happy and fulfilled (17%), being in good physical shape (12.3%), liking what I see in the mirror (12.3%), and being loved (11%). That's a start.

We can definitely turn to the wise women among us to guide us toward our goals. At just twenty-two, Jessica has already found a truth that others may never discover. "Confidence and having a good sense of self-worth are essential for feeling beautiful, because regardless of how you look or dress, there will always be someone who thinks you're not good enough. With confidence, you automatically demand that respect. It's not how hot I look that matters—it's how I display my confidence."

Brenda, a fifty-four-year-old grandmother of Mexican descent, has made it her goal to provide an example to her granddaughter. "Taking into mind my own negative experiences growing up Latina, I am already teaching my granddaughter to have a positive self-image. Latinas need to be proud of all aspects of being Latina. There are plenty of Latina role models and success stories in most areas of American society today—something that was not the case when I was growing up. We need to encourage our *Latinitas* to dream big. We need to teach them how to network and become resourceful in their efforts to develop their talents and skills, and in pursuing their future careers. Every Latina should learn early to find role models and mentors in successful Latinas: older sisters, aunts, famous Latinas, teachers, counselors, family friends, et cetera. That way, they can hitch their own stars to the Latina pioneers who are paving the way. *Latinitas* should also be taught that each one of them has a uniqueness to contribute to their own and future generations."

eight

Five Journeys to Success

ole models and mentors provide invaluable emotional, spiritual, intellectual, and social support. But how many of us had Latina role models or mentors to admire? How many of us had successful Latinas around us whom we could emulate? Over the course of doing the interviews for this book, I heard from many women who wished they had had Latina role models; I also heard from young women who yearn for these role models now, as they're currently experiencing major change and growth in their lives. Many of the women I interviewed make an effort to serve as role models, because they understand how significant their influence can be on young Latinas—who more than likely have been fed a line or two about the limits of their potential.

For my interviews, I sought out several successful Latinas whose work and lives provide inspiration for young Latinas. Their walks are varied, and in some cases their views may not be in line with our own, but their personal stories are fascinating and inspirational.

COMPASSIONATE CONGRESSWOMAN

Born in Orange, California, as the sixth of seven children to immigrant parents from Mexico, California Congresswoman Linda

Sánchez learned to be a trailblazer by following the example set by her parents, who packed up their family and moved to Anaheim to escape gang violence.

"We were the first Mexicans to live on our block," Linda recalls, "and there was maybe a handful of other Latino students at our school." At first, she felt right at home in her new environment. "I was very fair as a child. In many respects, I blended in with all my other classmates. It wasn't until I was older that I realized kids labeled each other. That's when it got more difficult for me, because my friends had different rules than my family."

The difficulties were compounded by the family's move to a new school district. There, Linda developed her ability to speak out for justice when her classmates were critical of Latinos. "I was somewhat confrontational about the fact that I was a Latina, and that we weren't all gang members," she says.

There were other frustrations for Linda during her high school years. She was a curvy girl, but not fat. Yet she received messages that made her feel otherwise at the time. "I remember this intense pressure from my mother, who had been thin all of her life and then gained weight after my brother was born. Some of the things she would say were related to being marketable to find a boyfriend or a husband. I remember being completely defiant and eating what I wanted. I was always rebellious, but I still thought I was fat. I look back at photos of high school, and I am amazed at how normal I looked. At the time, I felt like I was grossly overweight and thought I needed to be thinner in order to be liked or accepted," she recalls.

Linda was not just frustrated with the standards she was given about her weight. She was also frustrated with the differences between her parents' and her friends' expectations. "I had a dear friend who I played on the soccer team with, and she was Irish and Italian. When she turned sixteen, her parents bought her a car, and they bought her brother a car when he turned sixteen. They treated the two of them equally. I remember telling my parents that all my friends could go out until twelve, when I couldn't. My younger brother could go out as late as he wanted, and however many nights he wanted, and I remember thinking it was tremendously unfair and unequal. My mom would just say, 'This is the way it is.'"

When Linda started dating, the message from her parents was clear. "You remain a virgin until your wedding night," says the unmarried congresswoman. Her older sisters were the ones who talked to her about feminine issues and sex education. While Linda's parents were comfortable with her choices about whom to date, she did receive some critique from her grandmother. "I went through this spell of dating very tall, blond basketball players, and my grandmother nodded approvingly. And then once I started dating a short, dark Latino kid, she was horrified, and she said, 'You can have an American boyfriend—why do you want to date him?'" Linda recalls.

But dating was not the most significant part of her high school experience. During those years, Linda threw herself into her sports, playing softball and soccer. In many ways, her participation in sports provided her solace. "I was a big athlete and tomboy, so I stuck with my friends on the softball and soccer teams. This is why I am such a huge fan of team sports, because people don't look at you as your race."

In fact, it was on the athletic field that Linda learned to be more aggressive. Her soccer coach was a significant role model in her life. "My soccer coach said to me, 'When you're not on a soccer field, you are a lady, but the minute you step on the field, you cease being a lady, and you're a soccer player, and you need to focus one hundred percent of your attention on what you're doing on the soccer field.' That gave me permission to be aggressive and to compete, even against boys. Translating that from sports into my life has meant not thinking that just because I am a woman I can't compete. I want to show women that we can compete."

While developing that sense of competency and competition in high school, Linda was also learning about the political process. She volunteered for her first political campaign while she was in high school. After graduation, she went to the University of California, Berkeley, where she majored in Spanish literature with an emphasis in bilingual education. After obtaining her undergraduate degree, her sense of fairness and competitiveness led her to earn her J.D. from U.C.L.A. She practiced law and worked for groups like the International Brotherhood of Electrical Workers and the National Electrical Contractors Association.

During that time, Linda watched as her sister and role model, Loretta Sanchez, developed her career as a congresswoman. She came to realize that representing her community was work she was also well prepared to do. She was sworn into Congress on January 7, 2003, at age thirty-three, and is currently serving her third term as the representative of the 39th Congressional District of California. That swearing in was just the first of countless milestones in her congressional career. The Sánchez sisters are the first sisters—and the first women of any relation—to serve in Congress. Linda is the first Latina to serve on the Judiciary Committee, and she is the only woman on the Democrats' baseball team. But her successes have not come without their difficulties.

"One of the biggest stereotypes I face now is that I'm a quirky, nontraditional, irreverent person," Linda says. "When people describe me, they are trying to do it in a kind way, but they always use the term "hot-blooded Latina." I hate how that implies that Latinas are provocative women. We are not more disposed to being hot-tempered or promiscuous than other women. I think it is so insensitive. Within the Latin culture, there are the two extreme viewpoints of women: the nurturer, homemaker mother who keeps the family together, and the opposite, which is the promiscuous, irresponsible woman that men may fool around with but don't marry. In American culture, there is everything in between—thousands of permutations of what you can be—and so this dichotomy within Latin culture is hard for me to reconcile," says Linda.

Nonetheless, she is reconciling it, and she feels triumphant for having her whole self more recognized by others. "People are seeing me as more than just a Latina. With the work that I do in Congress, I don't think people see me as someone who only cares about Latino, women's, Californian, or young people's issues. Hopefully, people don't pigeonhole me anymore. Granted, I have unique perspectives. Young Latinas look to me as a role model, but so do young women and young people in general, and that's a huge triumph. I have a very multifaceted personality. I play on the congressional baseball team. I do stand-up comedy in my spare time. I shoot pool, play poker, and legislate. I love that I am many different things."

It's this depth that most informs what Linda sees as beautiful. "My definition of beauty is strength—someone who is confident and strong. When you are confident and strong, you have an aura about you that is beautiful. Healthy is beautiful, knowing that you can command your body because it's well nourished and you're giving it what it needs."

When asked how she would advise Latinas coming of age today, Linda says, "When you have to navigate between two cultures that may not be in agreement about certain things, you learn to have empathy for people, and you learn how to be a bridge between those two points of view—and that helps a lot in terms of diplomacy or the art of negotiation," she begins. "My father taught me—and this has proven to be invaluable—that when you start a new job, you work hard, absorb, and keep your mouth shut until you earn people's confidence in your work. Then you can express your views and ideas. People hate when someone comes into the job and just says, 'This is how you should do it.'"

And it's no surprise that Linda places an incredible premium on sports and how they help to develop a sense of confidence, satisfaction, and capability in participants. "Participate in team sports," she advises. "Women and girls who exercise are less likely to have depression, more likely to leave abusive relationships, and less likely to have children out of wedlock."

Linda is a living example of the type of woman she wishes every young Latina will become—strong, competent, and self-sufficient.

CULTURAL CREATIVE

Lucia Ballas-Traynor could not believe her good luck when, at age eleven, she found out her family was moving to the United States because of her dad's position as a Chilean diplomat. In the beginning, the move was just what it seemed—wonderful good fortune. But it wasn't too long before her bubble burst, starting with prejudices directed toward her family that came in the form of their home being vandalized. By high school, she felt uncomfortable about the fact that she wasn't really an immigrant or American.

"Our home was vandalized; someone spray-painted 'Spic' on our porch and burned our lawn chairs. I asked my mom, 'Didn't you know that this would happen?' And her response was just,

'You are the daughter of a diplomat.' But she was wrong in thinking that would give me any type of status or privilege. My peers
just saw me as a Latina; they didn't see me as coming from a high
socioeconomic class," Lucia recalls.

There were other tensions in high school for Lucia. "I went to a
public school. At the time, the only Latina on television was Charo,
and other students called me Charito. At first it was cute, but it got
stale fast. The few Latinos at my school were different from me.
They were from immigrant families that were in the service indus-
tries. I didn't hang out with any specific cliques, but I wasn't lonely
either," she says.

Lucia recalls that she started noticing what made her different,
and why she was having problems at school. "I was always taught
to wear makeup, look good, and flaunt my femininity. From an
American standpoint, I could be seen as a flirt, but I was so conservative and didn't understand where American guys got the idea that
they could hit on me and that I would go for something like that. In
Chile, men knew that flirting didn't translate to being loose, but in
the States, boys got mixed signals. At home, my parents didn't even
talk about sex, so I was naive about these sexual advances from
guys. I went to a guidance counselor for help, and the counselor
told me, 'Why can't you be like your sister and fit in?' and I replied
that it was because I wanted to be me. Which, I see now, was a
more difficult path."

Indeed, Lucia and her sister had chosen different paths as they
transitioned to their new life in the United States. Her sister was
quicker to assimilate. She changed her name so that it would have a
clearer English pronunciation. She joined the popular crowd.

Lucia remembers going back home to Chile for holidays and
vacations and feeling foreign there, too. She felt like she was *ni de*

aquí, ni de allá. "By the time I was fifteen or sixteen, I didn't feel Latin American anymore," Lucia says.

"In Chile, they told me I couldn't wash my hair when I had my period. I couldn't wear a tampon because I'd lose my virginity. The message was, 'Don't have sex with anyone until you're married.'" Growing up in the United States, though, she didn't relate to these ideas. She feels that growing up here was a benefit because she had exposure to opportunities she wouldn't have had as a female growing up in Chile. "My mom told me, 'You can accomplish as much as a male can, and you should pursue higher education.' This was an invitation I carried with me, and that made me very different from my cousins and friends in Latin America. And that message from my mom was all important to me."

Lucia went to college with the hope of becoming Chile's first female president, but her whole family in Chile was involved in politics, and as she got older, she began to see the way that politics complicated her family's life. So she decided against a return to Chile as a politician and instead signed on with a temp agency called Bilingual Concepts. She got a placement with Univision, and a career was born.

"As the years went by, Univision filled a cultural void I experienced because I was living in an American world. I climbed quickly through the ranks, and I found that there weren't a lot of young Latinas moving up. There were only a few Latinas attaining high positions in Univision. Years later, as Univision started hiring white, Anglo males, I found that my being Hispanic was an asset from a client perspective, but internally it was difficult. My male boss told me that I had three strikes against me: I was a woman, Latina, and short. I was accused of being too passionate or hysterical. These criticisms came most often from Anglo males. But my clients would tell me, 'You know this outlet inside and out.' After becoming the general manager of Galavision in 1999, some things happened in my life that started to change the way I felt about Univision. One was a personal crisis: My son was diagnosed as profoundly deaf, and it made me rethink everything. I was witnessing a lot of changes at Galavision around that time, and I decided to tender my resignation, which was probably one of the most difficult things I've done professionally, because I was the primary breadwinner, and because my mom kept telling me to stay."

Now Lucia is at MTV as a senior vice president and the general manager of MTV Tr3s. She is thrilled to be creating a network she has dreamed of for years. Tr3s is a bilingual and bicultural station with programming designed specifically for the station, including Mi TRL.

"I wanted to create a network for young Latinos, and this is where the Latina part of me comes in: I am a firm believer that *las cosas pasan para una razón* [things happen for a reason]. I realized the power of media. My grandparents relied on Univision for everything—and I realized how that could be both powerful and dangerous. With Galavision, I thought there was this opportunity to give young Latinos a destination that I never had—a destination that really reflects young people, beyond the single image of Charo that I had. I feel that it's our responsibility to empower young Latinos and give them alternatives." It's this sense of purpose that guides Lucia's decision-making in choosing programs that are both entertaining and empowering for young Latinos today.

This network was exactly the challenge that Lucia wanted next in her professional life. "When MTV interviewed me, they said they wanted to take MTV Español to a whole new level conceptually. We all had a similar vision."

MTV also gives Lucia something she has never had before: female mentors. "I had the same boss during my fifteen years at Univision. He is a brilliant, strategic guy, but from a management-style perspective, I wouldn't say he was a mentor. I really didn't have a mentor. Before I became the general manager, my boss sent me to Harvard for a weeklong class on leading groups, which helped me put together my thoughts about what to do and what not to do in terms of management and leadership. Unfortunately, there were no senior-level women I could look up to. Now it's a different story. MTV has quite a few women in higher-level positions—including my boss—which has been the greatest."

Lucia has two children and is working hard to help them value their experience as Latinos. And she says that living in New York City, with all its diversity, allows her to feel more comfortable about that in-between space of being "other" in the United States—not quite Latin American, not quite Latina, and not quite American.

"I am not sure that I would be able to live anywhere else," she says. "Being able to draw from two cultures and craft my own identity is my triumph. My Anglo friends tell me I am full of life and full of passion. Sometimes I think about what my life would be like if I lived back in Chile. But I love the independence I have here. I have a husband who supports that my career has taken off, and I think about how a lot of the Latino men I dated in the past wouldn't be so comfortable with my success. I have been able to pick and choose what I want and create an identity for myself that's allowed me to succeed. Growing up hybrid is a liability, but I try to remember that I am so fortunate that I can draw from the best of both worlds and create my own."

Lucia's advice to young Latinas stems from her own experiences: "It's important for young Latinas to be aware that some traditional Latin American thinking can be hard-line, and that it's okay to come up with something more relaxed, something that fits what's right for them. Nowadays, there are a lot more role models for Latinas, but it's important to remember that sometimes it's good to turn to someone outside of the familiar circles for advice."

TROPICAL TYCOON

Catholic high school in New Jersey wasn't easy for Nely Galan. Born in Cuba, she moved to the States with her family when she was four. She soon befriended two other Latina girls and managed her way through high school with them. But she ran into trouble her sophomore year, when she was falsely accused of plagiarism.

Frustrated by that in particular, but by school in general, Nely articulated her thoughts in an article on why parents should not send their daughters to all-girls Catholic high schools. Feeling satisfied by having written her truth, Nely sealed the article in an envelope addressed to *Seventeen*. The next thing she knew, she got an offer to have her piece published, and her high school administrators were up in arms when the article ran. They pushed for Nely to graduate early in an attempt to rid themselves of her and the scandal.

"I was so angry," she recalls. "I wrote the article, and it was a life-changing experience. When I got into trouble after *Seventeen* published it, I felt like this was clearly my calling. It was almost like *Seventeen* saw me. They knew who I was, and they got me."

Nely graduated that year, and *Seventeen* offered her a guest editor position, which she held for two years. From there, she was recruited by a producer who was launching a teenage version of *60 Minutes* for PBS. That gig took her to Austin, Texas. She reported for the show for two years before CBS hired her to work in their

Boston offices. There she met Norman Lear, who later approached her to be the station manager of WNJU TV Channel 47 in New York, which is how Nely, at age twenty-two, became the youngest station manager in the country. Channel 47 ultimately led to the launch of the Telemundo network, and Nely found herself—then just twenty-five years old—facing an incredible new opportunity.

"I was recruited by the president of CBS network to host a talk show, and I hated it. I just didn't feel like it was my calling in life. Having worked for a couple of moguls, I realized I wanted to start my own company. HBO was launching HBO Latin America, and they asked me to consult on how to launch it. Later, I got a call from Rupert Murdoch about wanting to launch six channels in Latin America."

After developing her relationship with Murdoch, Nely realized that this connection could lead to her dream of starting her own company. "I asked him to loan me the money," says Nely. "In 1994, he loaned me five million dollars, and I was able to pay him back in two years. Initially, we launched television companies in Latin America. Then, in 1998, I left my company to run Telemundo for three years. Since I came back in 2001, we have produced over six hundred TV episodes, including the series *The Swan*, which ran on Fox for two seasons and featured women undergoing extreme makeovers.

Galan Entertainment describes *The Swan* as a show where " . . . a team of experts help transform self-proclaimed 'ugly ducklings' to Swans with 'full-life' makeovers on the inside and outside, complete with plastic surgery. The finalists compete to be crowned America's Swan in a one-of-a-kind beauty pageant finale, in which a panel of judges vote for the Swan who had the most amazing transformation."[1]

The Swan evolved from an epiphany that Nely had just after the birth of her son. "I had a baby and had broken up with the father of my son, which was a mournful period, because the life I expected to have wasn't going to happen. I was in a very blue period and decided to go to Canyon Ranch [a health and wellness spa]. I kept thinking that I wished I could be there for months. When I got home, a friend had sent my son the complete works of Hans Christian Andersen. I read him 'The Ugly Duckling,' a story that says that all the ducklings are really swans and don't know it. Everything clicked. I took it to Fox, and they bought it on the spot," she says of her proposal. For her, the show was about giving women whom she felt she identified with a new life.

Though the idea for the show occurred to Nely spontaneously and all the pieces seemed to fall into place, it was not without controversy. Reactions from the public, especially, included criticism that the show was like a train wreck, so horrible that you couldn't peel yourself away from it. Many expressed disdain that these women, who had probably felt inadequate their whole lives, were given the chance to chase their dream appearance with plastic surgery, only to have their looks quantified by a pageant at the end of the show, reinforcing the notion that the most valuable thing these women had going for them was their looks. Moreover, the amount of plastic surgery the women on the show underwent sent the message to some that beauty comes from the exterior and should be measured by a certain standard. Galan acknowledges the criticism, but whether it's because she abides by a glass-half-full mentality or because it's denial or professional savvy, she's not giving in to it.

"I loved the controversy," she counters. "If you are an artist and you paint, and you think everyone is going to like your work, you shouldn't be an artist. When people get polarized by my voice, I feel like I succeeded. I was personally attacked because of *The Swan.* I made a collage of all the people who said ugly things about me, and I think that was a big lesson in growing up," Nely recalls.

When confronted about the problems surrounding the fact that some contestants on the show underwent so much plastic surgery, Nely points out that television is an entertainment medium.

It's likely that some of the contestants may have opted for more surgeries, because anything was an option. "They felt like kids in the candy store. Those are very personal choices—maybe not choices I would make, but I am content with those being their choices. And I am very nonjudgmental about other people's choices. I know not to judge people, because I am not living their life," Nely tells me.

She stands by *The Swan*—not just as a product, but also as a signal change in her own professional and personal life. "I never thought that I was particularly pretty, but I also never thought grin-gas were the prettiest. I thought Latinas were cuter, but I just wasn't the cute one. My problem was not loving myself enough. I feel very differently about the world today. In the last five years, I've started to love myself. *The Swan* was magical for me, because I know so many women who battle against low self-esteem. The concept for the show just clicked for me. It took me a long time to figure out that finding a husband and the right job isn't what the journey is all about. I am compassionate toward women, because I know how tough it is. I feel prettier and better at forty-two than I did at twenty-two and at thirty-two, which makes me a little sad that I didn't appreciate what I had back then," she says.

The reason *The Swan* has had such an impact on her life, and why she's so proud of the show, even though it makes plenty of women shudder, she says, is " . . . because it happened in my life at a time when it was a clear extension of my true voice. I had the age and wisdom to know how to truly appreciate making that show. I got to work with incredible women and have compassion for myself, as well as other women, and see that we were on a similar journey. It has also set up my path for the future, which I'm thrilled about."

Nely has now become a mogul in her own right. She has been dubbed the Tropical Tycoon by *The New York Times* and has found her place and her voice as a media entrepreneur. "I wanted to create a business that properly creates products that reflect my voice and my life experiences," she tells me. "For some years, the lion's share of my professional work was about being Latina."

Her work has clearly had an impact on Latinas, because it has tangible results in terms of how many Latinas are featured in modern media culture. Nely says, "You didn't see any Latinas ten or twelve years ago. If you did see them, they were not aspirational: maids, nannies—and not even well-told stories about those types of women, because those women have amazing stories. We are very lucky to have Salma, Jennifer, and Cameron, who have made us very hot. Let's not look a gift horse in the mouth, though. We are now seeing depictions that are aspirational. It could not be a hotter time to be a Latina. You are one of the hottest voices and people on the planet right now." Nely's voice is passionate when she speaks, which may have contributed to how successful she has been in winning the confidence of moguls in the United States and Latin America.

She feels that the browning of our media has altered the beauty ideal in America. "The American ideal of beauty used to be blond, stick thin, vanilla ice cream; I would say the Latina perception is more macadamia nut. We like women who are more juicy. There are a lot of skinny white girls, but it is not like everyone finds that beautiful."

As witness to this sea change in the depiction of Latinas in the media, Nely felt emboldened to broaden her pursuits and go after her goals of attaining more coverage of and for the Latino community where media are concerned. Now, with the success of *The Swan,* her outlook about what she'll do next is broader. "I am developing *telenovelas* in English for NBC prime time, because I want to cross over a Latino market product. Then, I'm going to do programming on health, wellness, and beauty. I just did a pilot for a show called *The New You.* It will be a multiplatform brand. My mission for the next ten years is going to be about women's wellness," she enthuses. "My voice in the last six years has changed a lot, because I became a single mom and because of the success of *The Swan.* My voice has become much more about women in general. You have to be very ballsy to do what I do for a living. You have to be someone who has the wherewithal. When people tell me no, I feel like I should do that thing they're telling me not to do."

Even though she is diversifying her productions, Nely credits her Latino upbringing for the invaluable perspective she has about her career. "It's given me a whole other dimension. I can equally live in both worlds and understand both sides, and it has made me a very good negotiator," she reflects.

For young Latinas, she offers the following insight: "Life is a puzzle, and different things happen to you—some good and some bad—and you don't understand why it happens to you, but it will all be revealed. When the puzzle starts coming together for you, you will know that you are on the right path. You have to have faith that you have been brought this far; you are not going to get dropped. You have to be looking under your nose. The answer is always under your nose. Your path, your voice, is always right under your nose."

TRAILBLAZING TEJANA

"This will not turn me away," Carrie Rodriguez sings in her sweet Texas drawl. The lyrics are from "Seven Angels on a Bicycle," the title track on her fall 2006 solo debut album. At twenty-eight, she sounds more Natalie Maines in the early Dixie Chicks years than Shakira, but the soulfulness of her voice and the depth of her lyrics reveal a Texas upbringing that wasn't without its tensions.

Carrie was born in Houston, Texas, to a father of Mexican descent who was a songwriter and an Anglo mother who was a painter. After her parents' divorce, she and her mother moved to Austin, where she spent her formative years.

"I grew up in a very white neighborhood in Austin. I didn't grow up with other Mexican Americans. I went to a school where they bussed Mexican Americans in from the east side of town. That was a strange dynamic. I felt like an outsider in both worlds," she recalls.

The tension was complicated for Carrie when she heard her white friends make derisive remarks about the Mexican American students, and when she saw the general separation between the two groups.

"I remember kids calling the Mexican American kids 'Spics,'" she says, though she hastens to add that not everyone behaved this way. "I had a few girlfriends who were great, who came from liberal families, and who would never have any type of racial hatred."

When Carrie was young, she wanted things to be easier for her. She wanted to fit in, and she came up with a simple idea that her mother didn't buy in to. This experience was a lesson Carrie never forgot. "I had a stable, happy childhood at my mom's house. She's a very knowledgeable, cultural person. She listens to all sorts of music; there's art around the house; she cooks all sorts of foods. She speaks Spanish better than my dad. She always made sure that I was proud of my heritage. At one point in elementary school, I wanted to change my last name to hers, because I was feeling like an outsider and I thought that would help. She wouldn't let me. She said I should be proud of my name."

At first, Carrie didn't understand her mother's message, but as time passed, she came to better grasp the significance of her full ethnic heritage. In the meantime, throughout junior high, Carrie still struggled to understand where she belonged. The tension between the two groups of students seemed to escalate. "I remember these Mexican American girls telling me, 'Get out of our way, white girl.' And I wanted to say, 'Wait, I am not a white girl!' It took me a while to find where I was going to fit in."

Carrie would eventually find a place where she did fit in, but it wasn't with one group over another. It ended up being a concept, an art. It was in music where Carrie found her sense of home and belonging. "I was fairly serious about music from the very beginning. I started playing violin when I was five, and I continued to play classical violin." She expected that her dedication to the violin would lead her to a career in classical music, and she began to focus her energies more on that dream. "In high school, I got a lot of respect for playing the violin. People recognized me for what I did. That became my identity more than my race or neighborhood."

Carrie was able to tune out the tensions around her as she increased her focus and attention on her future as a musician. She found that this allowed her to get through her high school years with a calm and confidence that she had struggled to find in those earlier years, when she felt like she didn't fit in. Her mother's parenting also instilled her with confidence and quelled self-doubt. "My mother didn't put too many restrictions on me. She certainly didn't try to stop the natural process of me finding my sexuality and becoming a woman. She let me wear makeup. I dyed my hair purple when I was thirteen, and she looked at me and said, 'Wow, Carrie, that was very creative of you.' I felt pretty comfortable about my femininity, body image, and sexuality."

After high school, Carrie studied at the prestigious Oberlin College Conservatory of Music in Ohio, seeking the training she needed to become a professional classical violinist. Shortly thereafter, she met Lyle Lovett, a family friend, and he invited her to play with his band while they rehearsed for a show. Even though she didn't feel she had done that well, Carrie realized that she wanted to play fiddle music instead of classical. She transferred to Berklee College of Music, in Boston, and found a professional mentor in Matt Glaswer, a bluegrass jazz fiddle player and a professor at Berklee. Being in Boston was good for Carrie, professionally and personally. The big city and different environment helped her reconcile some of the ethnic-identity issues she had suffered through in her youth.

"I became Latina in adulthood. Growing up in that neighborhood and feeling that racial tension made me push stuff to the back. Maybe I thought that thinking of myself as a Latina would make my life harder. I remember trying to make my hair straight, doing things that would make me look more Anglo. I wasn't doing it consciously, but now that I look back, I can see that that's what was going on. I'm not sure when I let go of that trauma and started to embrace my heritage. It had something to do with leaving Austin and going up north—and it is different up here. There is so much more interaction. It's such a big melting pot. I feel a sense of freedom up here."

After graduation, Carrie went back on stage with Lyle Lovett. She performed with him at a concert where Lovett sang a song Carrie's father had written for her mother. She was hooked on the experience, and her goal was to find a band she could perform with. She found that opportunity with a country band. Not too long after that, Chip Taylor, a veteran songwriter with hits like "Wild Thing" and "Angel of the Morning," saw Carrie playing at an Austin record store during the 2001 South by Southwest music festival.

"He asked if I could sing, and I said yes, because I really wanted the gig," she recalls. Over the course of three albums she made with the band, her role leapt from background vocalist to duet partner. The experience also freed her to embrace her own sort of beauty. She let go of the pressure she felt to achieve a certain type of look and began cultivating her own style. "When I played in the country band, the men all wore tight Wranglers, starched white shirts, and hats. I tried to be the country girl and wear cowboy boots and hat. Back then I thought that was what I was supposed to look like. But now I am making my own music, and I like to make my stage outfits as funky as I am feeling that day. But I still wear cowboy boots."

She reflects, "It doesn't matter how much makeup you put on or how great your figure is—the beauty won't come out. You have to feel your self-worth to be beautiful."

Carrie has come a long way with her music, her self-image, and her concept of who she is. "The challenges have been understanding where I fit in in the grand scheme of things. Understanding how I can preserve my history and my culture and still create a whole new life for myself. It took me a long time to even feel like I was Latina, growing up the way that I did. That has been a challenge. My husband is from Spain. Since we met, I have learned Spanish, and I am fluent. I can speak with my grandmother in Spanish now, and she's so grateful. The beauty of being a Latina is having that culture, and making it part of your everyday life in some way," she says.

She's also proud of her position in an industry that is usually dominated by men. "There are not a lot of female instrumentalists; it's really a man's world. I'm used to being the only woman in a band. We need more of us out there doing it. I am proud that I'm doing it, and hopefully inspiring other girls," she says. She's very mindful that she is now a role model to others, especially as she grew up without seeing female role models in the field she pursued. She also knows that her success in a difficult field is a source of pride for other Latinos, and she takes that seriously.

She offers one last thought about what her experience as a Latina has meant to her life. "It's given me a rich and diverse culture to draw on and pass down to my kids when I have them. My mother's side of the family comes from West Texas. People there are colorful, because it's so desolate. I have such a rich background. Having that enriches my life. The more cultures and more ways of looking at things, the better, as far as I'm concerned. I know I want to teach my kids to speak Spanish and English at the same time, in a natural way. It's going to be an asset to them to have that extra-strong connection to being a Latino, speaking the language. I just want to make sure that they feel pride in all the places they come from, and to project that to other kids. I want my kids to have what I didn't have. I didn't spend time with the Mexican American side of my family and didn't know much about my culture. If I had had a stronger sense of that culture, I could have had a stronger sense of confidence and pride in my Latina heritage earlier on."

OUTSTANDING OLYMPIAN

A birthday party changed Jennifer Rodriguez's life when she was four years old. Born in Miami to a Cuban father and a white mother in the late '70s, Jennifer's parents encouraged her to be active. "The birthday party was a [roller] skating party, and I just loved it. I picked it up really quickly," she says.

She started skating, and since she was already doing gymnastics, her parents made her choose between the two. She chose skating. "I took beginners' classes, private lessons, and went to competitions. Roller-skating transformed into Rollerblades," she recalls.

Jennifer was fifteen and ready when the sport of in-line skating went professional, and she became world champion in 1993. Her success as an athlete kept her shielded from some of the typical growing pains of adolescence. At age fourteen, she spent most of her time with other professional in-line skaters who were in their twenties.

"I hated school, but it wasn't like anyone picked on me. I would rather have been doing sports. I was always one of the guys, kind of like a tomboy. I had a small circle of friends, and only they knew what I did. I didn't really relate to a lot of the things that were going on in high school. I trained before school and after, so it didn't leave much time for a social life. I related more to the people I was skating with. I definitely had my school friends, but that was separate. Now I'm not in touch with anyone from high school. All of my tight bonds come from skating," she says.

In fact, Jennifer feels that skating is what kept her safe at a time when other teens around her were vulnerable to influences and peer-pressure. "Had I not done sports, I know that I would have gotten into a lot of trouble out of boredom. Not once did my friends try to peer pressure me into trying something. They just knew that I would just say no. I just had an excuse: I was skating and getting drug tested. But my friends never put me in a situation that made me feel uncomfortable," says Jennifer.

Skating on the level that Jennifer did kept her away from the harsh critiques that some high school girls endure. In some ways, Jennifer was insecure that her body hadn't developed yet when she was in her early teens, but her focus on skating and the strong physique it gave her helped temper her insecurities. "The best thing I found about sports is that it gives people goals and helps people work toward something to achieve. It kept me out of trouble. Kids get in trouble because they have no aspirations."

Jennifer always felt that she would date and marry a skater, probably due to the amount of time she spent with fellow skaters. This prediction turned out to be true, and she developed a relationship with ice skater K. C. Boutiette. K. C. encouraged Jennifer to transition from in-line skating to ice skating, where she would have a chance to compete in the Olympics. A year and a half later, she made the 1998 Olympic team and traveled to Nagano, Japan, as the first Cuban American winter Olympian. She surprised herself by finishing fourth in the 3,000 meter race.

Jennifer's experience at the Olympics resulted in an awakening for her as far as her ethnic identity was concerned. "When you are at the Olympics, you don't know what's going on back home. I came home to Miami when the season was done, and I realized how big a story I had become. It was a really big story for Hispanics. I had never really thought of it that way. I more thought of it like I had only been doing this sport for a year and a half before making it," Jennifer recalls.

At the Salt Lake Olympics in 2002, Jennifer won two bronze medals, and the interest among Latinos intensified. "I was being recognized on the streets. People knew me by name. As an Olympian, you get five minutes of fame, but I still sometimes get recognized. People say, 'We were so proud of you.' The people who get most emotional are the Cuban Americans. They say things like, 'I want you to know how much it means to us.' I realize that I'm not just skating for me. I'm skating for myself, my family, and a whole people. I am part of what their dream was to come here, and that means a lot to me. Growing up, being Cuban American didn't mean anything to me. It wasn't until the last ten years that I took a step back and started finding out more about my history. So I always make an effort to thank the people who stop to talk to me. It is very humbling when someone says that they're proud of me, especially because I'm Latina. I feel like a hypocrite that I am representing the Cuban community, and that I don't speak Spanish. I would love to one day do an interview in Spanish. But I also realize that it's not just about whether I can speak Spanish. It's not what you look like; it's what's in your blood," Jennifer says with conviction. "I always lightened my hair," she says. "I liked the surfer-girl look, like I had just come from the beach. I look Caucasian, like my mom. My brother is darker. People think my last name is my married name. They used to call me a 'Cuban cracker' because I was mixed. A lot of my friends were Hispanic and African American."

Now retired from speed skating, Jennifer has opened a bicycle shop in Miami with K. C., who's now her husband, and is becoming more involved in cycling. She's back in a Miami that's different from the one she grew up in. It's more Latino dominant, and she hears Spanish everywhere. She's also more sensitive to her own role as a Latina and how it has changed since when she was a girl.

Now Jennifer's Latinidad is a prominent part of her identity and her self-confidence. "I am really proud of my family. I take time to step back and think about the sacrifice my dad's family made to come to a new country and learn a new language. They made so many sacrifices so that I could have what I have today. I am a product of their strength. When I look at my grandmother, I think about how she made it possible for me to do what I want to do." Jennifer's voice radiates pride.

The confidence this realization has given Jennifer is apparent and makes her glow. "If you have self-confidence," she says, "you are beautiful. But you can't be cocky and overwhelming. It's important just to be happy with who you are, regardless. It doesn't matter so much about your weight, hair color, et cetera. I have seen some really pretty people who end up being jerks. Self-confidence and self-control are beautiful; they show that you are strong inside."

Jennifer's experiences as an Olympian have solidified her sense of her own ethnic identity and have made her sensitive to how others who share her background can struggle as they transition between their two cultural identities. "Being Latina in America keeps me humbled. Every American is an immigrant, but that hits close to home for me now, and that keeps me humble. My parents always said our situation could be worse, and yeah, it could be worse. A lot of times, people don't realize how good we have it here. My family is so proud of being American. My dad says the proudest moment of his life is when he became American. He flies the flag every day. To have it good doesn't mean you have to have it better. It means that you don't take everything for granted."

When asked what advice she would give to Latinas coming of age today, she doesn't hesitate. "The most important message to send to girls is: Be proud of who you are. Don't worry about what everyone else thinks. Don't do things because someone else wants you to do them. Do things because you want to do them yourself. Don't compare yourself to people in Hollywood. It's all about making yourself happy. A lot of people don't know what makes them happy. Set goals for yourself in everyday life. And figure out the steps that it will take to get there. It makes things easier in life. It ends up giving you more self-confidence and more self-esteem in the end."

LESSONS LEARNED

Congresswoman Linda Sánchez, Lucia Ballas-Traynor, Nely Galan, Carrie Rodriguez, and Jennifer Rodriguez are successful women who have aspired and achieved goals and lived rich lives, full of experiences. They have soul. They've found a way—whether it was through acculturation or retro-acculturation—to comfortably exist and excel in their hybrid lives. Several of them found role models or mentors early on, and others didn't find them until later in life. But their experiences along the way taught all five of them the value of having role models, of finding their passion at a young age, of using their voice, of standing up for their views.

These women found something they loved to throw themselves into, something that allowed space for their identity to come from within rather than from without. What struck me most clearly when I first talked to Carrie and Jennifer was their passion for their vocation, and how early they started doing what they loved: Carrie started playing violin at age five; Jennifer was skating on her fourth birthday.

These women and their families invested time and resources in building a deep relationship with one single passion, rather than encouraging their daughters to try everything a little bit. This focus is inspiring, particularly in a culture that values overachievement, in which so many parents try to build the most well-rounded child, all to fit the bill for future college applications.

I fell in love with each of these women as I talked to them—wanted to jet off to New York City, Miami, and Washington, D.C., to spend a weekend with them. I fell in love with them because they are so very real, so honest about their struggles and hopes.

Their experiences provide valuable lessons, and their advice is clear and true. We are not from here or there; we are from a blended place that is of our own making. But it's only when we find our true voices that we can have a sense of pride, comfort, and ease in who we are.

nine

Giving Up Beauty

Beauty is a vague concept, isn't it? What it means to me and what it means to you can be completely different. It's subjective, in flux, fluid. Yet oftentimes we treat it like it's not, like it's a formula, an absolute or a given. But ask any woman you know who she finds most beautiful, and you're bound to get different answers. Maybe it's time we change the question. What if who's the most beautiful didn't matter anymore? How refreshing would that be? What if the most critical question in our culture were how beautiful a person is on the inside? What if we validated what is beautiful about ourselves? These questions of inner beauty, after all, hold the answers that will serve us best in living our lives. Knowing and owning those answers are what can help us let go of the deathlike grip that traditional beauty definitions have on us.

SCARS SHOW CHARACTER

"It's not a malignancy." The doctor looked at his chart, nodding, not looking at me. I stared at him, squinting, trying to comprehend what he meant with these words.

I craned to see the chart, convinced that he must have the wrong one, reading me some other woman's good news. After all,

I was only in for a five-week follow-up to my breast-reduction surgery. My breasts were simply smaller—not broken, not tumorous, not possibly cancerous. They were the breasts of a twenty-six-year-old woman with no family history of breast cancer. Of course there was no malignancy.

My gown was open, revealing a left breast that was not as far along in its healing process as the right one. Several weeks earlier, the vertical seam that connected where point A and point B came together to mark point C, underneath which inches had been snipped away, had come undone. I discovered it one morning as I put on deodorant. In the humid haze of my bathroom mirror, I caught sight of what my insides looked like. At the doctor's office that afternoon, I'd expected more stitches, for this two-inch-by-one-inch gap to be zipped closed. Instead, the doctor looked at it a moment, pinched it shut with his fingers, and placed a Steri-Strip over it. I shuddered at the thought of having to use tape to pinch my skin closed each morning. "You can use two if you like," he added upon seeing my disturbed look, as if that would make it easier for me.

Now there I was, back at his office for a standard follow-up. There was a caterpillar-size scar that crawled up my left breast. The breast was red with tape burns and scabbing, and while it was by far the uglier of my two altered breasts, he glanced at my right breast furtively.

Sensing my confusion at his remark, my doctor explained that it's standard practice to send things from surgery to biopsy. "The biopsy revealed a significant cyst removed from your right breast," he told me. "We examined it, though, and it's not malignant."

I nodded, thinking about these words, thinking about how a cyst could hide in a breast, thinking about how I might have reacted if he had told me I had a tumor and cancer in the same breath. I stared down at these small breasts, perfect and round and scarred in ways that I could not have imagined a month ago. And for the first time following my surgery, I had no regrets. If I were not already thankful for the newfound freedom (and some days I was not), I had to be thankful for this discovery. The reduction of what I had formerly perceived as my womanhood revealed a dark spot that may not have been detected until it had grown too large to deny, and morphed into something that could harm me.

I certainly hadn't gone into surgery with a sense of relief. Each day, I struggled to figure out how I felt. Physically, it felt necessary; it *was* necessary. But it also felt like anticipating the loss of an old love or a best friend. And then, a week before the surgery, a college friend called—one with whom I shared an undeniable attraction over the years we studied together. He was coming to town and wanted to stay with me. I choked and then replied that I wouldn't be able to see him, since I was going into surgery the day he arrived. He asked if this was the surgery I'd always wanted. He'd remembered what I hated most about my body, but it was awkward, too, because we both knew it was what made me stand out physically. I hung up the phone, cold and shaking, uncertain whether I could be beautiful without large breasts and unsure that I had ever been beautiful, even with them.

I left home at 6:30 AM on the day of my surgery. In the surgical prep room, I talked with my nurse, who'd gone through breast-reduction surgery ten years earlier. I fought the urge to ask, "Did anyone ever look at you again? Do you feel sexy without them?" I wasn't sure I would be seen as sexy without them. I didn't know what I had in me, because I had always had these breasts on me.

My surgeon arrived and swiftly began the pre-op procedures. He diagrammed my breasts and chest in red and black permanent marker to ensure that when everything was carved and sewn, I would be even and congruent. During this time, I realized the magnitude of what was before me; I saw just how much of my body would no longer be with me a few hours later.

It's going to be fine, I told myself.

My surgeon finished outlining my chest and gathered my entourage, two nurses and the anesthesiologist, and we started down the hall toward surgery. I looked at them, heard them laughing and exchanging minute details of their lives, when the surgeon caught my eye.

"You will be beautiful," he said, "just beautiful."

We crashed through the doors of the operating room with incredible force, and the energy of the room immediately changed. The pace was fast, hands everywhere on my body, attaching different monitors. I thought about what he'd said and how shamefaced I'd been when I first came to his office. I hadn't wanted people to think I was going to see a plastic surgeon for vanity. But here I was now, terrified that in three hours I would no longer have an external indicator for beauty.

Give it up, I thought, and faded into sleep.

When I woke up, my chest was on fire, a white heat that I could not breathe through without wincing. The nurse noticed me stir and came over to my bed.

"I'll get your mother," she said, and disappeared.

But I was more than my mother could handle. She looked at me and fainted; I wondered whether it was, indeed, that bad. That moment alerted me to what I already subconsciously knew: My reaction to my own recovery would be the example for everyone else to know how to react. If I could not feel beautiful, graceful might be within my reach.

For the next few weeks, I shared my good cheer. I had a week off from work to rest and recover. I visited with friends and wrote thank-you notes. I learned to bandage my chest and clean the wounds. By the second week, I was walking more rapidly, trying to maintain some degree of fitness. In the third week, I began to lift light weights. A day later, I discovered that my breast had torn open, and a small part of my soul followed suit.

Each morning I would gently pull off the tape that was forcing the hole in my left breast shut, and wince as it reopened the wound. I washed it carefully, feeling slight weakness when I pinched it shut with one hand and taped it with the other. One morning, it was especially painful and unnerving. When my boyfriend arrived to take me to lunch, the defeat was etched on my face.

"What's wrong?" He asked, and I told him. He squinted at me and said, "I don't get this; it's going to heal. What's the problem?" I closed my eyes, wishing we had never begun this conversation. "Look," I replied, "I am just feeling a little scared, vain, and pathetic. Can you give me that?" He stared at me, astonished.

"I can't, because you have never been any of those things. It's not like you, and it's just a scar." His words reminded me of a scar that I had on my knee, a one-inch-long marking that had once been more than three inches wide. I once dated a man who looked at that scar, traced its outermost limits, and said, "Scars show character." He won me in that moment, affirming what I had always believed: It's the difficult things that make you rich and give your life personality and flavor in ways that the easy things cannot. I've gone back to that declaration since, and I've thought about how very true it's turned out to be for me.

I hated my left breast for not healing properly, but in critiquing it for beauty, I never considered my right breast and what it might be hiding. I didn't think of what it contained behind its walls, because it had turned out beautifully, the way my doctor had promised that it would. And yet it was my right breast that could have ultimately altered my world. It was my right breast that was conspiring against me.

On the examining table that morning, I looked down at my left breast, red with blood and healing and force, and then at my right breast, small and perky. In that moment, I knew it wouldn't matter if "beautiful" was a word I ever heard from anyone's mouth to describe me. I had two breasts and a life and a new start. I stepped out of my gown, pulled on my white cotton bra, and glimpsed at myself in the mirror. I stood straight and stared hard, assessing. Finally, I found myself looking at my scars and seeing healing where once I had seen only fullness and could never see myself.

WHAT IS BEAUTIFUL?

That experience in the doctor's office was an awakening for me. Today, though I sometimes still struggle with my weight or hair or self-image, I am gentler with myself than I once was. I now realize that beauty is character rather than blondness; personality rather than waist size. Beauty is about taking big bites of life, not small bites of food. After all, who decided that blond, tall, and thin is the standard for women? How did we even come to that? Does my shortness, darkness, or fullness erase my capabilities? Do they disqualify me in some way, make me less than? Do they dull my compassion or passion? Do they negate that I inherently—that we all inherently—have something of value to give? The reality is that beauty is not superficial—and that realization has given me more patience with myself.

One of my favorite parts of the interview process for this book was asking the women what they considered beautiful, because for so many, it was an *aha!* moment. They realized that they were often judging themselves based on pop culture standards, even though what they considered beautiful was more soulful.

Miranda is thirty-five, lives in New York, and is of Colombian descent. "I am rarely happy with my size," she admits in her phone interview.

"Do you compare yourself to women in the media or women around you?" I ask. She answers without hesitation. "I do if I see someone in the media with a great body. Especially women my age, or women who are in their early forties and look amazing. When I go to a club, I see these younger women who are underdressed and yet look beautiful. It does a little something to my ego."

There is quiet on the line. I wait a moment before asking my next question. "Are you secure in your appearance? Do you consider yourself sexy?"

"I still struggle as far as my weight." Pause. "I do consider myself sexy." Pause. "Interesting," she says, feeling the full impact of what she has just revealed. She laughs for a moment—the nervous giggle of clarity.

"So what do you believe is essential for being beautiful?" I continue. Her answer comes faster now, and with more certainty. "Confidence. It comes from inside. Being down to earth, humble. Being intellectual and politically and socially conscious. Being grounded and authentic."

She doesn't say "skinny." She doesn't say "being underdressed." She doesn't say "a rock-hard body." She answers with adjectives and descriptors that describe herself perfectly. I tell her what I appreciate about her interview and then hang up, hopeful that she'll realize that she exemplifies her own definition of beauty.

Confidence as a cornerstone to beauty turned out to be a common concept among my interviewees. Iris, a twenty-four-year-old of Colombian descent who lives in New Jersey and works in the arts, dispensed deep wisdom for her young age: "Love who you are. Love your culture and how you look. Everyone is different. No one is the same. Embrace the way you are, and be confident. In the end, confidence is what makes you more beautiful."

Enid, who's thirty-four and of Puerto Rican and Colombian descent, found that she gained confidence in her beauty, and thus in herself, from her college experience. "When I went to college, the impression I got from classmates was that I definitely fit the Latina look. I enjoyed college and left feeling self-confident about my look, because people made me feel beautiful." Given this experience, it didn't surprise me to hear how Enid now defines beauty.

"Self-confidence shines through, whatever your body shape or color. That to me is beautiful."

Laura is a twenty-six-year-old of Puerto Rican and Panamanian descent who lives in North Carolina. She has just recently come to appreciate her own beauty. She says the portrayal of more Latinas in mainstream media has helped.

"At this point in my life, I feel better than I ever have about myself. I am more comfortable with myself. When I compare myself to white women, I don't feel as worthy. When I compare myself to Latinas, I feel better. Now I tell people to be comfortable with themselves for who they are. If you can do that, most of the outside messages won't get in. Everyone is unique, and that uniqueness makes you who you are. That should be valued. The ability to love is essential for being beautiful."

Not letting the message in is imperative. If looking through a beauty or fashion magazine hurts your feelings and lessens your self-confidence, then you have to stop looking. Once you quit taking in the verbal and visual clutter of what society says is beautiful, you can make room for what you think and feel is beautiful.

LOVING YOUR LATINIDAD

Jesse is twenty-seven, and her heritage is a mix of Mexican, German, and French ancestry. She lives in San Francisco, where she practices both Catholicism and Buddhism. She feels most connected to her Latin roots. When I ask her what she loves about being Latina, her answer comes out in a rush.

"I love the female-centered aspect—worshipping mother figures, honoring women's wisdom, power, and strength. Latinas are honored for being strong women who feed the family. I love the fact that we are brought up with spirituality and sisterhood. There is a closeness among women in our culture. We also 'hold' a lot of the culture. We pass it down to people in our families. We maintain traditions. We have important roles that are often overlooked, but we all know that we hold it together."

Frances, thirty-five, grew up in New York City. She is of Colombian descent and also speaks with passion about loving her Latinidad. "I love being a person of color. I feel such a sense of affinity for other people of color. I love the history behind being Latina and the historical narrative of all of these cultures coming together. I love that sense of lineage that comes from different parts of the word. I love the flavor, fire, spirit. I feel such a connection in Colombia. I was amazed that so much of my spirit was there."

She also speaks about feeling connected to her upbringing in the United States. "I get the benefit of being an American woman with all the feminist work that was done before I was born, but I also get the richness of this Latino history and culture. I have always felt entitled to move freely, but I feel like being a woman of color is a passport. All of those layers open up my ability to connect with other people and other cultures, and it just makes my life that much richer."

Her advice to young Latinas is: "Find a female mentor, preferably a Latina, and if not, then a woman of color. It's important to have an adult confidante. It gets you through a lot."

Latinas exist in a dual universe, and it's important that our perception of beauty and our definition of it incorporate both our worlds. Defining beauty through just one lens leaves out a crucial element of who we are. We must define beauty by honoring our whole selves, our whole experience.

It's so easy when you're out with a group of women to run through a checklist of how you do or don't stack up. Dare yourself to stop that habit. After all, no one exists in the world as you do—with your realities, your concerns, your genes, your truths. Have a magnanimous approach to your self. Don't compare. Don't critique. Just be.

And to the women you love, offer acceptance freely. Challenge them to stop the self-critical conversations. No more "I need to lose five pounds" or "My thighs are too big." Fine the women you love a dollar for every self-critical remark they make. That can quickly add up to a nice bottle of wine. Then, while you drink it, compliment each other.

FEARLESS DUALITY

It was incredibly moving to listen to the interviewees consider who they've become, and how the duality of being Latina has positively shaped their lives.

When asked what growing up with two cultures has given her, Miranda, the thirty-five-year-old New Yorker, answers, "The family values and morals that I grew up with have really grounded me. They have encouraged me—made me strong, determined, and positive. I have been exposed to so many cultures, and I have come to understand our commonalities. I've been fortunate."

But there is something else she wants to add: "I do find that there's a lot of animosity among different Latinas," she tells me. "I don't feel like we're united. We're somewhat segregated—at least the more recent immigrants. There's all this underlying tension. We are divided, and it's why we are so underrepresented. We have to be pro-Latino. Period. Imagine the magnitude. Imagine the strength we could have collectively." Finally, she offers advice to other Latinas who are just now coming of age in the United States: "Aim for the stars. There's nothing that you cannot accomplish. Be proud of who you are and where you came from. You are beautiful and deserve the very best. Don't settle for anything less."

I love Miranda's advice, because it encourages us to grow, to take on new challenges. By pushing ourselves to accomplish things we never considered possible, we build the habit of impressing ourselves, which breeds confidence and clarity.

Brenda is now fifty-four, and as a Chicana who's spent her whole life in Texas, she has long considered her duality. "The positive aspect of having a dual cultural identity is that there is more to choose from. I love being bilingual, being able to understand Spanish when I hear it spoken. I love being able to identify with two cultures, two peoples, two languages, two heritages. It's like my life is automatically multiplied by two in everything I experience. The main thing to keep in mind is that each Latina is a mix and blend of their Hispanic and American heritage, and therefore they'll embrace differing degrees of both cultures and languages. With my Latina friends, we remind one another that we must be kind to ourselves and accept our differing degrees of blending of our two worlds, without pointing fingers at each other for not being either American or Hispanic enough. Oftentimes, we Latinas are the harshest critics of one another in this area. The other thing is to educate ourselves by reading and learning more about both worlds, and by being accepting of whatever and whoever each one of us has become."

Mia, the thirty-two-year-old *puertorriqueña,* has brief but direct advice for Latinas on how to be both American and Latina: "Accept who you are, be who you are, and accept your own identity. If you pretend to be someone you aren't, then you really aren't a Latina or an American. You are just a character in a play."

Mia's metaphor is great, because it speaks to being conscious of the ways in which we're malleable to what those around us want. Coming into our *own* understanding creates a sense of resolve that others will respect and appreciate.

Sarah, who's thirty and of Colombian and Cuban descent, talks about what worked for her in terms of navigating and celebrating her duality. "Get an identity mentor, someone whose worldview gives you a model for how to embrace your own identity. The question is not 'Are you a Latina?' It's 'What type of Latina are you?' How do you feel about language, politics? I feel comfortable with other Latinas who see the humor and silliness of living in all these worlds. Don't reject any part of yourself. You are not just one thing. It's important to be accepting of your Anglo part."

Marisa is thirty-three, and she is sensitive to how her upbringing would have been different if she had been raised in either of her parents' countries of origin—Colombia or Puerto Rico. "I have been able to live the dreams that my mom and dad never got to. I was the first to go to college. I had access to financial aid, and I could create a career for myself. I could provide for myself. I feel like I have full independence to travel and come and go as I please. I am able to speak freely."

Her insight for young Latinas? "Incorporate where you have come from into where you are going. Take as much opportunity as is available to you. Make yourself a better person, and give back to your community."

Nadia, a student in Minnesota, is twenty-one and of Paraguayan descent. She relishes her duality. "It gives me a unique perspective into two different worlds that I can understand and relate to. I can almost act as a peacekeeper. And it gives me a broader range of influences."

Asked how one can be American without betraying her Latina roots, Nadia gives us insight into the mindset of her generation of young women—a group that's grown up within the most diverse culture the United States has ever known. "Just acknowledge your roots, first of all, and then acknowledge the constant struggles of what it is to be a Latina and a minority in this country. Take pride in your culture, but also take pride in being an American. It's okay to be strong. It's okay to have an opinion. It's okay to speak your mind. Sex and sexuality aren't the only option you have."

Dahlia is twenty-five—of the same generation as Nadia—and also speaks to her experience of having grown up knowing diversity and opportunity. She's of Cuban and Colombian descent and is also acutely aware of how different her life is having been raised in the United States. "The educational opportunities you have are different. Being a minority in the United States plays a role in your life here. It would have been different growing up in Cuba or Colombia, where I would have been part of the dominant culture. Here I've grown up crossing two cultures, and the majority of my life has been spent translating. When you grow up like this, it frames who you are, because you're not part of the dominant group. But having been born in the United States, I know that I've had more access to resources."

In thinking about how her own experiences could inform someone else's life, she speaks with the passion and enthusiasm of someone who's witnessed a lot, and she has encouraging words to offer: "I would say to all women—and especially to Latina women—you need to be yourselves. If you love a sport, just do it. Don't let go of your dreams. Think big, accomplish big. There's no limit to what anyone can do, even though you may have had a hard life, hard times. You can't let anything get you down. Education is the most important thing in the world. Your biggest choice is to educate yourself and to be happy with who you are. Think of your family with pride and not as a burden. If someone breaks your heart, it's going to be okay. You will find friends along the way. Teenage years are tough, but you will get through it. Everyone should go to college. There is no reason not to succeed. Always ask for help."

Sonya is thirty-two years old and grew up in Boston. Her Peruvian and Polish/Scottish background informs her approach to life. "I have a larger understanding of what it means to be American, because I think this whole continent has a shared history—of colonization and genocide—and we have all been affected by that. U.S. culture is defined by capitalism—the American dream is about being greedy. Having been born here does not contradict my Peruvian heritage. What *does* conflict is this movement toward greed and isolation. The America I choose to be a part of is one of social change and social justice, and those values are in line with my Latin heritage. My work is about building community. My advice is that we look for each other. If we keep looking, we will find those bridges to the places we need to go. Look for the similarities, not the differences."

Joselyn, who's twenty-three and now lives in New York, grew up in a small town in Illinois. Her experiences are all about duality—as a Latina of Mexican heritage and an American, and as a small-town girl and a big-city dweller. All of these influences have shaped the woman she is.

"It's made me open to everyone else. It's made me more empathetic to other people's struggles. When you have two identities and two cultures, there are a lot of things you can't vocalize. It makes me more understanding and makes me appreciate the diversity."

Jessica's parents hail from El Salvador, and she lives in Chicago. At twenty-two, she's fortunate to already have such a deep appreciation for the opportunities she's been given. "The duality adds enrichment to my life. Being born here and raised half here and half there has been a humbling experience. I came to appreciate how hard my parents and other people work. It's allowed me to be more open and more receptive to other parts of Latino culture, and it's helped me view the world as I view it today. My parents always promoted a good sense of self-worth and confidence. I know what it feels like to be caught in the middle, not being good enough for either side, waiting for someone to tell me what to do."

When I ask her what advice she would offer young Latinas today, she responds, "Educate yourself. Know what you're saying before you open your mouth. Present yourself in a respectful manner, and be confident."

Jesse, mentioned earlier in this chapter, is wholly aware of how her duality shaped her. "Because we Latinas have a mixture of different ethnicities, I feel very complex. . . . Not only am I mixed, but Mexican culture is mixed. I love my complexities. I love being a feminist and adapting that to my cultural beliefs. I love my curiosity in life, my desire and my need to create—art, opportunities for myself. I love my need to be connected with others. I think that comes directly from my culture, which informs my sense of community and family. I also love my femininity and masculinity, being able to be in both worlds and connect with both parts of myself. I grew up with a lot of privilege, a lot of material things, a lot of resources. Had I grown up in Mexico, I would have relied on different resources, which essentially might have made me a happier person, because I would have lived more simply. But I wonder how easy, as a woman, it would be for me to be successful and driven professionally, and how, as a lesbian, I'd be able to negotiate my sexuality in Mexico. I think it would be a lot more difficult. My duality has allowed me to fit into many different worlds. It's allowed me to learn different values, beliefs, and traditions from so many different groups. I've been able to draw the positive from each group and adapt it in the way I want to my life. I have the option and opportunity to choose. I can take what I like and leave what I don't like."

Asked how she would encourage Latinas coming of age today, Jesse speaks emphatically. "Delve into the creative work of other Latinas who reflect your own life and experiences. Learn the stories of your roots. Seek out mentors who can reflect back to you what you want to become, who can guide you on your path."

Your situation may not easily lend itself to finding a Latina role model, but role models of any age or ethnicity can be beneficial.

When I was young, I didn't have any Latina role models outside of my family, because there weren't other Latinas around.

Initially, I found role models in books, and later, in teachers. In elementary school, I was captivated by Christa McAuliffe and devastated, like so many others, when she died in the *Challenger* shuttle explosion in 1986. In middle school, I admired Samantha Smith, a Maine fifth-grader who tried to broker peace with the Soviet Union during the Cold War. Samantha died in a plane crash three years after her first letter to Soviet Communist Party General Secretary Yuri Andropov earned her worldwide attention. Though they had their lives cut short by tragic circumstances, both of these heroines informed my sensibilities and love for activism. In college, I found female professors and administrators who provided me with the type of guidance I was seeking. They were all activists in some way. Not all of them shared my ethnicity, but they shared an understanding of what it was like to work hard, and to succeed when the odds are stacked up against you. Having this type of support and insight is a great benefit to all young women, and being a support to others as you gain experience is a worthwhile pursuit.

Yes, growing up looking and being different in America is hard. But for most of the women I spoke to, it contributed to their sense of self and their sense of place, both in U.S. culture and in their cultures of origin. All of the women recognized that growing up in the United States meant growing up far more privileged than they would have been otherwise.

The head start that most of us received because of the sacrifices of our parents or grandparents has afforded us the opportunity to be women of a different world order. In thinking about these opportunities, I've wondered whether our grappling with beauty, body-image, and self-confidence issues is easy compared to the issues that might be consuming us had we been brought up under different circumstances. Thinking about the larger problems I might have struggled with—human rights limitations and lack of work and food—gives me some perspective. Imagine what we could do if, instead of fighting and pining for the "most beautiful" label, we invested our collective energy in fighting for our rights and for issues of substance—for ourselves, our offspring, and our brothers and sisters.

LETTING GO

When I was teaching high school, there were times when I panicked at the idea of having my own children. I did not want the power, ability, or proximity to negatively affect someone whose care and development were wholly my responsibility. As a teacher, counselor, and mentor, I had nurtured other people's children for so long and taken such care and pride in what I did. I'd loved them unconditionally and paid so much attention to them—at the expense of my own health and lifestyle. When I imagined how much all that energy, care, compassion, and attention would be magnified if it were *my own child,* it was nearly paralyzing. What if I couldn't transfer all those skills and all that love? What if I couldn't save my son from ego and bravado and too much rough and tumble? What if I couldn't spare my daughter from her own inquisition at the mirror? What if I couldn't show my children how to be allied with the forces of good and truth in this world? Those fears would catch my throat whenever I thought of motherhood.

But lately, my thoughts have been less panicked and more proactive. It's not that marriage has changed me, or that motherhood is eminent. It's that I've come into this next part of my life with an awareness that I can be part of the solution. Changing what you see around you is not just a Pollyanna wish. It's a valid option.

What if there were no machismo, and what if there were no inquisition? To recall the question that led this chapter, what if we could create a world where beauty was understood to be something inside? What if we found a way to make comparisons around our personal growth, rather than around the way we look? What if we started loving our biology, rather than fighting it? What if we stopped stuffing ourselves or depriving ourselves or so altering the course of how our body evolves that it actually alters the course of the soul? What if we quit sacrificing ourselves and our health in pursuit of a standard that isn't adequate, fair, or even appropriate? What if we told our daughters and sons, sisters and brothers, friends and family that what's hot is loving yourself, caring for yourself and others, being kind and being true, fighting the good fight, and loving well?

If we gave up beauty, just imagine what we could do in place of that misused, misspent, and mismanaged energy.

ten

Raising Our Voices

Today I find comfort in my duality, in my ability to move around in this world with both earned confidence and established sensitivities and sensibilities.

I remember an incident years ago that stays with me as one of the first times I felt my confidence brimming over. I was learning best practices, the highest standards in youth-development work, from youth organizations that worked with gang-affiliated young people in Roxbury, Massachusetts. It was a cold January—crisp, with snowfall covering the streets. Graffiti was the only pop of color in an atmosphere otherwise filled with tones of gunmetal gray on tin. I walked those streets attentive, eyes straight ahead, taking in where I was and why I was there, that cold air energizing me with a sense of purpose and clarity. When I showed up at the youth center one morning, one of the young men asked me, "You walking these streets by yourself?" He didn't hide his surprise.

"Yeah," I answered. "Is that a problem?"

Just then, another young man I'd already worked with for a few days interrupted our conversation. "Bro, have you seen how this girl walks? Ain't nobody going to take her for a fool."

I felt confident and strong in that moment. I felt like I had finally arrived at a place where I wasn't second-guessing myself. Suddenly my reality, my duality, had crystallized. It was a profound experience, and it affected the way I saw myself from that day forth. I had arrived in my adulthood—crossed the boundaries that had once left me cautious—into a world of my understanding.

For years, I had felt isolated. At the time, I only understood what I was feeling as loneliness, but as I aged I realized that what I really felt was alone—which was something quite different. And I realized that to be okay with being alone was to embrace my own sense of self, to own my own self-confidence.

In the years leading up to that January in Roxbury, I had been discovering, collecting, and establishing the woman I wanted to be. Once I realized that the woman I wanted to be was someone I actually *could* be, and maybe already was, I started to make sense of my world. My life unfolded differently after that. In the space between isolation and clarity, I had learned how to value the things that were important to me, and how to pass over things that didn't feed my soul. Even though I wasn't always sure about where I was going or how things would end up, I had accessed something deep within, and it served as an unfailing compass as I continued—sometimes still stumbling—on my way forward.

THE GOOD LIFE

There's a lot to be said for growing up both Latina and American: Our world can be wider; we can move through groups and experiences that others might find difficult; we have acquired skills through a lifetime of being minorities that help us deal with traditional America; and we have a whole other world that is ours for the taking—the Latino culture, which represents the fastest-growing minority in the United States.

Many women I interviewed saw reason to celebrate this expansiveness. "I can navigate between two cultures. I have the ability to do so. It is easier for me to adapt to situations when I need to," says thirty-year-old Carolina, who's Puerto Rican and grew up in New York City.

How do we get to that comfortable place, though? Carolina suggests that young Latinas " . . . take it all in stride. Learn about yourselves. Love your unique qualities. Young Latinas are trying to compete with the media in terms of stereotypes. I see girls who are starving, who have ridiculous blond hair and blue contacts. I want to tell them to stop, because natural is the most beautiful form."

Clara is twenty-nine and lives in New York City. Her mother is Peruvian. When describing the triumphs of being a Latina in America, she can hardly hold back the stream of words: "We have an edge. When we go out into the workforce, we bring something special to the table. We have a lot to contribute: our upbringing, our culture. We teach people that life is not just about making money, and we represent a culture that speaks to how important our extended families are, how music can bring us up, bring us closer, and bring joy into our lives. My life would have been boring had I grown up in just one culture. We live a richer life. Having a dual culture, we get the best of both worlds."

Clara advises Latinas to speak up and not hide behind American culture. "Always stay as in tune as possible to who your people are. Learn about your history. Learn about the struggle that Latinos have had. Learn about your family's struggles. Understand how far they've come; learn about their journey; and look inside yourself for how you can contribute to that, and how you can take us to the next level as a people."

Jessica, the twenty-two-year-old of El Salvadoran descent, says of her duality, "It gives me a broader perspective, a broader outlook on myself and the way I live, the way I interact with people and treat others. It has a very positive effect on my life. I have so much I can rely on."

Blanca is a twenty-eight-year-old Dominican American in New York City. She says that being Latina has made her a better person. "I think I'm less materialistic than other Americans. I have always said that if you have never had something, then you don't need it and you shouldn't miss it."

Olivia, thirty-seven, is of El Salvadoran descent, and she acknowledges that being raised in the United States has broadened her perspective. "My views on gender are completely different. So are my views on class. We are a classist society here, but El Salvador is *really* classist. I value the family, but there is a value in the United States for the individual that I would not have adopted in El Salvador."

Thirty-seven-year-old Puerto Rican Marie Isabel, who lives in Pennsylvania, agrees. "I am much more open-minded because I have been exposed to other cultures. I am more accepting of differences."

And after struggling for years with her heritage and how others perceived her, Marie Isabel is relieved to see Latino kids garnering new confidence in the programs run by the nonprofit where she works. "I deal with kids now, and I find that they are actually having an easier time with the duality than I had as a kid. It's cool now, and more acceptable, to be who you are. We are teaching kids to be proud of their heritage. If we can instill girls with pride in their heritage when they're coming of age, life will be so much easier for them when they get older."

EXACTLY HOW WE'RE SUPPOSED TO BE

For some time now, I've been immersed in contemplating the body and all that comes with it. But I am not yet the type of body warrior I want to be, nor am I a woman untethered to the beauty machine.

I advocate self-acceptance and admire the female body in all its shapes and sizes, but I also have a drawer full of hair products that I'm convinced will do just the right thing for my unmanageable hair. I have way too much makeup, and yet I lack the ability to apply it artfully. I can look in the mirror with acceptance, and yet I'm ever aware of how I look in what I'm wearing. There are days when I feel lucky to have genes that have given me good skin, and yet I prefer the way I look with a tan than without one.

Talking to so many diverse, interesting, compelling women has been empowering and enlightening to me. I have always known that I'm not alone in the fact that I critique my body. The fact that we can be accepting and *are* accepting gives me a sense of hope— hope that we do not have to move forward alone in championing a more inclusive and realistic beauty and body ideal.

On both high school and college campuses, I worked with many young women who battled low self-esteem. I found that the way we feel about our body becomes intertwined with our self-image, coloring every move we make, so that little things seem impossible and insurmountable. Giving young women positive reinforcement about their ideas and their work became paramount to the way I approached my job.

One young woman in particular resisted the idea that there was anything positive, beautiful, or compelling about her. She would sit in the chair in my office crying, seething, hating herself. "You are creative," I would tell her, and she would roll her eyes. "You are strong," I would insist, and she would crumble. "You are so compassionate," I would remind her, and she would shrug it away. But I kept up my mantra. She didn't have to believe what I said, but she had to hear me.

As I became a more confident mentor, I encouraged my students to just say thank you when I complimented them, rather than deflect the sentiment. I pushed them to look at their strengths—physical strength, like the way their legs carried them in a soccer game; and emotional strength, like the way they supported their friends. I packed one young woman a healthy lunch for weeks until she finally agreed that respecting herself meant eating. I talked to other young women about choosing friends who celebrated them rather than demeaned them. I celebrated my college students whenever they walked into my office, and I made sure that I saw them—really *saw* them—so that I could mirror back to them their magnificence.

There are even more solutions out there, and the women I interviewed freely shared theirs. I asked them what they would say if a young woman they loved and admired came to them, revealed her long-suffering body dissatisfaction, and asked, "How do I start loving my body?" Their answers did not disappoint. They raised their voices to offer the following suggestions, and as I listened, I felt myself expanding with a renewed sense of hope and pride about how much we already know.

Sonya is a thirty-two-year-old who grew up in Boston. Her father is from Peru. She's long battled a negative self-image, and her advice reflects her growth over the years. "I would say that to begin loving your body, you must pay attention to it—not by comparing it to others, but listening to it yourself. When I stopped comparing my body to other women's bodies was when I truly began to believe and feel that God does not make mistakes. When I believed my body is exactly how it's supposed to be, I could finally begin to let go of my habit of negativity and shame. The two things I did differently to begin the process of undoing my negative self-image was to learn how to touch myself—not just masturbation, but paying attention to what felt good, what didn't feel good, where my mind went when I allowed myself time to explore these moments of just feeling good—and being a bit more open with other women about their issues. It was not surprising that I discovered many women have the same issues and fears as I do, and many even have the same problems. If we keep secrets—whatever that looks like to us—we can never be rid of the shame. So I stopped being secretive about my body. When I opened that door, it was simply amazing what came out."

Thirty-five-year-old Frances grew up in New York City and is of Colombian descent. She was motivated by the question posed; for her it is not a hypothetical situation. "Many female friends—Latina and otherwise—who I admire greatly have expressed dissatisfaction with their bodies. It's not only been verbally expressed to me, but I see that they express their lack of self-love in nicotine addiction and sexual promiscuity, and in pushing their bodies to perform without sufficient rest. It makes me feel that perhaps I haven't given enough attention to these complaints. In the future, I will lend a listening, nonjudgmental ear first and foremost. I would advise them to deepen their spiritual connection with God or a higher power, as perhaps the self-image issues stem from a deeper sense of emptiness or alienation. I might advise friends to seek counseling. I would advise them to list in a journal all the things that they love about their body or what their body can do, to treat themselves to some body TLC—a massage, yoga, a manicure, a pedicure. They might also list things that have brought their bodies joy, and do one [of those things once] a week. I would ask them to read for inspiration."

I often teach journaling workshops to people of various ages, from ninth-graders to senior citizens, and I have found that this tool alters how people view themselves and their problems. In fact, journaling is what saved me as a young Latina. In the quiet of night, I would grab paper and pour out everything that I couldn't voice to anyone. I learned so much about myself through the process, unveiling who I was as I went through volumes of college-rule paper. I found purpose on the page. I often suggest to young women I meet that they try journaling. The things you can uncover about yourself in the process are amazing. It opens up a different type of perspective—a window on things that perhaps are preoccupying you more than you know. For me, writing out my reality kept me aware of the real and important pieces of who I was and always would be—at thirteen, fifteen, eighteen, and twenty. Journaling is not just an activity. It can be a person's salvation.

Rosa is forty and from Peru. "These are good questions," she starts, "but very hard." Nonetheless, she offers her wisdom: "I would begin by asking her to describe how she sees herself, and how she thinks others see her. It has been my experience that these two points of view are very different more often than not. We are most often our worst critics, so learning to address what you consider your negative body image, or your bodily dislikes, is a difficult process. I would listen to how she describes herself, what she wanted to change and why. Merely suggesting ideas or making recommendations is not enough to help someone to take a first step in learning to like—then, eventually, love—herself as a whole. She has to want to change and be willing to work at it alone—with support from family and friends, of course."

Lucia, thirty-eight, is a Chicana living in Austin. She would advise her young Latina to "get to know yourself. Know who you are. Know what your likes are, where your values lie, what ethics you have. And don't let anyone else try to convince you or change your mind about who you are. We can only be true to ourselves after we know what is at our core."

Thalia is twenty-seven, Chicana, and an educator. Her advice? "Respect yourself. Don't rush into things. Let things happen when they should. Know who you are and the value of your mind, body, and soul. Don't let others try to break you. Be proud. Everything is there with you. Being Latina is part of your life. Accentuate it. God gave you dancing hips; shake them. God gave you full breasts; wear a good bra."

Twenty-seven-year-old Liza, who's Puerto Rican, would advise her loved one that "it's a long, hard road. And I completely sympathize. I would tell her about my own struggles of going through periods of not eating when I was younger, and how now I eat junk food like crazy, because I'm always stressed. I would offer her the advice that's worked for me—to find something physical that you can do with your body that no one can take away from you. This might be working out, yoga, running, salsa, merengue, *folklorico*, ballet, contemporary dance, sex, singing, playing soccer, dancing naked in front of your mirror to the best Hector Lavoe song ever, walking, sitting, meditating, hiking, biking, standing on the beach and breathing in the air, whatever. Something that makes you feel good. Keep on doing that, and know that many people don't have the gifts you have. Enjoy it."

She continues, "My best friend has struggled with her weight the entire time I've known her. So we go to the gym together at least twice a week, and then we feel good. And when she uses her true talents—painting and doing makeup—that's where she shines. When she puts on her crazy eye-shadow color combinations and wears low-cut shirts, she knows she looks good. So it's about doing what makes you feel good inside. The other thing is to admire women whose bodies are like your own. I have few skinny friends. I don't even know anyone whose [body is] physically perfect. You really have to work with what you have. And sometimes we get these messages from mainstream America that are like, *Skinny! Blond! Skinny! Feminine!* and it's frustrating. But then I actually look around at happy, smiling, laughing black, Islander, and Latina ladies around me, and I think, *Who really cares what you look like?* It's all in how you feel. If you hate your body, and wearing sexy lingerie makes you feel good—damn, wear it every minute under your clothes, and then parade around the house in it! If getting a tattoo makes you feel closer to your physical body, then do it. It's about doing what comes from within. What comes into your head—after you've been able to lay on your bed for an hour alone—that you would like to do to make yourself happy, feel good, and loved by yourself? It is not about what anyone else in the world is telling you to do."

Twenty-eight-year-old Josette is of Peruvian and Colombian descent and grew up in Queens. She says, "I would be as blunt as possible by telling her to travel. Why travel? Because in different parts of the world, different body images and characteristics are loved. I think it's because I traveled that I began to love my body. I dance salsa, and when I started going salsa dancing in Paris, I noticed really small-chested girls dancing without bras and looking absolutely fabulous and confident. They looked sexy to me. Then there are places like L.A., where I go salsa dancing and all I see are short skirts, breast implants, and lots of makeup. So by surrounding yourself with other cultures, you can begin to put less pressure on yourself to conform to the Americanized vision of beauty. In China, people came up to me and asked me to take a picture with them because they thought I was beautiful! Isn't that something? I was so surprised when this happened multiple times in different cities. They thought I was Indian and loved my features. Amazing. By seeing what other cultures love, you realize that beauty is very subjective. There is no one universal pattern. And you then realize that you can be very beautiful to others. Most important, you start being beautiful in your own eyes—and those are the most important eyes."

Miranda is thirty-five and lives in New York. Her heritage is Colombian. Her advice for a friend in need of some self-love and respect? "God doesn't make mistakes. You are exactly who you need to be and who God intended you to be: a beautiful, loving, and powerful woman. Every day, look in the mirror and tell yourself how much you love yourself. You have the power to create happiness and fulfillment in your life. You choose how to see yourself and, therefore, how others see you. Make time for yourself, do the things that you love most for yourself—read a book, draw a bath, get a massage, take a yoga class, exercise, meditate, play your favorite music. And do these things for yourself on a regular basis. Love yourself so that you can truly love and be loved."

A CALL TO ACTION

Here's your call to action: Take the time to feel the ideas presented in this book. Take time to ingest them. Let them resonate for you.

Then take a small piece of one particular thing that spoke to you and incorporate it positively into your life. All of us—regardless of what we suffered through because of our breasts, our hair, our noses, our skin, our family, our finances, our accents, our attributes—still have had so much entrusted to us. Our ancestors, grandparents, or parents bravely navigated a new land in the name of their futures and the futures of their offspring; in so doing, they paved the way for the lives that we're living. We have the option to take that hope and stretch further, reach higher, do more. The body and beauty revolution is ours to begin. It's time to give ourselves, and the girls and women around us, a wider lens through which to consider our beauty, and who we are beyond our beauty. We have to bite our tongues when a moment of self-loathing or criticism enters our minds. We have to encourage the women we love to talk about something other than their cellulite. We have to eradicate these limiting thoughts from our minds, because a change in our own minds leads to changes in our media and on our planet. On your bad days, call someone who loves you as you are, and bask in the respect they give you. If you don't have someone like that in your life, perhaps you need to examine why, and start looking.

The expectations we absorb can either encourage us or limit us. They can catapult us to possibility or keep us confined by our feelings of inadequacy.

There is an old saying that tells us we are only as strong as our weakest link, and it's true in this case. Body image isn't just the problem of the insecure girl. Having confidence does not mean that body-image issues will not affect you. If your child's teacher is plagued by low self-esteem, it affects how she champions your child; it affects you. The way women have been reduced in our world affects all of us, directly and indirectly. If the women of the next generation are crippled by their lack of confidence, their leadership will falter, and their ability to make change will be compromised.

Champion all women. We need to know that as long as one woman is crippled by feelings of inadequacy, then the world that we have created is inadequate. Supporting one another and freeing one another from the limiting messages that we internalize can be revolutionary. We make the choice whether to internalize these messages. We make the choice whether to build up or tear down. We can have power in our lives by not taking in negative messages, and we can empower other women by not sending out negative messages.

We are all beautiful and powerful women, and we must make the choice to always present our authentic selves. Don't box others in; don't relegate someone to a space she hasn't chosen for herself. If you're not already doing something you love, find something that you can throw your heart into, something that can pull your passion out. See yourself in that context—as a singer, a mentor, a dancer, a yogini, a teacher, a painter—and you'll soon see yourself as the competent, strong, authentic woman you already are.

We can and should acknowledge the vastness of all Latina experiences and realities—as well as the experiences and realities of our non-Latina sisters. When we begin to see women in all of their dimensions, we begin to eradicate confining stereotypes and worldviews. We start to see Latinas and all women as complex individuals, and not just as part of a larger stereotypical hold. Look wider, acknowledge more, think bigger. We are women of all colors and cultures, and we can make a world that does not relegate us to type and cast. We can choose to live in a world that celebrates wholeness and complexities in our women. We can choose to create a society that encourages women to be healthier and more whole, a society that unites us in our commonalities while acknowledging the depth of the individual. The more we challenge the limits we place on each other, the more open the world will be to all of us.

The women of *Hijas Americanas* are an inspiration, an acknowledgment of the real work it takes to come into one's own. They're an affirmation that we—as Latinas, as all women—are not just one identifiable thing to be categorized by others. We are dynamic and complex and not easily defined. By speaking their truths, these women are activists, and your call to action is to do the same by sharing your own truths. Discover yourself, share yourself, and encourage others to do the same.

Raise your voice and demand an end to a narrow beauty mystique. No matter where you have been on the journey to selfhood, start each day with the intention of championing yourself and others. It is never too late to claim yourself. The revolution—for all of us, of any upbringing—is about to crescendo.

❖ APPENDIX A ❖

Growing Up Latina Survey

DEMOGRAPHIC PROFILE

How old are you?

A. 18–20

B. 21–23

C. 24–27

D. 28–30

E. 31–34

F. 35–37

G. 38–40

From where is your Latino heritage? (You may mark more than one.)

A.	Argentina	K.	Guatemala
B.	Bolivia	L.	Honduras
C.	Brazil	M.	Mexico
D.	Chile	N.	Nicaragua
E.	Colombia	O.	Panama
F.	Costa Rica	P.	Paraguay
G.	Cuba	Q.	Peru
H.	Dominican Republic	R.	Puerto Rico
I.	Ecuador	S.	Uruguay
J.	El Salvador	T.	Venezuela

Which words best describe where you grew up between the ages of 10 and 18? If you grew up in more than one area, please answer for the location that had the most influence on your development.

A. rural

B. suburban: near a small- to medium-size city

C. suburban: near a large city

D. urban: small- to medium-size city

E. urban: large city

What region best describes where you grew up between the ages of 10 and 18?

A. Deep South: Alabama, Florida, Georgia, Louisiana, Mississippi

B. Mid-South: Kentucky, North Carolina, South Carolina, Tennessee, Virginia

C. Mid-Atlantic: Delaware, Maryland, New Jersey, New York, Pennsylvania, West Virginia

D. New England: Connecticut, Maine, Massachusetts, New Hampshire, Rhode Island, Vermont

E. Great Lakes: Illinois, Indiana, Michigan, Ohio, Wisconsin

F. South-Central: Arkansas, Kansas, Missouri, Oklahoma, Texas

G. Upper Plains: Iowa, Minnesota, Nebraska, North Dakota, South Dakota

H. Southwest: Arizona, Colorado, Nevada, New Mexico, Utah

I. Northwest: Idaho, Montana, Oregon, Washington, Wyoming

J. Pacific West: Alaska, California, Hawaii

What region describes your current permanent address?

A. Deep South: Alabama, Florida, Georgia, Louisiana, Mississippi

B. Mid-South: Kentucky, North Carolina, South Carolina, Tennessee, Virginia

C. Mid-Atlantic: Delaware, Maryland, New Jersey, New York, Pennsylvania, West Virginia

D. New England: Connecticut, Maine, Massachusetts, New Hampshire, Rhode Island, Vermont

E. Great Lakes: Illinois, Indiana, Michigan, Ohio, Wisconsin

F. South-Central: Arkansas, Kansas, Missouri, Oklahoma, Texas

G. Upper Plains: Iowa, Minnesota, Nebraska, North Dakota, South Dakota

H. Southwest: Arizona, Colorado, Nevada, New Mexico, Utah

I. Northwest: Idaho, Montana, Oregon, Washington, Wyoming

J. Pacific West: Alaska, California, Hawaii

How many siblings do you have?

A. 0   B. 1   C. 2   D. 3   E. 4   F. 5   G. 6 or more

How many sisters do you have?

A. 0   B. 1   C. 2   D. 3   E. 4   F. 5   G. 6 or more

Where are you in birth order?

A. oldest

B. youngest

C. in the middle

D. close to oldest

E. close to youngest

What is your employment status?

A. student

B. employed part-time

C. employed full-time

D. student and employed either full- or part-time

E. unemployed

What is your education?

A. some high school

B. high school graduate

C. technical school

D. some college (including those who are currently completing a degree)

E. bachelor's degree

F. some graduate work (including those who are currently completing their master's)

G. master's degree

H. doctorate

FAMILY INFLUENCE/ IMPACT

Are you satisfied with your family relationships?

A. very satisfied

B. satisfied

C. somewhat satisfied

D. somewhat dissatisfied

E. very dissatisfied

Did your mother demonstrate physical confidence when you were young?

A. yes   **B.** no

Did your mother demonstrate emotional confidence when you were young?

A. yes   **B.** no

Were you affirmed for your personality and intelligence when you were growing up?

A. yes   **B.** no

Were you affirmed for your appearance when you were growing up?

A. yes   **B.** no

Did you have physical confidence from childhood until age 10?

A. yes   **B.** no

Did you have physical confidence from ages 11 to 14?

A. yes   **B.** no

Did you have physical confidence from ages 15 to 18?

A. yes   **B.** no

Did you have emotional confidence from childhood until age 10?

A. yes   **B.** no

Did you have emotional confidence from ages 11 to 14?

A. yes   **B.** no

Did you have emotional confidence from ages 15 to 18?

A. yes   **B.** no

Did your father affirm your personality and intelligence when you were growing up?

A. yes   **B.** no

Did your father affirm your appearance when you were growing up?

A. yes   **B.** no

Do/did you feel that your family expects/expected you to become a wife?

A. yes   **B.** no

Do/did you feel that your family expects/expected you to become a mother?

A. yes   **B.** no

Do/did you feel pressure from your family to marry a Latino, or partner with a Latino/a?

A. yes   **B.** no

Which cultural traditions will you keep in your life?

_____

_____

_____

Which cultural traditions do not fit into your lifestyle?

_____

_____

_____

MEDIA INFLUENCE/ IMPACT

What has most influenced your view of what is beautiful in/for women?

A. my own personal experiences

B. my family's viewpoints

C. the viewpoints of my friends

D. print media

E. television and film

F. the viewpoints of men

Do you believe that women today are largely expected to be more attractive than women twenty years ago?

A. yes   **B.** no

Do you believe that women today are largely expected to use methods available to enhance their attractiveness?

A. yes   **B.** no

Do you see women who look like you portrayed in mass media?

A. yes   **B.** no

How do you feel about famous Latinas like Salma Hayek, Eva Mendes, Jennifer Lopez, Michelle Rodriguez, and Cameron Diaz?

_____

_____

_____

What do you consider the American standard of beauty?

_____

_____

_____

What famous Latinas do you most admire (listed in order)?

1. _____

2. _____

3. _____

4. _____

5. _____

List in rank order five well-known women whom you consider very beautiful.

1. _____

2. _____

3. _____

4. _____

5. _____

List in rank order (if different from above) five well-known women whom you consider very attractive.

1. _____

2. _____

3. _____

4. _____

5. _____

List in rank order the magazines you read most frequently.

1. _____

2. _____

3. _____

4. _____

5. _____

List in rank order the television programs you watch most frequently.

1. _____

2. _____

3. _____

4. _____

5. _____

SOCIAL INFLUENCE/IMPACT

What were your favorite childhood games? Please describe.

_____

_____

_____

Do you believe that there are negative stereotypes about Latina women in the United States?

A. yes   **B.** no

If so, what are the stereotypes that you believe exist?

_____

_____

_____

If so, have you been affected by these negative stereotypes?

A. yes   **B.** no

What are the major difficulties you face as a Latina?

A. having to reconcile growing up in a different situation than my parents, grandparents, etc.

B. having to fight stereotypes

C. issues in intimate relationships

D. having to reconcile my body image and beauty perception

E. having to reconcile my ethnic identity

F. having to prove myself

G. having to play multiple roles to please others

Have you ever had to deal with prejudice/discrimination because of your ethnicity and gender?

A. yes   B. no

If so, what type(s) of prejudice/discrimination? Select as many as are applicable.

A. discrimination by my peers in school

B. discrimination by my teachers or administrators in school

C. workplace discrimination

E. discrimination by the general public (for example, someone may have targeted you with a racial slur)

F. discrimination in services (at stores, restaurants, etc.)

G. prejudice from law enforcement

H. sexual harassment or assault

Have you ever discriminated against other Latinas?

A. yes   B. no

If so, can you provide examples?

_____

_____

_____

Do you change the way that you act in certain situations to elicit a more favorable response from non-Latinos?

A. yes   B. no

If so, what do you do?

A. emphasize my education

B. change my style of dress, makeup, or hair

C. change my way of speaking

D. talk about things that I perceive as interesting to the person I am with, as opposed to what interests me

E. other (describe):

Have you ever experienced discrimination from other Latinos?

A. yes   **B.** no

If so, please provide examples.

_____

_____

_____

What are the major difficulties you face as a Latina?

_____

_____

_____

Have you ever felt unwelcome as a result of being a Latina?

A. no   **B.** yes (describe)

_____

_____

_____

Most of my life experiences have been in:

A. settings that are predominantly Latino

B. settings that are racially mixed

C. settings with very few Latinos

Are you satisfied with your friendships?

A. very satisfied

B. satisfied

C. somewhat satisfied

D. somewhat dissatisfied

E. very dissatisfied

My friends are predominantly:

A. Latino

B. racially mixed

C. not Latino

How do you define the term "feminist"?

_____

_____

_____

Do you consider yourself a feminist?

A. yes   **B.** no

If you went to college, could you please describe that experience's effect on your sense of beauty, self, and confidence?

_____

_____

_____

FAITH INFLUENCE/IMPACT

What faith tradition, if any, guided your upbringing?

A. Buddhism   **F.** evangelical Christianity

B. Catholicism   **G.** Islam

C. Hinduism   **H.** Santería

D. Judaism   **I.** Other

E. Protestantism   **J.** None

What influence did your faith tradition have on you during the years between ages 10 and 18?

_____

_____

_____

Are you currently an active member of a church or religious community?

A. yes   **B.** no

Do you consider yourself deeply spiritual and influenced by your faith practice?

A. very

B. somewhat

C. not at all

If so, are you satisfied with your spirituality or faith practice?

A. very satisfied

B. satisfied

C. somewhat satisfied

D. somewhat dissatisfied

E. very dissatisfied

BODY IMAGE/BEAUTY PERCEPTION

Choose the word that most accurately describes your overall look.

A. attractive   **F.** feminine

B. average   **G.** gorgeous

C. beautiful   **H.** natural

D. cute   **I.** pretty

E. exotic   **J.** sexy

What about your looks led to your answer in the previous question?

_____

_____

_____

What makes you feel beautiful?

A. being more attractive than others

B. taking good care of myself

C. being in good physical shape

D. having a committed circle of friends

E. being loved

F. doing something about which I am passionate

G. having a strong partnership with a significant other

H. receiving compliments

I. liking what I see in the mirror

J. being successful financially

K. being successful professionally or academically

L. having a rich spiritual practice

M. investing in my community

N. having a sense of personal style

O. having a sense of humor

P. having a sense of confidence

Q. feeling happy and fulfilled

What products do you use on a regular basis (four or more days a week, or at appropriate regular intervals for some products)? Mark all that apply.

A. deodorant

B. hair-care products

C. perfume

D. body lotion

E. face-care products

F. full makeup

G. some makeup

H. hair coloring or bleaching

I. nail-care products

J. skin-tanning products

K. teeth-whitening products

L. skin-lightening products

How much do you spend a month on beauty products/procedures?

A. less than $25

B. $25–$50

C. $50–$75

D. $75–$100

E. $100–$150

F. $150–$200

G. more than $200

What do you regularly do in terms of personal maintenance (if "regularly" is defined as at least ten times a year)?

A. eyebrow wax

B. bikini wax

C. Brazilian wax

D. lip wax

E. facial

F. manicure

G. pedicure

H. massage

I. other

Have you had cosmetic surgery?

A. yes   B. no

If yes, what procedure(s)?

_____

_____

_____

If yes, did you make the right decision?

_____

_____

_____

If no, have you considered plastic surgery?

A. yes   B. no

How do you prefer to wear your hair?

A. natural texture, which is curly or wavy

B. natural texture, which is straight

C. straightened or relaxed

D. curled or permed

Do you dye your hair?

A. yes   **B.** no

If you dye your hair, how do you dye it?

A. lighter

B. darker

C. same color; just to cover the grays

Have you ever entered a beauty pageant?

A. no   **B.** yes (describe)

_____

_____

_____

Are you satisfied with your skin color?

A. very satisfied

B. somewhat satisfied

C. unsatisfied

D. very unsatisfied

Are you satisfied with your hair texture?

A. very satisfied

B. somewhat satisfied

C. unsatisfied

D. very unsatisfied

Are you satisfied with your body shape?

A. very satisfied

B. somewhat satisfied

C. unsatisfied

D. very unsatisfied

Are you satisfied with your weight?

A. very satisfied

B. somewhat satisfied

C. unsatisfied

D. very unsatisfied

Have you ever dieted?

A. yes   B. no

If yes, at what age did you first diet? _____

If yes, how often have you dieted?

A. rarely

B. occasionally, but no more than once a year

C. sometimes, but no more than two or three times a year

D. often (four to five times a year)

E. very often (more than five times a year)

Do you currently have, or have you ever had, an eating disorder?

A. no   B. yes (describe)

_____

_____

_____

How physically active are you?

A. inactive

B. moderate (three to four days a week, 30 minutes a day)

C. vigorous (more than five days a week, more than 30 minutes a day)

Attractive women are more valued in society.

A. strongly disagree

B. disagree

C. agree

D. strongly agree

Attractive women have it easier in life.

A. strongly disagree

B. disagree

C. agree

D. strongly agree

I am satisfied with my beauty.

A. strongly disagree

B. disagree

C. agree

D. strongly agree

I am satisfied with my physical attractiveness.

A. strongly disagree

B. disagree

C. agree

D. strongly agree

I am satisfied with my facial attractiveness.

A. strongly disagree

B. disagree

C. agree

D. strongly agree

I am satisfied with my body shape.

A. strongly disagree

B. disagree

C. agree

D. strongly agree

I am satisfied with my body weight.

A. strongly disagree

B. disagree

C. agree

D. strongly agree

I feel uncomfortable describing my looks in a positive way (i.e.: "attractive," "gorgeous," "sexy," "beautiful," "pretty").

A. strongly disagree

B. disagree

C. agree

D. strongly agree

I consider myself:

A. very overweight

B. slightly overweight

C. average weight

D. slightly underweight

E. very underweight

I feel concern about my weight:

A. all of the time

B. often

C. sometimes

D. rarely

E. never

I feel guilty about eating:

A. all of the time

B. often

C. sometimes

D. rarely

E. never

When I get depressed, I:

A. eat more

B. eat about the same

C. eat less

Are you satisfied with your health?

A. very satisfied

B. satisfied

C. somewhat satisfied

D. somewhat dissatisfied

E. very dissatisfied

Do you currently play organized sports?

A. no   **B.** yes (describe which sports)

_____

_____

_____

Have you played organized sports in the past?

A. no   **B.** yes (describe which sports)

_____

_____

_____

If so, how did your family react to your involvement in sports?

_____

_____

_____

Describe your sense of style. What informs your sense of style?

_____

_____

_____

What do you consider beautiful in a woman?

_____

_____

_____

SEXUALITY/INTIMACY/ROMANCE

What is your sexual orientation?

A. heterosexual

B. lesbian

C. other

Have you ever dated outside of your race?

A. yes   B. no

Will you only date Latino/as?

A. yes   B. no

How old were you when you when you had your first kiss? _____

How old were you when you had your first date? _____

How important is it for a woman to marry?

A. very important

B. important

C. not important

D. very unimportant

How important is it for a woman to be a mother?

A. very important

B. important

C. not important

D. very unimportant

Have you had sexual intercourse?

A. yes   B. no

If no, how old are you? _____

If yes, at what age did you become sexually active? _____

If yes, describe your first sexual experience.

A. involuntary

B. voluntary but unwanted

C. voluntary and desired

If yes, did you have sex before marriage?

A. yes   **B.** no

If yes, have you ever been pregnant?

A. yes   **B.** no

Do you use birth control?

A. yes   **B.** no

If so, what form?

A. pills

B. condom

C. IUD

D. diaphragm

E. rhythm method

F. withdrawal

G. the patch

H. other (describe)

_____

_____

Have you ever had an STD?

A. no   **B.** yes (please identify which STD or STDs)

_____

_____

_____

Have you ever had an orgasm?

A. yes   **B.** no

Do you feel sexually adventurous?

A. yes   **B.** no

Do you prioritize your performance over your pleasure?

A. yes   **B.** no

Are you familiar with your body?

A. yes   **B.** no

Have you ever downplayed your abilities or strengths to Latino men?

A. yes   **B.** no

Have you ever been physically/emotionally threatened by a partner?

A. yes   **B.** no

Have you ever been physically/emotionally abused by a partner?

A. yes   **B.** no

What is your marital status?

A. single

B. living with a partner

C. married

D. separated

E. divorced

F. widowed

If you are currently in a relationship, are you satisfied with it?

A. very satisfied

B. satisfied

C. somewhat satisfied

D. somewhat dissatisfied

E. very dissatisfied

Do you have children?

A. yes   **B.** no

If so, were you married when you had your children?

A. yes   **B.** no

If so, at what age did you have your child(ren)?

A. 13–16

B. 17–19

C. 20–23

D. 24–27

E. 28–30

F. 31–34

G. 35–40

From the list below, please mark everything that is important for an intimate partner to do:

A. be your companion

B. raise a family

C. give you love and affection

D. do physically demanding work around the house

E. make major household decisions

F. offer professional advice

G. engage in debate

H. give physical protection

I. support you financially

J. be sexually intimate

K. receive personal advice

What do you most want from a partner in a marriage or long-term relationship? (Mark all that apply.)

A. respect

B. pleasure

C. someone who comes from a respected family

D. good provider

E. intimacy

F. equality

G. emotional satisfaction

This was a web-based survey completed by 520 women from February to June 2006.

⚜ APPENDIX B ⚜

Phone and In-Person Interview Questionnaire

Name: _____

Ethnicity: _____

Occupation: _____

City, state of residence: _____

Age: _____

Educational background: _____

Marital status: _____

Birthplace: _____

Religion: _____

Current financial situation: _____

QUESTIONS

1. What do you love about being a Latina?

2. What do you love most about yourself? About what are you most confident?

3. How do you believe your life is different by growing up in the United States instead of growing up in the country (or countries) of your ethnic heritage?

4. Describe your overall experience of being a Latina in America. What are the triumphs and the challenges?

5. Tell me about your relationship with your parents in your home as you grew up both American and Latina.

6. What was your hometown like as you grew up? What is it like at this time? Where did you find your place in it?

7. What was the message you received inside/outside your home about femininity, body image, and sexuality? Did you notice a difference between the messages you received from your family, boys in your peer group, and girls in your peer group?

8. What stereotypes (if any) did you face as you grew up? What stereotypes do you face now?

9. Did you have a *quinceañera*? If so, what was that experience like?

10. In your romantic relationships, which rules and expectations from your parents' traditions applied, and which ones didn't?

11. Is machismo a major force in your life?

12. What do you believe are the beauty ideals in the Latino community?

13. What do you believe are the beauty ideals in American mainstream or pop culture?

14. What messages have you received about your style, hair, skin, body size, shape, and clothing?

15. Were you ever involved in beauty pageants? If so, tell me about those experiences and what role they played in your self-development.

16. Are you secure in your appearance? If not, why not? Do you consider yourself sexy?

17. What do you believe is essential for being beautiful?

18. Have you ever seriously considered or had plastic surgery? If so, on what and when?

19. What role does food play in your life?

20. Have you ever been treated as inauthentic by other Latinas or members of other racial groups? How did that affect your self-image and identity?

21. Did/do you ever feel that you have to stifle your true self when you are in the company of non-Latinas?

22. How much Latino influence from people, events, media, etc., do you encounter regularly?

23. Do you consider yourself a feminist? Why or why not?

24. How satisfied are you with how Latinas as a whole are treated in U.S. society?

25. What advice, insights, books, movies, websites, etc., have most helped you in your development as a Latina in America?

26. How has your duality—being both Latina and American—positively shaped your life?

27. How can one be Latina and American without betraying her roots?

28. What advice or insight do you have for Latinas who are just beginning their coming of age, or what advice or insight will you provide your daughters, nieces, or Latina mentees?

This interview was conducted with more than eighty women between February and April 2006.

⅗ RESOURCE GUIDE ⅗

As I interviewed women for this book, I asked them what media (books, websites, movies) had been helpful in their development. The following is a list of their suggestions, as well as other options I picked up along the way.

BOOKS

Isabel Allende. *House of the Spirits* (New York: Bantam Books, 1986).

Julia Alvarez. *Homecoming: New and Collected Poems* (New York: Plume, 1996).

Julia Alvarez. *How the Garcia Girls Lost Their Accents* (Chapel Hill, NC: Algonquin Books, 1991).

Julia Alvarez. *In the Time of the Butterflies* (New York: Plume, 1995).

Julia Alvarez. *Something to Declare* (New York: Plume, 1999).

Gloria Anzaldua. *La Frontera/Borderlands* (San Francisco: Aunt Lute Books, 1987).

Gloria Anzaldua, editor. *Making Face, Making Soul/Haciendo Caras: Creative and Critical Perspectives by Feminists of Color* (San Francisco: Aunt Lute Books, 1990).

Gloria Anzaldua and Cherríe Moraga, editors. *This Bridge Called My Back: Writings by Radical Women of Color* (New York: Kitchen Table: Women of Color Press, 1984).

Elena Avila and Joy Parker. *Woman Who Glows in the Dark: A Curandera Reveals Traditional Aztec Secrets of Physical and Spiritual Health* (New York: Tarcher, 1999).

Jennifer Baumgardner and Amy Richards. *Manifesta: Young Women, Feminism, and the Future* (New York: Farrar, Straus, and Giroux, 2000).

Susan Bordo. *Unbearable Weight: Feminism, Western Culture, and the Body* (Berkeley, CA: University of California Press, 1993).

Ana Castillo. *Massacre of the Dreamers: Essays on Xicanisma* (New York: Plume, 1995).

Ana Castillo. *Peel My Love Like an Onion* (New York: Anchor, 2000).

Veronica Chambers. *Mama's Girl* (New York: Riverhead Press, 1996).

Sandra Cisneros. *The House on Mango Street* (New York: Vintage Books, 1991).

Sandra Cisneros. *Loose Woman: Poems* (New York: Vintage Books, 1995).

Sandra Cisneros. *Woman Hollering Creek and Other Stories* (New York: Random House, 1991).

Judith Ortiz Cofer. *The Latin Deli: Telling the Lives of Barrio Women* (New York: Norton, 1995).

Orlando Crespo. *Being Latino in Christ: Finding Wholeness in Your Ethnic Identity* (Doumers Grove, IL: Intervarsity Press, 2003).

Angie Cruz. *Soledad* (New York: Simon & Schuster, 2001).

Susan J. Douglas. *Where the Girls Are: Growing Up Female with the Mass Media* (New York: Three Rivers Press, 1994).

Ophira Edut, editor. *Body Outlaws: Rewriting the Rules of Beauty and Body Image* (Emeryville, CA: Seal Press, 1998).

Eve Ensler. *The Good Body* (New York: Villard Books, 2004).

Laura Esquivel. *Like Water for Chocolate: A Novel in Monthly Installments with Recipes, Romances, and Home Remedies* (New York: Anchor, 1995).

Nancy Etcoff. *Survival of the Prettiest: The Science of Beauty* (New York: Anchor Books, 2000).

Angela Jane Fountas, editor. *Waking Up American: Coming of Age Biculturally* (Emeryville, CA: Seal Press, 2005).

Rosa Maria Gil, D.S.W., and Carmen Inoa Vazquez, Ph.D. *The Maria Paradox: How Latinas Can Merge Old Traditions with New World Self-Esteem* (New York: Perigee Books, 1996).

Paula Goldman, editor. *Imagining Ourselves: Global Voices from a New Generation of Women* (Novato, CA: New World Library, 2006).

Sandra Guzman. *The Latina's Bible: The Nueva Latina's Guide to Love, Spirituality, Family, and la Vida* (New York: Three Rivers Press, 2002).

Daisy Hernández and Bushra Rehman, editors. *Colonize This!: Young Women of Color on Today's Feminism* (Emeryville, CA: Seal Press, 2002).

Ada María Isasi-Díaz. *Mujerista Theology* (Maryknoll, NY: Orbis Books, 1996).

Belisa Lozano-Vranich, Psy.D., and Jorge Petit, M.D. *The Seven Beliefs: A Step-by-Step Guide to Help Latinas Recognize and Overcome Depression* (New York: HarperCollins, 2003).

Margo Maine, Ph.D. *Body Wars: Making Peace with Women's Bodies* (Carlsbad, CA: Gurze Books, 2000).

Cherríe Moraga. *Loving in the War Years* (Cambridge, M.A.: South End Press, 2000).

Robyn Moreno and Michelle Herrera Mulligan, editors. *Borderline Personalities: A New Generation of Latinas Dish on Sex, Sass, and Cultural Shifting* (New York: HarperCollins, 2004).

Sonia Nazario. *Enrique's Journey: The Story of a Boy's Dangerous Odyssey to Reunite with His Mother* (New York: Random House, 2006).

Mary Pipher, Ph.D. *Reviving Ophelia: Saving the Selves of Adolescent Girls* (New York: Riverhead Books, 1994).

Esmeralda Santiago. *Almost a Woman* (New York: Vintage Books, 1999).

Esmeralda Santiago. *When I Was Puerto Rican* (New York: Vintage Books, 1993).

Alisa Valdes-Rodriguez. *The Dirty Girls Social Club* (New York: St. Martin's Griffin, 2004).

Emily White. *Fast Girls: Teenage Tribes and the Myth of the Slut* (New York: Penguin, 2002).

Naomi Wolf. *The Beauty Myth: How Images of Beauty Are Used Against Women* (New York: Harper Perennial, 2002).

Naomi Wolf. *Promiscuities: The Secret Struggle for Womanhood* (New York: Ballantine Books, 1997).

MOVIES

Frida (2002)

Girlfight (2000)

A Guide to Recognizing Your Saints (2006)

Hangin' with the Homeboys (1991)

I Like It Like That (1994)

La Bamba (1997)

Mad Hot Ballroom (2005)

Mi Familia (1995)

Mi Vida Loca (1993)

Quinceañera (2006)

Raising Victor Vargas (2003)

Real Women Have Curves (2002)

Selena (1997)

Stand and Deliver (1988)

Tortilla Soup (2001)

West Side Story (1961)

Yo Soy Boricua, Pa'que Tú Lo Sepas/I'm Boricua, Just So You Know (2006)

WEBSITES

www.4women.gov
Federal website for women's health information.

www.campaignforrealbeauty.com
Dove's campaign to encourage a wider, more inclusive view of beauty.

www.edreferral.com
Eating-disorder information and referral center.

www.girlscouts.org
The Girl Scouts' Uniquely Me! program aims to champion the self-esteem of young girls.

www.instituteofpleasure.org
Dr. Charley Ferrer is considered the Latina Dr. Ruth.

www.lascomadres.org
An Internet-based networking and support group for Latinas.

www.latinitasmagazine.com
A bilingual online magazine for Latina girls.

www.latinoculturalcenter.org
Features the details of Chicago's annual Latino film festival.

ORGANIZATIONS

The Body Image Counseling Center
1545 Landon Avenue
Jacksonville, FL 32207
(904) 737-3232
www.bodyimagecounseling.com

Serves Northeast Florida in the treatment of eating disorders and related mental health issues.

Chica Luna Productions
1690 Lexington Avenue, 2nd Floor
New York, NY 10029
(212) 410-3544
www.chicaluna.com

The Chica Luna mission is "to identify, develop, and support women of color who strive to use popular media to engage social justice themes and are accountable to their communities."

Girls on the Run
500 East Morehead Street, Suite 104
Charlotte, NC 28202
(800) 901-9965
www.girlsontherun.org

A program that uses running to help girls escape "the girl-box." Locations nationwide.

Girl Talk Foundation
801 East Morehead Street, Suite 105
Charlotte, NC 28202
(704) 335-5885
www.girltalkfoundation.org

A program designed to help girls make positive choices.

Solomon House
200 South Main Street
Huntersville, NC 28078
(704) 875-7727

The Solomon House is a faith-based organization that helps low-income individuals with the healthcare process by providing advocacy, information, and referrals to community health resources. They offer bilingual service programs and have Spanish-speaking staff.

True Body Project
500 Reading Road
Cincinnati, OH 45202
(513) 470-5548
www.truebodyproject.org

A nonprofit organization that empowers girls and women to connect to their voices and bodies through writing and movement.

NOTES

CHAPTER 1: TURNING GRINGA

1. Michael Finnegan and Robert Salladay. "'Hot' remark prompts apology: Schwarzenegger caught on tape." *The Charlotte Observer*, September 9, 2006, 16A.

CHAPTER 2. DOUBLE LIVES

1. Rosa Maria Gil, D.S.W., and Carmen Inoa Vazquez, Ph.D. *The Maria Paradox: How Latinas Can Merge Old Traditions with New World Self-Esteem* (New York: Perigee Books, 1996), 26.

2. Ibid., 11.

3. Ibid., 22.

4. Louis Tornatzky, Ph.D., Jongha Lee, Ph.D., Olga Mejia, Ph.D., Stephanie Tarant, M.S. "College Choices Among Latinos: Issues of Leaving Home." The Tomas Rivera Policy Institute, June 2003, 6.

5. Olga Vives. "Latina Girls' High School Drop-Out Rate Highest in U.S." *NOW Times,* fall 2001. Found online at www.now.org/nnt/fall-2001/latinas.html.

6. Ibid.

7. U.S. Census Bureau, U.S. Census of Population, U.S. Summary, PC80-1-C1 and Current Population Report, 20–550.

8. U.S. Census Bureau, Fact Finder. Found online at http://factfinder.census.gov. (Access this information by going to Fact Sheets and choosing "Hispanic" as a group.)

9. U.S. Census Bureau Statistical Abstract of the United States. Table 266: College Enrollment by Selected Characteristics: 1990–2002. Found online at www.census.gov/prod/www/statistical-abstract.html.

10. Ibid.

CHAPTER 3: IN THE NAME OF THE FATHER

1. You can learn more about Liberation Theology with these online resources: http://en.wikipedia.org/wiki/Liberation_theology and www.liberationtheology.org.

2. Ada María Isasi-Díaz. Mujerista Theology (Maryknoll, NY: Orbis Books, 1996).

CHAPTER 4. AY, MAMI

1. Mary B. Adam, M.D., M.A.; Jennifer K. McGuire, Ph.D., M.P.H.; Michele Walsh, Ph.D.; Joanne Basta, Ph.D.; and Craig LeCroy, Ph.D. "Acculturation as a Predictor of the Onset of Sexual Intercourse Among Hispanic and White Teens, Archives of Pediatrics and Adolescent Medicine 159 (2005): 261–265.

2. Alexandra M. Minnis and Nancy S. Padian. "Reproductive Health Differences Among Latin American and U.S.-Born Young Women," Journal of Urban Health: Bulletin of the New York Academy of Medicine Vol. 78, No. 4 (December 2001): 627–637.

3. These statistics and other resources can be found online at www .advocatesforyouth.org/publications/iag/latina.htm.

4. Laura F. Romo, Ph.D., Eva S. Lefkowitz, Ph.D., Marian Signam, Ph.D.S., and Terry K. Au, Ph.D. "A Longitudinal Study of Maternal Messages About Dating and Sexuality and Their Influence on Latino Adolescents," Journal of Adolescent Health Vol. 31, Issue 1 (July 2002): 59–69.

CHAPTER 5. THE LATINA MYSTIQUE

1. For these statistics and others, visit www.girlscouts.org/research /publications/original/healthy_living.asp.

2. Ibid.

CHAPTER 6. HOW LATINA ARE YOU?

1. Veronica Chambers. *The Joy of Doing Things Badly: A Girl's Guide to Love, Life, and Foolish Bravery* (New York: Broadway, 2006), 201–202.

2. Rosa Maria Gil, D.S.W., and Carmen Inoa Vazquez, Ph.D. *The Maria Paradox: How Latinas Can Merge Old Traditions with New World Self-Esteem* (New York: Perigee Books, 1996), 36–37.

3. Michael Lassell and Elena Georgiou, editors. *The World in Us: Lesbian and Gay Poetry of the Next Wave* (New York: St. Martin's Press, 2000), 95–97.

4. You can learn more about retro-acculturation and Latino teens online in the Cheskin market study "The Wonderful and Lucrative Enigma of the Hispanic Teens." Found online at www.cheskin.com/view_articles .php?id=15.

5. Michael Quintanilla. "Why We Can't Get Enough of Mia Maestro," *Latina* magazine, June/July 2006, 140.

6. These figures are made available by Nationmaster.com. Found online at www.nationmaster.com/graph.

CHAPTER 7. MARÍA DE LA BARBIE

1. You can find the image and comments online at http://offtherack.people
   .com/2006/09/what_do_you_thi.html.

2. Ibid.

3. Perry Tannenbaum. "Review: Torches," Backstage.com, February 21,
   2006. You can read this review online at www.backstage.com/bso/news
   _reviews/southeast/.

4. Naomi Mandel and Dirk Smeesters. "Positive and Negative Media
   Image Effects on the Self," Journal of Consumer Research Vol. 32, No. 4
   (March 2006): 576–582.

5. These figures are based on research from the American Society of Plastic
   Surgeons and are available online at http://plasticsurgery.org/media
   /briefing_papers/Ethnic-Patients.cfm.

6. These figures were compiled by the American Society of Plastic Surgeons
   and are available online at http://plasticsurgery.org/media/statistics.

7. These figures were provided by the American Society of Plastic Surgeons
   and are available online at www.cosmeticplasticsurgerystatistics.com.

8. These figures are made available by Nationmaster.com and are available
   online at www.nationmaster.com/graph.

9. These figures are made available by Nationmaster.com and are available
   online at www.nationmaster.com/graph/hea_pla_sur_pro_percap-plastic-
   surgery-procedures-per-capita.

10. Eve Ensler. *The Good Body* (New York: Villard, 2004), xii–xv.

11. These figures are made available by the National Eating Disorder
    Association and are available online at www.nationaleatingdisorders.org.

12. Laura Donnelly. "Latina Girls: Helping with Body Image Issues,"
    Daughters, January/February 2005.

13. Marian Fitzgibbon and Melinda Stolley. "Minority Women: The Untold
    Story." Available online at www.pbs.org/wgbh/nova/thin/minorities.html.

14. Nancy Hellmich. "Do thin models warp girls' body image?" *USA Today,*
    September 26, 2006. Found online at www.usatoday.com/news/health
    /2006-09-25-thin-models_x.htm.

CHAPTER 8. FIVE JOURNEYS TO SUCCESS

1. From the Galan Entertainment website: www.nelygalan.com/tv.htm.

❧ ACKNOWLEDGMENTS ❧

When I was growing up, my Papito took me to the library on Saturdays and let me spend hours selecting the books I wanted to check out. He never told me that I had too many books when I stumbled toward him with a stack I could barely handle. He never said a word when he found me reading under the covers with a flashlight. He and my mom indulged my love of reading. They made sure I could buy whatever I wanted at school book fairs, handing me their hard-earned dollars that certainly would have been useful elsewhere in the family budget. More than twenty years later, this generosity brings me to tears, because they opened the world to me by making me a reader. They gave me the tools I needed to be courageous, kind, and creative. Thank you, Papito and Mamacita.

My love affair with books deepened and grew more intense when I was introduced to characters with whom I could identify. I don't have any idea where Ms. Patricia Grimes is today, but the books she assigned to my junior year English class were revolutionary for me, and the writing assignments she gave to accompany them were my first exposure to the idea that I might want to be a writer. When I read the pages of Richard Wright's *Black Boy,* followed by Toni Morrison's *Song of Solomon,* I cried because of how much I could relate to those stories. I connected with the characters' otherness in a way that I hadn't been able to articulate. The other. It has often been my place, but I have never been able to just sit in it. I have always had to act from that place, and I am thankful for the educators and role models in my life who fueled that fervor for justice in me.

To my students at Garinger High School and Davidson College: Thank you for helping me see the world as it is, helping me to take off my rose-colored glasses and see your realities. You empowered me to fight for you and the world that you'll inherit. The roots of this book were inspired by you. I carry each one of you with me, and I am better for it. Thank you for sharing your lives with me. You are loved.

To my families—both the one that raised me and the one that I married into: Thank you for your patience and support, your cheer-leading and curiosity. I am a lucky woman. My husband, Michael, is true and dear, and I have two families who respect my ethics, honor my passions, and support my dreams. Sonia, you are my favorite sister and best friend.

I grew up without the Latina *comadres* my mother has always cherished, but I have wonderful friends who have loved me my whole life—who have cared for, nurtured, and inspired me—and I am both thankful for and indebted to each one of them for helping me and loving me along the way: Jenny, Lylen, Jen, Sean, Braulio, Heather, Ken, Julie, Ben, Jill, Ruth, and Chris.

When I started graduate school, I was a fledgling poet. My first adviser, Jaime Manrique, encouraged me to write prose, insisting that I had enough to say in the longer form and telling me honestly it would take time before I would be able to say it well. Kim Addonizio and Michael Klein were equally skilled in their advising, and coached me as I wrote the manuscript that's the autobiographical sister to this work. I am grateful to the three of them and their vision, tireless guidance, and honesty.

Mima Stojanovic and Jenna Padilla were my enthusiastic and hardworking research assistants. I am so appreciative of their careful work, keen minds, good humor, thoughtful creativity, and tireless research. They made this work stronger, and I am heartened that they are out in the world making it better.

I first witnessed Brooke Warner's editorial work with *Waking Up American,* an anthology to which I contributed an essay that was later adapted for *Hijas Americanas.* Brooke had the foresight to sense that there was a need for a book like this, and her sharp eye and good instincts have been a delightful part of this experience.

Finally, I am grateful to the brave and beautiful women who made this book real, who were honest with someone they didn't know because they cared about something bigger than themselves: voicing the female experience and the experience of being "other." I am absolutely overwhelmed by the keen insights, rich friendships, and divine truths I have had the good fortune to experience with the creation of this book. As someone who grew up without Latina *comadres,* I now have an embarrassment of riches when it comes to m'ijas.

❧ INDEX ❦

⁂ ABOUT THE AUTHOR ⁂

After careers in secondary and higher education, Rosie Molinary, M.F.A., began writing and teaching writing full-time. Her poetry and nonfiction have won numerous awards and have been published in various literary magazines and books, including *The Circle, Caketrain* literary magazine, *Snake Nation Press* literary magazine, *Jeopardy, Coloring Book, Waking Up American: Coming of Age Biculturally,* and *Wishing You Well.* She has also contributed to various magazines, including *Health, Women's Health, deep, Our State, Charlotte,* and *Lake Norman Magazine.* In addition to her writing, she teaches creativity, journaling, and creative writing workshops for various book clubs, schools, colleges, conferences, and nonprofits.

In her free time, she paints, enjoys the outdoors by running and biking, and works on social justice issues in her community. She chairs a nonprofit initiative to provide emergency home repair for low-income families and serves on the board of an affordable-housing coalition. Rosie lives in Davidson, North Carolina.